1985

GEN
Master
Speech

W9-DFQ-854

3 0301 00085853 6

SPEECH
COMMUNICATION

SPEECH COMMUNICATION
THEORY AND PRACTICE

JOHN T. MASTERSON
University of Miami

STEVEN A. BEEBE
University of Miami

NORMAN H. WATSON
University of South Dakota

HOLT, RINEHART AND WINSTON
New York   Chicago   San Francisco   Philadelphia
Montreal   Toronto   London   Sydney
Tokyo   Mexico City   Rio de Janeiro   Madrid

LIBRARY
College of St. Francis
JOLIET, ILL.

PHOTOGRAPH CREDITS

1 (opp.), Gilles Peress/Magnum. **7,** Spencer Carter/Woodfin Camp. **18,** David Hurn/Magnum. **26,** L. Pelaez Collection. **30,** Wayne Miller/Magnum. **37,** Martin J. Dain/Magnum. **42,** Cornell Capa/Magnum. **47,** Patt Blue. **53,** Ken Heyman. **65,** Elliott Erwitt/Magnum. **68,** Dick Swift. **88,** Charles Gatewood/Magnum. **92,** Mary Ellen Mark/Archive Pictures. **98,** Abigail Heyman/Archive Pictures. **116,** Jim Anderson/Woodfin Camp. **119,** Richard Kalvar/Magnum. **121,** Dennis Stock/Magnum. **135,** Mark Godfrey/Archive Pictures. **151,** Thomas Godfrey/Woodfin Camp. **156,** Sepp Seitz/Woodfin Camp. **168,** Michal Heron/Woodfin Camp. **174,** Bill Binzen. **179,** Thomas Hopker/Woodfin Camp. **196,** Bill Stanton/Magnum. **197,** Charles Harbutt/Archive Pictures. **205,** Bill Stanton/Magnum. **207,** Alex Webb/Magnum. **209,** Charles Harbutt/Archive Pictures. **226,** Mark Godfrey/Archive Pictures. **230,** Burk Uzzle/Magnum. **251,** Philip Jones Griffiths/Magnum. **257,** Perrier/Great Waters of France, Inc., Greenwich, CT. **281,** Bettye Lane.

Photo research by Marion Geisinger
Text design by Barbara Bert/North 7 Atelier Ltd.
Cover design by Nancy Kirsh

Library of Congress Cataloging in Publication Data

Masterson, John T., date
   Speech communication.

   Includes index.
   1. Oral communication.   I. Beebe, Steven A., date.
II. Watson, Norman H.   III. Title.
P95.M37   1983   001.54'2   82–15794

ISBN 0-03-060599-7

Copyright © 1983 by CBS College Publishing

Address correspondence to:
383 Madison Avenue
New York, NY 10017

All rights reserved
Printed in the United States of America
Published simultaneously in Canada

3 4 5 6 7   090   9 8 7 6 5 4 3 2 1

CBS COLLEGE PUBLISHING
Holt, Rinehart and Winston
The Dryden Press
Saunders College Publishing

808.56
M428

PREFACE

Speech communication is, at one and the same time, the oldest and one of the newest academic disciplines. Scholarship in the field is characterized by enormous diversity—diversity in philosophical assumptions, theoretical approach, research methodology, and focus of study. In an introductory survey course in speech communication, it is appropriate to expose the student to the broad scope of the areas investigated by scholars in the discipline. It is equally important to stress that, as eclectic as we may seem, we are all concerned with one central underlying phenomenon—the spoken word as it functions in our lives.

In this book we have addressed ourselves to the diversity as well as the unity within our discipline. Our strategy has been to focus on one element that is found in *all* contexts of speech communication: the individual human being. We hope to foster awareness and appreciation of the general functions of speech communication in the life of the individual. More specifically, we examine the influence of various contexts on the processes of communication and we suggest ways toward increased effectiveness within those contexts.

The book is divided into five units. Unit I presents an overview of speech communication principles, models, and concepts and the basics of a single theory of speech communication that focuses on the individual communicator. This focus provides an organizing principle for the rest of the book. Unit II examines the intrapersonal processes of self-awareness and the relationships between language and perception. Units III through V concentrate on the influence of context on communication. Chapters in Unit III include discussions of interpersonal communication, listening, and interviewing. Unit IV presents the area of small-group communication from both prescriptive and descriptive perspectives. The final unit contains chapters on public speech communication. The book closes with an epilogue that reviews the content of the book and extends the discussion to the role of mass communication in society.

We believe an understanding of speech communication theory is essential to a comprehension of the relationships between and among the various areas examined by speech communication scholars. A solid theoretical foundation provides a framework from which communication in a variety of contexts can be viewed.

Awareness and understanding, though, are merely the first important steps in helping the reader to improve his or her effectiveness as a communicator. We have attempted in this volume to take theoretical material and make it relevant and practical. We hope that through reading this book and participating in the course for which it is intended the student will not only gain an appreciation of the potential power of the spoken word, but will also see more clearly the choices available in every communication situation. We have tried to provide an *awareness of alternatives* and the likely consequences of various selections from among these alternatives. Though theoretical foundations are stressed, the utility of these foundations is our primary concern. Toward this end, the bulk of the book

v

H6, 405

is aimed toward helping the reader to *apply* theoretical knowledge to *practical* situations. Thus, while some chapters are more theoretically oriented than others, *each* chapter ends with a section on *putting theory into practice*. A further aid in applying theoretical knowledge is the suggested activities section that follows; the activities emphasize practical applications. In addition, there is an *Instructor's Manual* that includes discussion questions and suggestions for class exercises.

We see no inherent conflict between theory and practice; theory *informs* practice. We hope that this book will help you to attain increased understanding as well as increased personal effectiveness as a communicator. We invite your comments.

We sincerely appreciate the efforts of those individuals who have contributed directly to this effort. We wish to acknowledge the extremely competent and professional assistance and direction of the editorial staff of Holt, Rinehart and Winston.

We are grateful to these reviewers of the manuscript, who have helped to make it a better book: Martin H. Brodey, Montgomery College; Diane O. Casagrande, West Chester State College; Blanton Croft, Northern Virginia Community College, Woodbridge Campus; Suzanne P. Fitch, Southwest Texas State University; Harry Hazel, Gonzaga University; Michael J. Hyde, University of Alabama; David J. Magidson, University of New Hampshire; V. A. Smith, Texas A&I University; Flavil R. Yeakley, Jr., University of Tulsa.

We are especially appreciative of our "in-house" editors, Nancy Masterson and Susan Beebe, whose skills have been invaluable to us.

J.T.M.
S.A.B.
N.H.W.

CONTENTS

Preface   v

UNIT I   INTRODUCTION TO SPEECH COMMUNICATION THEORY AND PRACTICE   I

I   SPEECH COMMUNICATION THEORY AND PRACTICE   3

What Is Speech Communication?   4
Some definitions   5
Principles of Speech Communication   6
Communication is not a thing; it is a process   6 / Communication is complex   8 / Communication is irreversible and unrepeatable   8 / Communication involves the total personality   9
Components of the Communication Process   9
Source (encoder)   10 / Message   10 / Channel   10 / Receiver (decoder)   10 / Noise   10 / Feedback   11
Speech Communication Models and Perspectives   11
The Shannon-Weaver model: the transmissional perspective   11 / The interactional perspective: Berlo and Schramm   13 / The transactional perspective   15
Speech Communication: Theory and Practice   17
Theory defined   17 / Uses of theory   17 / What has speech communication theory to do with practice?   20

SPEECH COMMUNICATION THEORY AND PRACTICE **PUTTING THEORY INTO PRACTICE**   *21*
SUGGESTED ACTIVITIES   *22*

2   A FUNCTIONAL THEORY OF SPEECH COMMUNICATION   23

What Can We Say About Speech Communication That Is True Whenever It Occurs?   24
The Functions of Human Communication   24
The linking function of speech communication   25 / Speech communication and the development of higher mental processes   28 / Speech communication and the regulation of behavior   31
The Levels of Speech Communication   32
The intrapersonal level of speech communication   33 / The interpersonal level of speech communication   34 / The group level of speech communication   35 / The public level of speech communication   35 / The levels of speech communication: interrelationships   36
Speech Communication and Roles   37
The Modes of Speech Communication   39

A FUNCTIONAL THEORY OF SPEECH COMMUNICATION **PUTTING THEORY INTO PRACTICE**   *40*
SUGGESTED ACTIVITIES   *41*

UNIT II THE INTRAPERSONAL LEVEL OF SPEECH COMMUNICATION 43

3 SELF-AWARENESS 45

What Is a Self? 46
Self-reflexiveness 46
Self-Concept 47
We, ourselves, and us 48 / The material self 49 / The social self 49 / The spiritual self 50
Speech Communication and Self-Concept 51
Self-concept and interpersonal communication 52 / Self-concept: an ongoing process 54 / Self-concept: consistency and change 56 / Self-image and self-esteem 56
Effects of Self-Concept on Communication 57
Self-fulfilling prophecy 57 / Selection of messages 58
Roles and Self-Concept 58
Self-Awareness 59
SELF-AWARENESS PUTTING THEORY INTO PRACTICE 61
SUGGESTED ACTIVITIES 62

4 PROCESSING INFORMATION: LANGUAGE AND PERCEPTION 64

The Barker Model of Intrapersonal Communication 66
Stimuli 66 / Reception 67 / Perceptual processes 68
Beliefs, Attitudes, and Values 69
Beliefs 69 / Attitudes 69 / Values 70
What Is Perception? 70
What Individual and Situational Variables Influence the Perception Process? 72
Physiological influences 73 / Contextual influences 73 / Psychological influences 74
How Can We Increase Our Accuracy of Perception? 76
Perception and Communication 76
What Is Language? 77
The Power of Words 78
Words have power to create 79 / Words have power to affect attitudes and behavior 79
Word Barriers 80
Barrier 1: Bypassing 81 / Barrier 2: Polarization 81 / Barrier 3: Allness 82 / Barrier 4: Static evaluation 82 / Barrier 5: Fact-inference confusion 83
Overcoming Word Barriers 83
Avoid signal response to symbols 84 / Avoid rigid, nonprocess orientations 84 / Try to clarify fact-inference confusion 84 / Realize that meanings are in people, not in words 85
PROCESSING INFORMATION: LANGUAGE AND PERCEPTION PUTTING THEORY INTO PRACTICE 85
SUGGESTED ACTIVITIES 86

UNIT III   THE INTERPERSONAL LEVEL OF SPEECH COMMUNICATION   *89*

5   INTERPERSONAL COMMUNICATION: RELATING TO OTHERS   *91*

The Baker Model   92
Reciprocal identification 93 / Psychic tension and silence 94 / Field of language 94
The DeVito Model   94
Competence and performance 94 / Field of experience 95 / Effect 96 / Communication context 96
Interpersonal Attraction   96
Physical attraction 96 / Similarity 97 / Complementarity 97 / Proximity, contact, and interaction 97
Interpersonal Communication: "Getting to Know You"   98
What isn't interpersonal communication? 99 / What is interpersonal communication? 99
Self-Disclosure   99
The dyadic effect 100 / Risk, trust, self-disclosure, and intimacy 101 / Self-disclosure and self-awareness 101
Relational Stages and Interpersonal Communication   102
Initiating 103 / Experimenting 104 / Intensifying 104 / Integrating 104 / Bonding 104 / Differentiating 104 / Circumscribing 105 / Stagnating 105 / Avoiding 106 / Terminating 106
Defensive and Supportive Speech Communication   106
Evaluation vs. description 107 / Control vs. problem orientation 107 / Strategy vs. spontaneity 107 / Neutrality vs. empathy 108 / Superiority vs. equality 108 / Certainty vs. provisionalism 108
Confirming and Disconfirming Responses   108
INTERPERSONAL COMMUNICATION: RELATING TO OTHERS
PUTTING THEORY INTO PRACTICE   110
SUGGESTED ACTIVITIES   111

6   NONVERBAL COMMUNICATION   *113*

What Is Nonverbal Communication?   114
Approaches to the Study of Nonverbal Communication   114
Why Learn About Nonverbal Communication?   115
1. Nonverbal communication plays a major role in our overall communication with others 115
2. Nonverbal communication is the primary way we communicate our feelings and attitudes toward others 116
3. Nonverbal cues are usually more believable than verbal messages 117
Functions of Nonverbal Communication   117
Relationships between nonverbal and verbal communication 117 / Dimensions of nonverbal communication 119
Describing Nonverbal Behavior   120
Sign language 120 / Action language 121 / Object language 121

Interpreting Nonverbal Messages   122
1. *Context can affect the meaning of the nonverbal communication   122*
2. *People respond differently to a common experience   122*
3. *What is appropriate in one culture may not be appropriate in another   123*
Applications of Nonverbal Communication Research   123
Meeting people: nonverbal communication and impression formation   123 / Speaking to an audience: nonverbal communication and speaker effectiveness   126 / Working in groups: nonverbal communication and group decision making   127 / Teachers and students: nonverbal communication in the classroom   129

*NONVERBAL COMMUNICATION **PUTTING THEORY INTO PRACTICE**   130*
SUGGESTED ACTIVITIES   132

7 IMPROVING LISTENING AND FEEDBACK SKILLS   134
Are You a Good Listener?   135
What Is Listening?   136
Selecting   137 / Attending   137 / Understanding   137 / Remembering   137
Types of Listening   138
Listening to enjoy   138 / Listening to evaluate   138 / Listening to empathize   139 / Listening to gain information   140
Listening Barricades: Why We Don't Listen Well   141
Suffering from information overload   141 / Deciding that the topic is not interesting   141 / Becoming wrapped up in our personal concerns   142 / Outside distractions   142 / Speech-rate and thought-rate differences   143 / Criticizing the way the message is delivered   143
Suggestions for Improving Your Listening   144
1. *Look for information you can use   144*
2. *Listen for ideas, not just facts   144*
3. *Try not to be distracted by an emotion-arousing word or phrase   145*
4. *Adapt to the speaker   145*
5. *Be an aggressive listener by adapting to the speaking situation   145*
6. *Practice your listening skills   145*
7. *Decide what your listening objective is   146*
8. *Try to anticipate the speaker's next major idea   146*
9. *Try to identify how the speaker is supporting the major ideas in the speech   146*
10. *Mentally summarize the key ideas   147*
Feedback: Responding to What You Hear   147
Suggestions for Improving Feedback   149
1. *Effective feedback should be descriptive rather than evaluative   149*
2. *Effective feedback should be specific rather than general   149*
3. *Effective feedback should take into account the needs of both the receiver and the sender   149*
4. *Effective feedback should be directed toward behavior that the receiver can do something about   149*
5. *Feedback is most effective when it has been solicited, rather than imposed on the listener   150*
6. *Feedback should be well-timed   150*
7. *Effective feedback should be constructive rather than destructive   150*
8. *Effective feedback should not overwhelm the receiver   150*
Active Listening: Combining the Best of Effective Listening and Feedback Skills   150

*IMPROVING LISTENING AND FEEDBACK SKILLS PUTTING THEORY
INTO PRACTICE* 152
SUGGESTED ACTIVITIES 153

8 INTERVIEWING 155

What Is an Interview? 156
Why Interview? 157
Purposes of an interview 157 / *Information-gathering interviews* 158 / *Information-
sharing interviews* 158 / *Problem-solving interviews* 159 / *Persuading interviews* 159
What Are the Responsibilities of the Interviewer? 160
Training 161 / *Preparing* 163 / *Questioning* 165 / *Listening* 167 / *Recording
information* 168
What Are the Responsibilities of the Interviewee? 169
Preparing 169 / *Listening* 170 / *Responding* 171
INTERVIEWING PUTTING THEORY INTO PRACTICE 171
SUGGESTED ACTIVITIES 172

UNIT IV THE GROUP LEVEL OF SPEECH COMMUNICATION 175

9 GROUP DYNAMICS: A DESCRIPTIVE APPROACH 177

How Is a Group Defined? 178
What Are the Characteristics of a Group? 180
Group structure 180 / *Group task* 187 / *Group climate* 188 / *Situation* 191 / *Group
phases* 193 / *Individual group member variable* 194 / *Communication* 195
What Are Some Types of Groups? 195
**What Are Some Disadvantages and Advantages of Working
in Groups?** 198
Disadvantages of groups 198 / *Advantages of groups* 199
What Are Some Group Communication Problems? 200
*GROUP DYNAMICS: A DESCRIPTIVE APPROACH PUTTING THEORY
INTO PRACTICE* 201
SUGGESTED ACTIVITIES 202

10 GROUP DISCUSSION: A PRESCRIPTIVE APPROACH 204

How Do Groups Solve Problems and Make Decisions? 206
Steps in Problem Solving/Decision Making 206
What Are Some Problem-Solving Formats? 211
The reflective-thinking format 211 / *The ideal-solution format* 211 / *The single-question
format* 212 / *Nominal group technique* 212
How Are Decisions Reached in Groups? 213

How Can You Increase Group Communication Effectiveness?   214
Developing an intrapersonal perspective toward group communication   215 / Developing an interpersonal perspective toward group communication   216 / Developing a group perspective toward group communication   218
How Can Groups Manage Conflict More Effectively?   220
How Can Leadership Effectiveness Be Increased?   222
*GROUP DISCUSSION: A PRESCRIPTIVE APPROACH **PUTTING THEORY INTO PRACTICE**   223*
SUGGESTED ACTIVITIES   224

UNIT V   THE PUBLIC LEVEL OF SPEECH COMMUNICATION   227

11   THE ESSENTIALS OF PUBLIC SPEAKING   229
1. Analyze Your Audience   230
Demographic audience analysis   232 / Psychographic audience analysis   232 / Environmental analysis   232
2. Select a Topic   232
3. Develop a Purpose   233
4. Gather Supporting Material   235
Types of supporting material   235
5. Organize Your Ideas   240
Preparing a speech outline   240 / Patterns of organizing a speech   245
6. Rehearse and Deliver the Speech   248
Styles of speech delivery   249 / Gestures   250 / Eye contact   250 / Movement   251 / Vocal cues   252 / Managing your anxiety   252

*THE ESSENTIALS OF PUBLIC SPEAKING **PUTTING THEORY INTO PRACTICE**   253*
SUGGESTED ACTIVITIES   255

12   PERSUASIVE SPEAKING   256
Persuasion Defined   257
How Does Persuasion Occur?   258
What Happens When You Experience Dissonance?   259
Needs as Motivators   260
Speaker Credibility   262
Preparing the Persuasive Message   264
Persuasive speech organization   264
Using Emotional Appeals to Motivate Listeners   266
Using Logical Arguments to Persuade Listeners   268
Facts   268 / Examples   268 / Opinions   269 / Statistics   269 / Types of reasoning   269
Adapting the Persuasive Message to the Audience   271
Adapting to a friendly audience   272 / Adapting to a neutral or apathetic audience   273 / Adapting to an unfriendly or hostile audience   274

PERSUASIVE SPEAKING *PUTTING THEORY INTO PRACTICE* **276**
SUGGESTED ACTIVITIES **278**

Epilogue   **SPEECH COMMUNICATION IN SOCIETY**   **279**

Mass Communication in Society   **280**
Summary and Conclusion   **281**

Index   **283**

SPEECH COMMUNICATION

UNIT 1

INTRODUCTION TO SPEECH COMMUNICATION THEORY AND PRACTICE

There are essentially two kinds of knowledge in the world: theoretical knowledge and practical knowledge. Theoretical knowledge is knowledge *about* things—why the sun comes up (or seems to) each morning, what will happen to water if its temperature drops to 32°F., what the likely consequences will be if you do not study for your next examination. Practical knowledge, on the other hand, involves *how to do* things—dunk a basketball, thread a needle, build a nuclear reactor, give an effective public speech.

These two forms of knowledge are not mutually exclusive. The technical (practical) knowledge needed to build a nuclear reactor was impossible to gain until the scientific (theoretical) knowledge of nuclear fission was generated. Students of surgery are required to master a theoretical understanding of the anatomy and physiology of the human body before they are instructed in the practical skills of that profession. While we do not intend to draw a direct analogy between nuclear physics or medicine and speech communication, we use these familiar examples to make a point: In nearly every case, *theory informs, guides, and improves practice.*

This book was written to help you improve your skills as a communicator. Its writing has

2

been guided by the conviction that a solid grounding in theoretical understanding will not only help to improve your communication skills in classroom activities, but will also make those skills more flexible and adaptable when you leave the college environment and move into your chosen career. Therefore we have sought to give our presentation a balance between theory and practice.

Unit I is heavily weighted in favor of theoretical concerns. In Chapter I we provide an overview of speech communication principles, concepts, and models and the relationship between speech communication theory and practice. Chapter 2 presents the basics of a single theory of speech communication that focuses on the individual communicator, and thus provides an organizing principle for the remainder of the book.

SPEECH COMMUNICATION THEORY AND PRACTICE

After studying this chapter you should be able to:

Explain, compare, and contrast three definitions of speech communication

Give examples that exemplify four principles of speech communication

Discuss three perspectives from which speech communication processes may be viewed and explain a theoretical model that has grown out of each

Identify five objectives of a good theory

Explain four steps in improving communication skills as these steps relate to the objectives of theory

---

"Professor, I am really upset."

The student's mother certainly seemed agitated, fidgeting in my office, looking and acting out of place, wringing her hands.

I believed her.

"My son says he wants to study speech communication," she continued. "Time and again his father and I have told him to study something he can get a good job in; to learn something *practical*! I'm sorry; I know it's your field of interest, but the boy has been *talking* for most of his nineteen years. He already *knows* how to do that. He doesn't need to *study* it. Surely you can understand."

This is a book about you, the reader. It is about your thoughts, your feelings, your relationships with others. It is about your ability to speak—to utter sentences to yourself and others—and the consequences for you, and them, when you do so.

There is a story about an old fellow who worked for years in a tool-and-die factory in the Midwest. About once a week, at 5 o'clock, old Charlie would leave the factory through the main gate pushing before him a wheelbarrow filled with sawdust. The guard at the gate, sure that Charlie was stealing from the factory, would sift through the sawdust but consistently come up empty-handed, whereupon he would allow Charlie to pass through without further detention. Finally, Charlie retired. As he passed through the gate after his final day at work, the guard stopped him one last time. "Charlie?" said the guard. "All these years I've had the feeling you've been stealing something, but I can't figure out what it is for the life of me. There's nothing I'd do now because you're retired. Tell me: What were you stealing?"

The answer: "Wheelbarrows."

Nothing so escapes detection as the obvious. Perhaps the most obvious (and the most elusive) fact of our human existence is that we spend a large portion of our lives talking, listening, thinking, and otherwise trading in verbal symbols (words). Novelist Walker Percy once observed that the first thing a Martian visiting earth would notice about us humans is that we

> . . . are forever making mouthy little sounds, clicks, hisses, howls, hoots, explosions, squeaks, some of which *name* things in the world and are uttered in short sequences that *say* something about these things and events in the world.

He goes on to note:

> This behavior seems a good deal stranger to the Martian than it does to us. This is the case because language is the very mirror by which we see and know the world and it is very difficult to see the mirror itself, to see how curiously wrought it is.[1]

In the brief dialogue with which we opened this chapter, the student's mother was failing, as most of us do, to grasp the obvious: *Speech communication is at the very heart of who and what we are. In a very real sense our success or failure in life is determined by our ability to use the spoken word effectively.* This book was written to help you increase your awareness and appreciation of the functions of the spoken word in your life, and to help you improve the communication skills you need to be a more competent human being.

WHAT IS SPEECH COMMUNICATION?

SCENE FROM A FAMILY REUNION

Uncle Harry   So, how's school going?
You   Pretty well, Uncle Harry.
Uncle Harry   What kind of courses are you taking?
You   I'm studying speech communication.
Uncle Harry   What's that? Helping people who stutter and stuff like that?
You   No . . .

Nearly everyone who has taken a course in speech communication has encountered a situation similar to the one above. While study of the spoken word has its roots in antiquity, the contemporary study of speech communication is a relatively new discipline. The Uncle Harrys of the world simply aren't familiar with it. It's going to be up to you to educate them. In this section we'll give you some ammunition for that next family reunion when the inevitable question arises, "What is speech communication?"

Some definitions

A brochure published by the Association for Communication Administration entitled *Communication Careers* says the following:

> Speech communication is a humanistic and scientific field of study, research, and application. Its focus is upon how, why, and with what effects people communicate through spoken language and associated nonverbal messages. Just as political scientists are concerned with political behavior and economists with economic behavior, the student of speech communication is concerned with communicative behavior.[2]

This description is suggestive of the broad range of interests held by speech communication scholars and students. The spoken word is a pervasive phenomenon; it occurs in a variety of settings and contexts from poetry readings and public speeches to informal conversations and business meetings. To observe the usage and effects of the spoken word in such a variety of contexts requires differing observational methods. While a structured, scientific approach may be appropriate for observing the dynamics of a problem-solving group or measuring the attitude change effected by a Presidential address, a more aesthetic approach is demanded by the reading of a Shakespearian sonnet. These diverse interests and methodologies are brought together through and by their common focus on the *spoken word*.

Another important phrase from the above definition is "research and application." In speech communication, we are concerned with both *description* and *prescription*. Through our research, we attempt to describe how the spoken word functions in a variety of settings. But we go beyond this and attempt to draw on the research knowledge we gain to apply it to real situations such as public speeches and group discussions in an effort to improve our skills in these areas. We not only find out what's happening, but we apply that knowledge to make it happen better. This makes speech communication exceptional among academic disciplines.

Speech communication is a human process through which we make sense out of the world and share that sense with others.[3]

In this (our own) definition we allude to the pervasive nature of speech communication. We will discuss more thoroughly in Chapter 2 the fact that it is through speech communication that we are linked conceptually with the world. We use words to organize our experiences into meaningful concepts and it is through words that we share our meanings with others. Speech communication, then, provides the foundation for all of our human relationships.

Speech communication: The process (or the product of the process) of the fusion of genetically determined speech with culturally determined language.[4]

When Uncle Harry asks, "What is speech communication?" this definition will probably end the conversation. Nevertheless, it is one of the best definitions we have found, because it addresses itself specifically to the core phenomenon of our area of study. Let's look at this definition more closely.

The linguist studies the structures of and changes within human language systems (French, German, Italian, Swahili, etc.). The speech pathologist studies the anatomy and physiology of the speech mechanisms (the diaphragm, larynx, vocal folds, tongue, teeth, lips, hard and soft palate, etc.). The speech communication scholar studies what happens when speech (our ability to produce, control, and articulate sound) comes together with language (a system of word-symbols). According to the last definition given, Dance and Larson's, appropriate areas of study for the student of speech communication include both the *process* through which speech and language come together (language acquisition and development) and the *product* of that process (the spoken word as it is used in a variety of contexts).

As we asserted at the beginning of the chapter, this is a book about you. Our focus is on you, the individual human being, and the ways in which the spoken word functions in your life: in developing and maintaining your self-concept, in establishing interpersonal relationships, in problem solving and decision making in small groups and also in organizations (as you send and receive messages publicly and through the mass media). We hope this book and the course for which it has been assigned will give you increased appreciation and understanding of the centrality of speech communication in your life as well as enhanced effectiveness as a communicator.

PRINCIPLES OF SPEECH COMMUNICATION

So far we have given you an introduction to the field of speech communication and provided some definitions. In this section, we are concerned with general principles—assumptions about the communication process that offer further insight into how the spoken word functions in our lives.

Dean Barnlund has suggested four principles that he says reflect characteristics of the full range of human communication phenomena from communication within the self (intrapersonal communication) to mass communication.

Communication is not a thing; it is a process

Unlike an earthworm, communication cannot be pinned to a tray of paraffin and dissected to determine the relationships among its parts. It is more like the

weather. It is ongoing and reflects dynamic interrelationships among many simultaneously occurring variables, just as the weather reflects complex interrelationships among such variables as the jet stream, position of the Earth, ocean currents, pressure belts, high- and low-pressure systems, mountains, and oceans.

Communication is *dynamic;* it is something which is *happening.* It is continuous, with no real beginning or ending. For example, as I sit here at my type-writer communicating with you, I cannot separate this communication from all of the communication which led to this moment—the decisions, socialization, education, and so on, which led me to be a college professor who writes books. Likewise, as you read these words, you are connected to all of the communicative processes which have led you to where you are at this moment. Thus we may say that communication is a *transactional* process.

The prefix "trans-" means "across." To say that communication is a *transactional* process suggests that the communication process cuts across or extends beyond the action of the moment. We cannot fully understand a communication event merely by examining the messages which pass back and forth between communicators. Rather, we need to view the event from a broader perspective that includes the past and future, communicators' intent, the context in which the event takes place, and a host of variables which will be discussed throughout this book.

To summarize briefly, communication is a transactional process which should be seen as a dynamic interrelationship of simultaneously occurring variables.

Communication is complex

As we discussed in the last section, when we study speech communication we are dealing with a lot more than who says what to whom. There are many variables which affect and are affected by the communication process. Take a conversation between friends over a cup of coffee in the student union cafeteria. Obviously the sex of the persons, how long they've known one another, their ages, their cultural and ethnic backgrounds, how much they know about each other, and how noisy the cafeteria is at that time of day will all affect the conversation. But consider this: If you are having a conversation with your friend there are, in a way, not two but six people involved in the conversation.

1. Who you think you are
2. Who you think your friend is
3. Who you think your friend thinks you are
4. Who your friend thinks he or she is
5. Who your friend thinks you are
6. Who your friend thinks you think he or she is

As we say, communication is a complex process. This book is designed to help you sort out some of the complexity.

Communication is irreversible and unrepeatable

Prosecuting Attorney Ladies and gentlemen of the jury, my plea to you to find the defendant guilty would not be as fervent were it not for the fact that he

went free last year after being indicted on not one, not two, but *fifteen* counts
of rape . . .

Defense Attorney *(Leaping to his feet)* Your Honor, I object!! The defendant's
prior record is inadmissible in this court!

The Judge Objection sustained. *(To the jury)* The jury is instructed to disregard
the previous comment.

Have you ever tried to take back something you've said? Even as you did so you
probably sensed the futility of your actions. The damage was done. In many respects the human mind is like a tape recorder that can't be shut off. The "tapes"
we make cannot be erased. We can only make new "tapes."

In the example above, the prosecuting attorney knew exactly what she was
doing. She knew that the evidence she was bringing forward was inadmissible
and that the defense attorney would object. She also knew that communication
is irreversible—that the jury would be unable to disregard her comment completely even though instructed by the court to do so.

Communication is also unrepeatable. Any teacher can give testimony to the
fact that the same lecture is never received by any two classes in quite the same
way. The context in which communication takes place is never static. The world
is in process. It's like the observation made by the Greek philosopher Heroclitus
that you can never step in the same river twice. Rivers are flowing and changing
from moment to moment. Each moment it is a different river than it was in the
preceding moment. (Students of Heroclitus went on to observe that in fact the
river's nature is such that you really can't step in the same river once!) This leads
us back to our assertion that communication is not a static *thing* but a dynamic
process.

Communication involves the total personality

Speech communication is more than a facet of human behavior. Speech communication affects our behavior at all levels. It is the primary tool with which
we develop and maintain a self-concept. It is through speech communication
that human relationships are built and sometimes destroyed. In other words, we
cannot separate speech communication from the person who uses it.[5]

COMPONENTS OF THE COMMUNICATION PROCESS

Analysis of any process involves "breaking down" that process into its constituent
elements and examining the relationships among those elements. So it is with
the process of communication. While there are many approaches to the study of
human communication and many theories related to different facets of the process, various components appear with enough regularity to be considered the
basic: Source (encoder), Message, Channel, Receiver (decoder), Noise, and
Feedback.

Source (encoder)

Communication involves information. The point at which information originates is the *source*. Loosely speaking, the source could be anywhere in the environment—your pet, a beautiful sunrise, your stomach, anything that serves as a stimulus to your senses. Usually, though, source refers to a human being who *encodes* a message. Encoding is the process through which messages are cast into a system of signals. If you wish to inform your friend that you are hungry, you must take that idea and put it in the form of words or gestures that will be recognizable by the other person. You may point to your stomach or your open mouth, or you may simply say, "I'm hungry." Either way you have encoded your message. Your success or failure, of course, depends on whether your friend shares the same code (i.e., the gestures you use or the English language).

Message

Messages are the components within a communication system to which we assign meaning. Messages may be sent verbally ("I love you") or nonverbally (a long gaze, a warm smile, and a soft stroke on the cheek), intentionally (you meant to send it) or accidentally (you didn't intend to send it, at least not consciously; for example, a blush might fit this category).[6]

Channel

A *channel* is a pathway through which messages pass on their trip between source and receiver. Telephone lines are one example of channels. In face-to-face communication the primary channels are the light and sound waves through which we can see and hear one another.

Receiver (decoder)

The characteristics of the *receiver* are essentially those of the source. In human communication the receiver is the person for whom the message was intended. Once again, the receiver's ability to understand the message depends on her or his sharing the same linguistic or nonverbal code as the sender.

Noise

Usually we associate *noise* with sound. In communication theory, though, noise is anything that interferes with clear reception of a message. Therefore noise can take many forms. A baby crying while you deliver a speech would disrupt your message and therefore constitute a source of noise. Less obvious is the fact that a room that is too hot can be equally disruptive. Noise can be visual. Distracting mannerisms or inappropriate style of dress can interfere with communication. Noise can also be internal. Receiver prejudice or bias toward the speaker or the topic can interfere significantly with the speaker's ability to "get the message through."

As you can see, anything can be a noise source if it gets in the way of effective communication.

Feedback

Effective communication is virtually impossible without *feedback*. Feedback is the response of receivers to our messages which allows us to gauge our effects on those receivers. Have you ever, as a prank, "deadpanned" someone who was telling a joke—stared at him blankly without responding at all? If you were successful, you probably generated a lot of frustration in the joke teller. Without feedback, we have no way of knowing if we are understood or if our message has had the intended effect.

In face-to-face communication, feedback can be positive or negative, verbal or nonverbal. Positive feedback (an affirmative nod of the head or "I understand what you're saying") lets us know that our message is understood and that we can proceed. Negative feedback (a frown and a negative head nod, or "What on earth are you talking about?") tells us that we need to revise our message and try again.

There are more subtle, sometimes unintentional, forms of feedback as well: a blush or a yawn, for example. We professors assume that no one *intends* to fall asleep in our classes, but when it happens, it provides some interesting feedback.

SPEECH COMMUNICATION MODELS AND PERSPECTIVES

Models are useful to the student of speech communication because they provide a way to define the key components of the communication process and examine the relationships among them. As you examine the models that follow, keep in mind that they are not important in themselves. Their significance lies in their ability to represent a process in which you are engaged at this moment.

The Shannon-Weaver model: the transmissional perspective

One of the earliest models in the field, the Shannon-Weaver model,[7] depicts communication as a linear flow of information from source to receiver—see Figure 1.

This is a *message-centered* model in that its focus is on what happens to messages from their inception to their receipt. It is a linear, *transmissional* model in which information (a message) is passed through a sequence of elements between source and destination. Let's apply the model to a couple of hypothetical situations: a telephone call and a public speech.

Suppose you have just suffered a vicious attack of the "hungry horrors" (known in some regions as the "munchies"). You dive for the phone and dial the number of Guido's Pizzeria. The phone at the other end of the line rings twice and an Italian tenor voice answers: "Guido's."

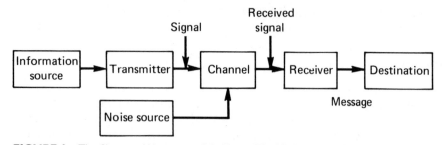

FIGURE I The Shannon-Weaver model. (From *The Mathematical Theory of Communication* by Claude E. Shannon and Warren Weaver. University of Illinois Press, 1949. Reprinted by permission.)

Source: You, your stomach, your brain, your entire nervous system, interacting and culminating in an intense desire for pizza.

Message: "I'd like a large pepperoni, mushroom, pepper, and onion (no anchovies) pizza to go."

Transmitter: Your telephone, which takes your message and recodes it as a set of *signals*—electrical impulses that are transmitted into the system.

Channel: The phone lines that now connect you and Guido's Pizzeria.

Receiver: Guido's telephone, which reconverts the electronic *signals* to a fair likeness of your original message.

Destination: Guido.

Noise source: When Guido hears your request for a pizza, what he hears does not quite sound like you; it sounds more like you with your nose held and your hand in front of your mouth. Something has happened to your message: the resistance in the phone lines and the elements of the phone system (amplifiers, microphones, etc.) have introduced *noise*.

At this point we have followed your message all the way through the model, and it is here that the model begins to lose its effectiveness as an explanatory tool. While it has identified and explained part of this communication event, it fails to include other important components of the communication process. Suppose when you have completed your order, the voice at the other end of the line says, *"Mi scusi, io non parlo Inglese."* Depending on the severity of your munchy attack, you will experience varying degrees of frustration when you learn that Guido doesn't speak English. This brings up two deficiencies of the Shannon-Weaver model and the transmissional perspective as they are applied to human communication:

(1) This perspective does not consider the nature of the source (you) and the destination (Guido). In our example, the effectiveness of your communication was dependent, in part, on your sharing the same linguistic code (language) with Guido. More than a linear tracing of your message through the phone lines is necessary here if we are to understand what is going on between you and Guido. Communication is more than a simple transmission of messages. The receiver's needs, beliefs, attitudes, values, language competence, and a host of other variables all affect the communication process.

(2) The absence of the *feedback* component described in the previous section of this chapter is noticeable in the Shannon-Weaver model.

The transmissional perspective represented here has made a significant contribution to our understanding of the communication process, particularly as it relates to information science. But it has limited applicability to human, face-to-face interaction. Let's follow it through one more example, this time eliminating the telephone to see how the basic components apply to face-to-face communication.

You have just received a glowing introduction and a warm welcome from the faculty senate at your college. You approach the lectern, preparing yourself mentally to greet this august body and begin your speech on "A Student's Perspective on General Degree Requirements." You are very nervous and rather tired, having just completed an afternoon of student teaching in a first-grade classroom. You calm yourself by thinking of the children you just left. You face the faculty and begin: "Good afternoon, children. . . ."

Source: Again, you.

Message: "Good afternoon, children. . . ."

Transmitter: All of your speech mechanisms—larynx, vocal folds, tongue, teeth, hard and soft palate, etc.—which generate signals, in this case sound waves, which are transmitted.

Channel: The air between you and the faculty senate through which the sound waves pass.

Receiver(s): The hearing mechanisms of your audience (ears and the neural pathways to the brain) which allow them to reconvert the sound waves into the meaningful words you transmitted.

Destination: The minds of the members of the faculty senate.

Noise source: There could be many here. The public address system may be faulty. The room may be too hot or too cold. The faculty may be tired and not want to listen to a speech. Then, of course, there's the inappropriateness of your opening remarks.

Given the various elements of the communication process, even in an incomplete model, we can see how communication can go awry at any point in the process. The opportunity for message distortion can take place within the source or the receiver or at any place in between. Given all of the possibilities for miscommunication, it's a wonder that we puzzle over "communication breakdowns," and a marvel that the process works at all.

The interactional perspective: Berlo and Schramm

In 1968, the Speech Communication Association adopted as its definition of speech communication "spoken symbolic interaction."[8] This definition has guided much of the thinking and research in the field since that time. It suggests, as we do, that the spoken word is the central phenomenon under investigation. It further suggests that the spoken word is best understood as it functions in human *interaction;* that is, as if affects the thinking, feeling, acting, and relationships between the senders and the receivers of speech communication.

The *interactional perspective*, then, views speech communication as two-way, reciprocal interdependence in which feedback from the receiver elicits further responses from the sender and vice versa. Thus all participants in the communication process are both senders and receivers of messages.

One of the earliest proponents of this perspective was David Berlo, who described the ideal communication relationship as follows:

> When two people interact, they put themselves into each other's shoes, try to perceive the world as the other person perceives it, try to predict how the other will respond. Interaction involves reciprocal role-taking, the mutual employment of empathic skills. The goal of interaction is the merger of self and other, a complete ability to anticipate, predict and behave in accordance with the joint needs of self and others.[9]

Berlo's model of communication takes the core elements we saw in the Shannon-Weaver model and expands them to include what Berlo saw as the essential characteristics of each component—see Figure 2. Berlo's model begins to get at many of the variables—especially the human variables—that affect speech communication. As we mentioned earlier in the chapter, speech communication is complex and involves the total personality.

A different interactional model was proposed by Wilbur Schramm.[10] Whereas Berlo's model presented a body of related concepts, Schramm's model focused on underlying process—see Figure 3. Here in this model we can see a circular process of interaction in which messages are decoded and interpreted, then serve as the basis for the encoding of new message, and so on.

These interactional models probably relate better to your everyday experience than did the transmissional model presented earlier.

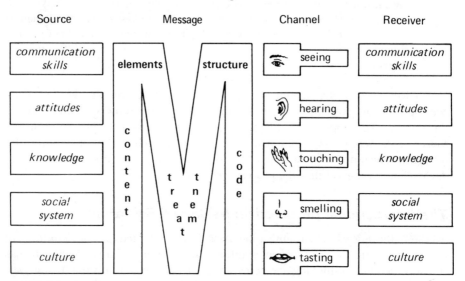

FIGURE 2 The Berlo model. (From *The Process of Communication: An Introduction to Theory and Practice* by David K. Berlo. Copyright © 1960 by Holt, Rinehart and Winston, Inc. Reprinted by permission of Holt, Rinehart and Winston, CBS Educational and Professional Publishing.)

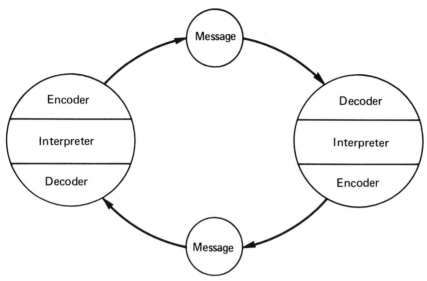

FIGURE 3 The Schramm model. (From *The Process and Effects of Mass Communication* by Wilbur Schramm. University of Illinois Press, 1954. Reprinted by permission.)

> **Don:** "Wanna go out with me on Saturday night?"
> **Josie:** "Sorry, I'm busy."

Even in this simple piece of dialogue (which is familiar to most of us), we can see the interactional process in action. Don encodes a message, probably based on his observations and prior communications with Josie. Josie receives and decodes Don's message, interprets it (Don could mean many things by his question), and then encodes her response. Josie's response serves as a stimulus and structures the possibilities for whatever Don will say next. You may write the end of the drama.

The transactional perspective

The transactional perspective is the newest and most comprehensive approach to speech communication. Here the spoken word is viewed as it is interrelated with the total communication situation. Jabusch and Littlejohn state that "(T)he transactional perspective emphasizes three important aspects of communication: context, process, and function."[11]

Context In order to be understood fully, speech communication—what we say—must be viewed within the context in which it occurs. The same behavior may be interpreted very differently as the context changes. The index and middle fingers, spread and raised over the head, have meant at various times "V for Victory" and "Peace." The word "gay" has undergone a shift in meaning over the last several years. These are examples of *historical* context as it relates to communication.

Cultural context is another important consideration in examining speech communication. Different cultures have different norms for communicative behavior. What is appropriate in one culture may be inappropriate in another. For example, most of us would consider it polite to admire and comment on an object of art in someone's home. But in many Arab countries to do so would prove embarrassing, for your host would be obliged to give you the object of your admiration. There are many such cultural differences that affect communication— norms about who speaks first, how far apart you stand from one another, the amount of eye contact you maintain, whether or not it is gauche to arrive an hour late for a meeting. These are important variables when you are communicating with someone of a different cultural background.

Physical context is another important variable. You know from your own experience that a conversation begun in the hallway changes dramatically when you step into a crowded elevator. Some environments are conducive to conversation, while others are not. Have you ever been in an "*unliving room*," a room that is beautiful but impossible to get comfortable in? Everything from color and decor to the placement of furniture has an effect on our ability to communicate comfortably and effectively. How do you feel in the waiting room of your doctor's office?

Process We have already discussed communication as a *process.* The important thing to remember is that communication is never static; it is a flowing interrelationship of simultaneously occurring variables.

Function Speech communication functions to make us who and what we are— thinking, reflective, symbol-using beings. By *function* we mean that certain phenomena are the *inevitable* result of our use of speech communication. Thus far three functions of speech communication have been identified and supported:

1. Through speech communication we are symbolically linked with the environment.
2. The development of our higher (cognitive) mental processes is functionally related to speech communication.
3. Speech communication functions to regulate our own behavior and, to an extent, the behavior of others (through persuasion, for example).[12]

These three functions will be explored fully in Chapter 2.

The transactional perspective is the most comprehensive of the three perspectives we have discussed. Communication does not exist in a vacuum. It is a vibrant human process in which we are engaged nearly every minute of every day. Viewing this process from a transactional perspective allows us to take into account all of the important variables that affect this process. The most productive way for many of us to examine these variables and the interrelationships among them is through the use of theories. Theory and the relationship between speech communication theory and our practice of speech communication is the subject of the next section of this chapter.

SPEECH COMMUNICATION: THEORY AND PRACTICE

Theory defined

Any good discussion of "theory" should include a definition.

Theory: A proposition or set of interrelated propositions that purports to explain a given social phenomenon.[13]

In other words, a theory should explain under what conditions and with what results a social phenomenon occurs. But a really useful theory does more than this.

Uses of theory

We believe that theory should provide: (1) a method of organizing and categorizing "things"; (2) increased understanding of a phenomenon; (3) adequate explanation of the phenomenon; (4) increased accuracy of predictions; (5) some potential control of the phenomenon.[14]

In an attempt to describe how a theory might accomplish these five objectives, let's look at an example of a social phenomenon we all experience: grocery shopping.

Suppose you are a college student (this is the easy part) in a speech communication class that meets from 3:00 to 4:00 P.M. on Mondays, Wednesdays, and Fridays (more difficult?). One Friday morning you decide that it's about time to restock your refrigerator. After your communication class, you stay around for a while talking with your friends, making plans for Saturday night. You then stroll off to your car and drive to the supermarket, arriving at 5:00. You grab a cart (the one with the flat wheel), and wander up and down the aisles, making impulsive choices but also nutritional choices that require much label-reading. Finally you estimate that you've used up this week's food budget—plus most of next week's. You head for the checkout lanes. It's now 5:45.

To your great surprise, you find that the lines at the checkout lanes are l-o-o-o-o-ng. About half the town's population seems to be in them. You recall that when you came in, there were no lines.

While standing at the end of a line snaking along the dog-food aisle, you begin to reflect on your plight. It's now 5:55 on a Friday afternoon at a large supermarket in a populous section of town where most people get off work at 5:00. By considering these observations—the time, the day, and the setting—in a sense you are developing a "theory" concerning the ins and outs of grocery shopping. You are in the process of devising your own *perspective* or *viewpoint*. Basing your "theory" on the observed facts, you conclude that in this supermarket late Friday afternoon is not the most opportune time to do grocery shopping when you are in a hurry.

1. Organizing and categorizing At the least, we should expect a theory to provide us with a way of identifying, categorizing, and labeling those variables or concepts which a theorist believes to be crucial to the understanding of a phenomenon. This selection process, it should be remembered, is dependent upon the perspective, training, and interests of the theorist. Without this labeling-and-defining process, how would other theorists know the content of a particular theory? An explanation of theoretical concepts provides this basic understanding. Such theoretical concepts as day of the week, time of day, flatness of shopping-cart wheel, number of cashiers on duty, and size and location of the store might be included as parts of a theory of grocery shopping efficiency.

2. Increased understanding As the organizing and categorizing objective of a theory attempts to answer a "What" question ("What concepts or variables are crucial to the understanding of the phenomenon?"), the understanding objective of a theory attempts to answer a "How" question: "How are these variables related to one another as they influence the phenomenon being studied?" These relationships are generally expressed in terms of propositions. An example of such a proposition from our grocery shopping theory would be "The time of day and the day of the week combine to influence grocery shopping efficiency." We might observe that grocery shopping efficiency is not at the same level at 10 A.M. on Saturday as it is at 10 A.M. on Thursday. Why? The next objective of a theory attempts to answer this question.

3. Adequate explanation   This aspect of a theory attempts to answer "Why" questions, such as "Why are these variables related to one another and to the phenomenon in a particular manner?" These explanations are expressed in the form of axioms or theorems: "The number of people in a supermarket, and thus the efficiency of grocery shopping, will be influenced by time of day and day of the week *in combination* because the number of people available for grocery shopping is influenced by time and day." In other words, more people will be shopping at 10 A.M. on Saturday than at 10 A.M. on Thursday because on Thursdays many people are usually working at 10 A.M. Thus, this axiom attempts to explain why *both* time of day and day of the week work in combination to influence grocery shopping efficiency. By developing a number of these axioms, one should be better able to predict the conditions under which grocery shopping might be most efficient.

4. Increased accuracy of predictions   This is the major objective of any scientific endeavor. The aim of most scientists is to know the conditions under which particular events will occur. A prediction about the occurrence of an event under specified conditions is called an hypothesis. An hypothesis for our grocery shopping example might be: Grocery shopping will be most efficient at 10 A.M. on Thursday, with three or more cashiers working, in a large store, when shoppers use grocery carts with four round wheels. You might want to test this hypothesis for the accuracy of its prediction next time you go grocery shopping. Only through observing the phenomenon and testing its accuracy of prediction will you (the theorist/researcher) know the usefulness of your theory.

5. Increased control   This is the final objective of a theory. To the extent that a theory is able to make accurate predictions about the occurrence or nonoccurrence of an event under a specified set of conditions, it is useful in allowing us to exert some amount of control or influence over the phenomenon. If, after observation and experience in grocery shopping, we find that the most efficient grocery shopping can be done in large stores at 10 A.M. on Thursdays, we can then control our choice of store, time, and shopping cart to increase our own grocery shopping efficiency. We might find that 10 A.M. on Thursdays is not *invariably* the best time to do grocery shopping, but it might *generally* be the best time. Theories do not always predict phenomena correctly, but they are stated in terms of "generally" or "usually" in an attempt to increase the *accuracy of the predic-*

tions. A question still remains: What has all this to do with speech communication skills?

What has speech communication theory to do with practice?

Many people would maintain that since most of us have been speaking since the age of 12 to 15 months there should be no need, after so much practice, to be concerned about speech communication theory. Such is not the case with many skills, however, including the practice of speech communication. As we discussed earlier, theory-based and theory-enlightened practice usually improves grocery-shopping efficiency. This relationship also holds true for speech communication. We may all have had several years of *adequate* speech communication practice or performance, but each of us could *improve* our practice by learning more about theory and applying it.

How theory aids practice   Learning to become a more effective speech communicator involves four steps: (1) awareness, (2) understanding, (3) recognition of alternatives, and (4) choice. To see how theory relates to improved practice, we can examine this four-step learning process in terms of the five objectives of theory (organizing and categorizing, understanding, explanation, prediction, and control or influence).

1. Awareness   By organizing, categorizing, and labeling constructs which are crucial to a theory, we become *more aware* of the numerous variables that influence the speech communication process. When we become aware, for example, that language style and bodily movements may influence audience members' perceptions of a public speech, we have taken the first step toward improving our public speaking skills. We then have some concepts or constructs to look *for* and *at* when attempting to improve our communication effectiveness. Thus, the awareness step in the learning process is accomplished by *knowing what to look for* in trying to decide how to improve speech communication practice.

2. Understanding   As you may remember, the understanding and explanation objectives of theory attempt to answer the "how" and "why" questions concerning a phenomenon. By answering (or attempting to answer) these questions, a theory of speech communication helps us to more fully *understand* this complex skill. These objectives attempt to tell us *how* the theoretical concepts or influences are related to one another, as well as *why* they influence the speech communication process the way they do. As you begin to understand, for instance, *how* some group members prefer to handle conflict in the group, and why some methods of conflict management are constructive and others are destructive, you have engaged in the second learning step.

3. Recognition of alternatives   The fourth objective of theory—increased accuracy of predictions—aids us in the third step of the learning process, *recognition of alternatives.* We should all recognize that "Your side of the room looks like a pigsty!" is not the only alternative available to us in encouraging our room-mate to clean his or her side of the room. Through the process of theory build-ing, theory testing, and theory revision, a theory of speech communication should enable us to realize that certain communication strategies are available and are likely to work under certain conditions, and other strategies might have a greater probability of working under another set of conditions. Increased recognition of alternatives should help us improve our speech communication practice by in-creasing the possibility of *predicting which strategy is most useful under a given set of conditions.*

4. Choice   The final step in the learning process, that of *choice,* is up to you. You alone have the choice of influencing your own speech communication behav-ior. Whether you are talking with your parents about that dent in the new car, preparing for a group discussion about student government elections, or present-ing a speech to the local Rotary Club, the choice from among alternative com-munication strategies is yours. Only you can choose the most effective way to gain control over your own speech communication behavior and increase the in-fluence that your speech communication may have on others.

In these ways, then, theory can help you improve your speech communi-cation practice. Organizing and categorizing concepts aids in becoming *more aware* of the complexity of the skill. Explanation of the relationships among the-oretical concepts can help you to *understand* the process better. *Recognition of alternatives* is accomplished through a theory's predictions concerning which communication strategies will work under a given set of conditions. And finally, we are better able to make *choices*—theory-enlightened choices—about our speech communication behavior by wielding *influence* over which alternative(s) to use, once we know all we can about the "what," "how," "why," and "how many" in the communicative situation. It's up to you.

SPEECH COMMUNICATION THEORY AND PRACTICE

PUTTING THEORY INTO PRACTICE

In this chapter we have introduced you to some definitions, perspectives, and models of speech communication. We have also discussed the relationship between speech communication theory and the practice. We have explained how speech communication theory *in general* is useful in your attempts at improving your communication skills. The purpose of this section in the remaining chapters is to offer some suggestions for translating the content of the chapter into improvements in *specific* speech communication skills. Look for these sections; read them. Above all, *use* them. We believe that speech communication theory is translatable into more effective practice. We hope you, too, will find this to be so.

SUGGESTED ACTIVITIES

1. Develop your own speech communication model. Include all concepts which you believe are necessary to fully explain the phenomenon whenever and wherever it occurs. Present your model pictorially as well as in written form.
2. Think of a communicative situation in which you have at one time participated—a classroom lecture, a conversation with a friend in the student union, a group meeting. List all the sources of potential noise present in that situation. Then briefly explain why each of these interferences were noise and how each reduced the effectiveness of the communication.
3. We have discussed a four-step learning process that should aid you in improving your speech communication skills. Using these four steps as a basis, take the role of your instructor in this course. Outline some of the communication alternatives available to you for teaching this course, and explain which alternatives you might choose. Why would you make certain choices and not others?

NOTES

[1] Walker Percy, *The Message in the Bottle* (New York: Farrar, Straus and Giroux, 1975), p. 12.

[2] *Communication Careers* (brochure). Falls Church, VA: Association for Communication Administration, 1981.

[3] Thanks to our friend and colleague Ralph Thompson for the inspiration for this definition.

[4] Frank E. X. Dance and Carl Larson, *Speech Communication: Concepts and Behaviors* (New York: Holt, Rinehart and Winston, 1972), p. 11.

[5] Dean Barnlund, "Toward a Meaning-Centered Philosophy of Communication," in Kenneth G. Johnson, et al., *Nothing Never Happens* (Beverly Hills: Glencoe Press, 1974), pp. 211–215.

[6] We are speaking somewhat loosely here in the interest of simplicity. Strictly speaking, messages are not *sent* at all. Messages are technically *encoded* by the sender into stimuli that are "sent." Messages based on these stimuli are then re-created (decoded) by the receiver.

[7] Claude E. Shannon and Warren Weaver, *The Mathematical Theory of Communication* (Chicago: University of Illinois Press, 1949), p. 7.

[8] R. J. Kibler and L. Barker, eds., *Conceptual Frontiers in Speech Communication* (New York: Speech Association of America), 1969, p. 18.

[9] David Berlo, *The Process of Communication: An Introduction to Theory and Practice* (New York: Holt, Rinehart and Winston, 1960), p. 14.

[10] Wilbur Schramm, *The Process and Effects of Mass Communication* (Urbana: University of Illinois Press, 1954), pp. 4–8.

[11] David Jabusch and Stephen Littlejohn, *Elements of Speech Communication* (Boston: Houghton Mifflin Company, 1981).

[12] Frank E. X. Dance and Carl Larson, *The Functions of Human Communication: A Theoretical Approach* (New York: Holt, Rinehart and Winston, 1976).

[13] Bailey, Kenneth D., *Methods of Social Research* (New York: The Free Press, 1978), p. 439.

[14] Reynolds, Paul D., *A Primer in Theory Construction* (Indianapolis: The Bobbs-Merrill Company, 1971), p. 4.

2 A FUNCTIONAL THEORY OF SPEECH COMMUNICATION

After studying this chapter you should be able to:

Distinguish between the concepts of "function" and "purpose" in human communication theory

Discuss the relationship between speech communication and thought

Identify ways in which speech communication functions to regulate human behavior

Explain the interrelationships among four levels of speech communication

Describe the influence of role expectations on speech communication

Explain how "role taking" can help in the management of interpersonal conflict

Identify situations in which modal contradiction either impedes or facilitates effective communication

This text began with an assertion that this is a book about you—that the theory, principles, and suggestions presented within these pages can help you to gain a better understanding of your own communicative behavior and how it relates to a variety of contexts and situations. We discussed in general how communication theory is related to communication practice. Throughout the remainder of this book we will discuss a variety of theories which relate to specific contexts—theories of interpersonal communication, persuasion, and so forth. But this chapter is different. Here we want to discuss what we can say about human communication *wherever it occurs*—in the bathtub, over coffee, in a public speaking situation, in the committee room, over the airwaves. To do this we need a theory that explains the individual communicator rather than a specific communication context. We need to describe *you* and how speech communication functions in *your* life, because you are the common denominator in all of the contexts of communication.

WHAT CAN WE SAY ABOUT SPEECH COMMUNICATION THAT IS TRUE WHENEVER IT OCCURS?

Consider the sentence above. Do you sense an ironic quality here? Here we authors are in our present moment writing a book, and there you are in yours, reading it. The subject with which we are both wrestling is speech communication—a fundamental human process through which we are doing the writing and you the reading. And yet here we are talking about the subject as if it were a third party.

Do you ever talk to yourself? Who is the speaker? Who the listener? We ask: What can we say about speech communication? Whatever the answer, we are using that which we are describing in order to describe it! Yet if we didn't stop to think about this now, the original question would not seem odd at all. It would merely be another question about another body of academic material.

At the core of all the above questions, at the heart of any conceptual pursuit, is our capacity to use symbols. Our symbolic capacity so dominates our lives that we don't really notice it until someone or something draws our attention to it. The question we will address in this chapter is: How does spoken symbolic interaction (speech communication) function in your life? It is not enough to define speech communication as "spoken symbolic interaction"[1] or "the process by which sensory data is organized, transmitted, and interpreted."[2] Such definitions, while extremely useful for many purposes, still treat speech communication as something outside of us, a process to be described apart from our usage of it. The approach we will use in this book is guided by the pioneering work of Frank E. X. Dance and Carl E. Larson, to which we make grateful acknowledgment.

THE FUNCTIONS OF HUMAN COMMUNICATION

Speech communication functions so importantly in the life of a human being that the understanding and study of speech communication are at the core of a liberal education.[3]

In the heading and the quotation above, the word "functions" appears. It is important at this point to examine this concept, as it will be used throughout this book. We often confuse "function" with "purpose" and use the two terms interchangeably. To do so here, however, would be misleading. "Purpose" refers to goals, objectives, aims. Your purpose in a public speech, for example, might be to persuade your audience that the grading system at your school should be abolished. The term "function"—as it is used throughout this book—refers to a necessary, inevitable relationship between two or more variables. This usage of the word is similar to its use in mathematics, wherein "function" refers to "a variable so related to another that for each value assumed by one there is a value determined for the other."[4]

CONCEPTUAL DEFINITION

Function: A relationship wherein one quality is so related to another quality that it is dependent on and varies with it.[5]

In this chapter we will discuss three functions of speech communication. This is not to imply that there are *only* three, "but rather that only three functions have thus far been sufficiently isolated to warrant statement and adequately supported to warrant belief."[6] The functions are: (1) the linking of person and environment; (2) the development of higher mental processes; and (3) the regulation of behavior. These three functions define, in part, the centrality of the spoken word in our lives.

The linking function of speech communication

Helen Keller is probably a familiar name to you. Perhaps you've seen the play or film *The Miracle Worker*. Perhaps you've read Helen Keller's own book, *The Story of My Life*. You probably know the story. Having been unable to see, speak, or hear since infancy, 8-year-old Helen discovers the world of human symbolic language through her teacher, Anne Sullivan:

> We walked down the path to the well-house, attracted by the fragrance of the honeysuckle with which it was covered. Someone was drawing water and my teacher placed my hand under the spout. As the cool stream gushed over one hand, she spelled into the other the word *water,* first slowly, then rapidly. I stood still, my whole attention fixed upon the motion of her fingers. Suddenly I felt a misty consciousness as of something forgotten—a thrill of returning thought and somehow the mystery of language was revealed to me. I knew then that "w–a–t–e–r" meant the wonderful cool something that was flowing over my hand. That living word awakened my soul, gave it light, hope, joy, set it free! There were barriers still, it is true, but barriers that could in time be swept away.
>
> I left the well-house eager to learn. Everything had a name, and each name gave birth to a new thought. As we returned to the house every object which I touched seemed to quiver with life. That was because I saw everything with a strange, new sight that had come to me. On entering the door I remembered the doll I had broken. I felt my way to the hearth and picked up the pieces. I tried vainly to put them together. Then my eyes filled with tears; for I realized what I had done, and for the first time I felt repentence and sorrow.
>
> I learned a great many new words that day. I do not remember what they all were; but I do remember that *mother, father, sister, teacher* were among them— words that were to make the world blossom for me, "like Aaron's rod with flowers." It would have been difficult to find a happier child than I was as I lay in my crib at the close of that eventful day and lived over the joys it had brought me, and for the first time longed for a new day to come.[7]

116, 405

LIBRARY
College of St. Francis
JOLIET, ILL.

A beautiful story, yes, but it's more than that. It's a stunning glimpse at the dramatic change in awareness or consciousness effected by the *word*. In Helen's case it was obviously not the spoken word. Indeed it was her inability to see, hear, or speak that prevented her from learning to use symbols earlier in her life. But look at what happened here. The sudden flood of awareness that came when Helen associated a verbal symbol with a simple experience changed her "from the good responding animal which behaviorists study so successfully to the strange name-giving and sentence-uttering creature who begins by naming shoes and ships and sealing wax, and later tells jokes, curses, reads the paper, writes *La sua volontade e nostra pace,* or becomes a Hegel and composes an entire system of philosophy."[8]

Speech communication functions to link us—through verbal symbols—with our environment. Take a moment to listen to the sounds around you, wherever you're reading this book. What do you hear? Voices in the next room? A typewriter down the hall? Music? The hum of fluorescent lighting? Now look around you. What do you see? Think about yourself for a moment. Who are you? Are you a nice person? Shy? How would you describe yourself to someone who asked, "Who are you?" Throughout each of these experiences—identifying sounds, sights, ourselves—we use verbal symbols, words, to organize and interpret our experience. If an airplane were to fly overhead right now, how would you respond to the sound or sight of it if you had no word for it?

Here's an interesting mental exercise: You're a science fiction writer, telling a story of a strange creature discovered in the far reaches of the galaxy. It is a creature that bears no resemblance to any other organism known to Earth people. Try to describe it. Can you? Can you create a mental picture of something for which you have no words? It's difficult, at best.

The limits of my language are the limits of my world.

—Wittgenstein

In a very real sense, the meaning of our experiences is *created* through our use of symbols. The tree outside your window has no particular meaning in and of itself. It simply exists as a configuration of cellular and molecular processes. But when a human being confronts that tree something new happens; the tree may appear as romantic or sad, as shade on a hot day, as the site of a first kiss, as an arboreal playground. But these meanings do not reside in the tree itself. Their home is in that peculiar symbolic linkage between person and environment which our capacity for speech communication provides. It's little wonder that Helen Keller found the discovery of her symbolic capacity so exciting!

In the Beginning was the Word . . .

—John I:I

CONCEPTUAL DEFINITION

Displacement: Speech signals may be employed without reference to the immediate situation. Individuals can employ speech signals to talk with each other about things entirely removed from the time or the place in which speech communication occurs. Indeed, man is probably the only animal capable of constructing for himself and others a reality entirely of words.[9]

Displacement is a unique feature of the linking function of speech communication which warrants some scrutiny. It's one of those obvious things about us humans which is so obvious that we don't notice it. With speech communication we can "step outside of ourselves" and move rather freely through time and space. We can think about what is going on on the other side of the world, we can reflect on the past and plan for the future. This is one of the features which makes *human* communication so unique. Unlike the other members of the animal kingdom, who are tied to the perceptual present (that is, they can respond only to stimuli which are physically present in their environment), we can use the experiences of yesterday or even of past generations to guide our actions today. This simple fact of our existence goes a long way toward explaining why it is that we humans have built elaborate social institutions—communities, cities, governments, nations—while the other animals continue a repetitious cycle from generation to generation.

In a way, our whole sense of time is an artifact of our speech communication ability. What we think of as time—minutes, hours, days, weeks, and so forth—really describes a relationship between space and motion—the hands on the clock, the movements of heavenly bodies in relation to one another. The only moment which ever really exists, then, is the present one. Yet we know that we can reminisce about the past and look to the future. But what is the locus of the past? Where is the future? The only reality we can point to with certainty is the present. We can think about yesterday, but our thoughts are still in the present. What, then, are we thinking about when we remember past events?

Again, it is the symbol that permits us to retain the past. What we think of when we remember yesterday is actually our symbolic representation of yesterday's events—events that are quite outside of our perceptual present. Our symbolic linkage with the environment, the linking function of speech communication, provides an important key to understanding human communicative behavior: because we interact with the environment symbolically, we can displace—step outside of ourselves—into other times, other places, other people's symbolic worlds. We carry with us our symbolic representations of the past, which inform the present and help us plan for the future. This function of speech communication provides the basis for all of our social relationships, beginning with our relationship with ourselves:

> . . . once the individual is constituted as "self," then the central operation of the linking function is in an individual's social environment. That is, human communication links people with other people. It is the process through which social bonds are established and maintained, human relationships are defined, and almost all forms of social behavior are manifested.[10]

Speech communication and the development of higher mental processes

Try to recall how the world looked to you when you were 15 years old. How about when you were 10? Five? Three? Obviously there have been many changes in your life over the years between your birth and now. Our concern here is with your symbolic representations of the world around you over that time (and indeed into the future). Think back to your first year in elementary school. What do you remember? Do you feel that you have more control over your life now than you did then? How specific are your recollections?

CONCEPTUAL DEFINITION

Higher mental processes: Activities identified by the term "higher mental processes" include memory, planning or foresight, intelligence or cognitive insight, thinking, judgment, and speech communication and its derivatives reading and writing.[11]

Logically, language can no more be a basis for itself than thought can think itself.

—*Brice Parain*[12]

The quotations here suggest the functional relationship between speech communication and thought. Try to think about something without using words. It's difficult, if not impossible. At the same time, to say that language and thinking are one and the same is illogical. Languages do not arise in a vacuum. There must be some mental operation on which they are based. Neither conceptual thought nor language can take place exclusive of the other. Thus, there is a functional relationship.

Given this functional relationship between speech communication and higher mental processes, we should be able to see the development of one reflected in the development of the other. Indeed, this seems to be the case.

> ... The most important discovery is that at a certain moment at about age two, the curves of development of thought and speech, till then separate, meet and join to initiate a new form of behavior. ... [At] this crucial instant ... speech begins to serve intellect, and thoughts begin to be spoken.[13]

Now return to the development of your own thinking processes. When you were 2 or 3 years old it is quite possible that Mom or Dad pointed to a furry, four-legged animal that had whiskers and purred, and asked, "What's that?" and you said, "Doggy." Although now you know that the furry little beast was a cat, your assumption that it was a dog was not unreasonable at the time. You had learned from your experience with books and pets the concept "dog." You were able to generalize that concept to include St. Bernards, beagles, dachshunds, and a variety of mutts. But if you did not have a separate, mental, symbolic category for "cat," the animal before you would appear to fit all or most of the criteria for "dog" and would thus be identified as such. Here we can see the function of the symbol in delineating a thought category into which we fit our experience. Your failure to recognize a cat as a cat was not a perceptual failure but a conceptual one. You simply didn't have enough symbolic categories to see it as something different.

As we grow, learn, accumulate experience, and pass through various educational processes, we continuously elaborate our symbolic category systems. The process is primarily *deductive;* that is, we tend to notice first generalities and then specifics. Thus objects we once identified as "tree" are now oaks, palms,

and maples. Where once the people in the world were Mommy, Daddy, people we know, and people we don't know, there are now a myriad of categories into which we place others.

The development of higher mental processes and their functional counterpart, speech communication, continue (with luck) throughout our lifetimes. Our perceptions continue to elaborate and become more specific as we acquire new symbolic categories. This leads us to the following point: *our thoughts and perceptions are only as accurate as our ability to represent or express them.*

We will discuss language and perception more fully in Chapter 4. For now, let's look at it this way: Because of our uniquely human symbolic linkage with the world, we interact not only with reality but with our representations of reality. Insofar as these representations influence our behavior, they themselves are, in fact, part of reality (the fact that we use words to communicate with each other is certainly real). Speech communication—spoken symbolic interaction—is the primary means through which we acquire, elaborate, and refine our thoughts and perceptions. Given the functional relationship between speech communication and higher mental processes, improvement in our speech communication abilities should result in a concomitant improvement in those mental operations identified as "higher mental processes."

Speech communication and the regulation of behavior

Through speech communication we regulate our own behavior and, to an extent, the behavior of others. There are of course some obvious and blatant examples of this, as when a political candidate delivers a stirring campaign speech that brings his believing audience to its feet. Or when the young father instructs his toddler, "Tell the nice man your name," and the child does so. But there are also more subtle ways in which speech communication functions to regulate human behavior.

Sticks and stones can break my bones, but words can never hurt me.

Even when we were children we knew that this rhyme, usually chanted in an emotional moment of attempted retaliation, was untrue. Words—the building blocks of our social reality—are very powerful regulators indeed. They can help or hurt, facilitate or impede. Speech communication in a public setting can anger, soothe, stimulate thought, entertain, inform, persuade, bore. At a committee meeting it is used to help solve problems or prevent their solution. In our interpersonal relationships we use spoken words to build intimacy, warmth, and trust, or to disengage ourselves from those relationships. Within ourselves we use speech communication to regulate our own behavior.

Think, for a moment, about a problem in your life. What happens in your body when you think of this problem? Does a "hollowness" appear in your stomach? Does the heart beat faster? Through speech communication we can literally "talk ourselves" into a variety of physical and emotional states. Will you have to give a formal speech in the class for which you're reading this book? What you say to yourself about the prospect (whether vocally or silently) not only reflects your thinking about the situation but will have a powerful effect on your performance as well. If you say to yourself, "There is nothing in this world worse than having to get up and talk in front of a group of people," this will probably be reflected in your speech. If, on the other hand, you say to yourself, "It's scary, but I know I can do it," you are likely to give a stronger speech. It's rather like the story of "The Little Engine That Could," who literally talked himself over a steep mountain while pulling a heavy train ("I think I can, I think I can, I think I can . . .").

There are many ways in which behavior is regulated through speech communication. Such regulation may be of the self by others, of the self by the self, or of others by the self. Dance points out that "The regulation of behavior through speech communication commences from the outside in and then is internalized, so as to provide self-regulation, and finally is consciously expanded as an instrument to control others."[14] We are born into a symbol-producing world. Our adaptation to that world is regulated by its language and social structures. As we internalize these symbolic codes to the point that we can use symbols to reflect on ourselves, we begin to use speech communication to regulate our own behavior.

> When a child subordinates himself to the verbal order of an adult, he assimilates this method of organizing actions. He himself begins to form the pattern of his own future actions. . . . Speech, addressed as an order to oneself, quickly becomes one of the most important methods of regulating behavior in the development of the child.[15]

Eventually, we learn to influence others in our environment with speech communication and, in time, to use speech communication as a powerful persuasive tool.

There is one point that we must not lose sight of through all of this discussion: We have asserted a *functional* relationship between speech communication and the regulation of human behavior. Whether speech communication is taking place within the individual, between individuals, or through the mass media, *whenever speech communication is taking place, behavior is being regulated.*[16]

Let's stop for a moment and look at where we've been so far in this chapter. We have been trying to answer the question, "What can we say about speech communication that is true wherever it occurs?" At the core of our answer is you, the individual human being for whom speech communication functions in at least three significant ways: your symbolic linkage with yourself and the rest of your environment, the development of higher mental processes, and the regulation of behavior. Because of your symbolic link with the world you can move mentally through space and time. You can learn, not only from your own experience but also through the experience of others. The ability to displace gives us a past, a history that informs the present and helps us to plan for the future. What happened 10 minutes ago we retain as a symbolic construct and use to guide our actions now. The three functions of speech communication are thus working in concert. The effectiveness with which we regulate our behavior is dependent on the degree of development of our higher mental processes, which, in turn, is made possible through our uniquely human symbolic linkage with the world.

THE LEVELS OF SPEECH COMMUNICATION

Speech communication is, obviously, a tremendously complex phenomenon that is at the very core of our humanity. We have been discussing the functions of speech communication within the individual human being. Now we turn our attention to four basic levels of relationship that influence and are influenced by speech communication and the individual.

In Chapter 1 we identified several components of the communication process, including communication *context* and the notion of *senders* and *receivers* who *encode* and *decode* messages. In discussing the levels of speech communication, we are looking at how different classes of senders, receivers, and contexts interact with the basic processes we have been describing.

The basic levels of speech communication are (1) *intrapersonal,* (2) *interpersonal,* (3) *small group,* and (4) *public.* While these levels are interconnected, each contains features sufficiently unique to that level to warrant separate discussion. One feature which is common to all four levels and yet different in each is the level of *intentionality* in the speech communication act as it occurs at each level. As we move through our discussion of each level, note the steady progression of the degree to which speech communication is a planned, purposive event.

The intrapersonal level of speech communication

We derive the prefix "intra-" from the Latin word *"intra,"* which means "within" (as in intramural, "within the walls"). Thus, intrapersonal speech communication is speech communication within the person.

On this level, sender and receiver are the same person. In one sense, then, intrapersonal communication is talking to yourself, as when you mentally discuss with yourself the pros and cons of sleeping an extra hour and skipping that early morning class, or when you approach the lectern, look out over the audience, and think to yourself, "Oh, boy, here it goes. I hope no one notices that my knees are shaking. . . ."

Yet intrapersonal communication is more than this. The way in which we communicate within ourselves constitutes much of our uniqueness as individual humans. Each of us processes the information we receive through our senses in different ways, according to the symbolic structures through which we receive it. Self-concept, beliefs, attitudes, and values are all built and maintained, in part, through intrapersonal communication.

While all of us in a particular language group (e.g., speakers of English) use the same system of symbols (language) to link us to our world, each of us brings a unique interpretation of those symbols to each communicative event. The process through which we interpret communicative stimuli, either from within or outside of ourselves, takes place on the intrapersonal level. This process will be discussed in greater detail in Unit II.

At the intrapersonal level we are usually conscious of no particular intentionality behind our actions. Our interpretations of events seem to "just happen." Thoughts seem to come to us randomly. There are times when we may intend to solve a particular problem or plan a particular activity, but we do not, even then, plan our messages with a particular effect in mind. Not so as we move on to other levels of speech communication.

The interpersonal level of speech communication

What does it mean when you say that you are "getting to know" another person? What is it about that person that you are learning? The recognition of a face and a name comes quickly, but what is beyond that? Through speech communication (and associated nonverbal messages) we are "linked" with others, but what within us is being linked with what within them?

While we do not wish to downplay the aesthetic or spiritual beauty of love and friendship, interpersonal communication (communication between two persons) bears a striking resemblance to theory building as it was described in Chapter 1! When we say that we are "getting to know" another person, it means (in part) that the person is becoming predictable to us—that we have a growing certainty that under certain conditions in certain situations there is a probability that the person will respond in a particular way. To know someone well is to carry a "theory" of that person that is consistently supported by the observed behavior of the other. We may then choose our own communicative behaviors with some knowledge of how they are likely to be received. It's little wonder that we are more comfortable around people we know.

Interpersonal communication is a process of discovering the uniqueness of the other person. It is learning what sets that person apart from all other persons. As we have noted in our discussion of Level I (intrapersonal) communication, the uniqueness of each individual (other than the obvious physical differences) resides in that person's particular way of representing the world to himself. Interpersonal communication, then, is a linkage between two "inner worlds"; it is entry into another person's interiority.

CONCEPTUAL DEFINITION

Interpersonal communication: When predictions about outcomes are based primarily on a cultural or sociological level of analysis, the communicators are engaged in non-interpersonal communication; when predictions are based primarily on a psychological level of analysis, the communicators are engaged in interpersonal communication.[17]

This definition of interpersonal communication by Miller and Steinberg points to speech communication that is aimed at discovering and responding to the uniqueness of the other individual. Such an aim implies much more intentionality at this level than we found in Level I communication. Our experience tells us that this is so. When we engage in conversation with the different people we know, we formulate messages and adapt them to each person and the level of our relationship. Whether we are simply passing the time of day, trying to seduce the other, attempting to elicit information, or negotiate a marriage contract, we choose those messages which are most likely to be effective according to our predictions of that person. You may feel that you are simply "yourself" in your communication with all the people you know, and in a way you are. But think about it. Think of your two closest friends. Do you communicate about exactly the same things in precisely the same way with both of them?

We will explore the whole realm of interpersonal communication further in Unit III.

The group level of speech communication

When three to about fifteen or twenty people meet and, by using mutual influence through speech communication, attempt to accomplish some task agreed upon by the members of that group, speech communication is occurring at the group level. Whether the task is entertainment (a sailing club), information sharing (a study group), planning (a community action group), or problem solving/ decision making (a corporate board of directors), all groups use speech communication in an attempt to reach some goal. The interrelationships among the group members (nature of the receivers) and the reason for group interaction (intentionality) again distinguish group communication from the other levels.

If you have ever worked in a group, you probably already know some of the problems associated with trying to make a decision—any decision—in such a situation. You try to convince one person you are right, and everyone else chimes in at once. You try to talk to the whole group, and someone claims you are trying to hog the floor. No one in a group ever seems satisfied with what is happening. If you have every experienced anything akin to this, you know that what you say in a group has to satisfy not one, not two, not three, but *all* members of the group. If even one person disagrees, the whole group will know it. Every member of a group is a critical listener and a potential speaker. When communicating in a group setting, you need to base your message(s) both on what you know about the uniqueness of individuals in the group and on what you know about the common interests of the group members. This is one of the factors which distinguishes group communication from interpersonal communication, and from the next level, public communication.

Because of the complexity of message production for a group of unique individuals who have a common goal in mind and who are all potential respondents to all messages, the level of *intentionality* related to group messages increases above that at the interpersonal level. Any message in a group—even a less formal one—must take into account the unique characteristics of the individual group member(s) that the message is intended for, *as well as* consider the individual feelings, interests, and goals of all group members. When George responds to Carmen's idea, and Thelma responds to George's attitude toward Carmen, and Jose yells at Thelma for picking on George, the complexity of speech communication at the group level becomes evident. We will discuss the group level of speech communication further in Unit IV.

The public level of speech communication

Toward the end of this book we have included two chapters on public speaking. Units and courses in public speaking are aimed at enhancing your knowledge and skills in preparing and delivering formal spoken messages to groups of individuals.

In comparison with the other levels of speech communication there are both similarities and differences at the public level. On one hand at all four levels we can see the formulation (encoding) of messages by the sender with a particular receiver in mind. All of the processes of Level I (intrapersonal) are still operating at the fourth level; we are still perceiving, thinking, feeling, interpreting. There are two essential differences, however, between public speech communication and the other three levels. Again, they are defined by (1) the nature of the receiver(s) and (2) the level of intentionality.

In contrast to the interpersonal level, where the individual addresses the receiver in terms of the person's *uniqueness*, at the public level the speaker looks for *commonalities* among the individuals in the audience. For the speaker attempting to analyze an audience, the goal is predictability, just as it was at the interpersonal level. The speaker, to be effective, needs to have some idea of how the message will be received. While each member of the audience is a unique individual, research in group behavior has shown that members of particular groups (based on age, sex, political affiliation, educational level, etc.) share many common characteristics. It is these common characteristics which give groups some degree of predictability in terms of response to our messages.

Public speech communication, whether it occurs in a face-to-face context or through one of the mass media, is basically a highly structured form of something we do quite naturally—talk to one another. But this formal structure sets it apart. In public speech communication the highest level of intentionality is manifested. Messages are planned, often well in advance, before they are delivered. Audiences and situations are carefully analyzed. We are highly conscious of the intended effect of our messages. Our mode of delivery is thoroughly planned and often thoroughly rehearsed.

The levels of speech communication: interrelationships

The levels of speech communication we have described do not exist separately but are *dynamically interrelated*. Activity at one level can, and usually does, affect activity at the other levels. For example, consistent rejection by members of the opposite sex at the interpersonal level may have an effect on our intrapersonal communication; we will probably be troubled by it. Likewise, consistent success in public speaking may help to restore our confidence somewhat. Our self-confidence (or lack thereof) at the intrapersonal level will probably be evident in our communicative behavior in interpersonal, small-group, and public situations.

The point to remember here is that communication at any one level is influenced by the other three. If you are going to understand, for example, your communicative behavior as leader of a small-group problem session, keep in mind that in that situation you are influenced by what you say to yourself, alone in your room, in the dark of night.

SPEECH COMMUNICATION AND ROLES

How do you communicate with your mother? Your clergyman? The store clerk? Your best friend? Your professor? Have you ever had a teacher who became your friend? How did that shift affect your communication with that person?

CONCEPTUAL DEFINITION

Role: ... [T]he pattern of expectations regarding the occupant of a position.[18]

Do you communicate differently with women than you do with men? Do you feel that your self-identification as male or female has an influence on how you communicate with others? How would you feel if your doctor began to discuss his personal problems during your visit?

Roles, socially determined patterns of expectations, have a powerful influence on our speech communication behavior. Earlier in the chapter we suggested that we perceive the world through the symbolic categories (words) we have for it. Our symbolic categories give us a predisposition to respond to the world in certain ways. If we have one symbolic category such as "snow," when the white stuff falls we will say, "It is snowing." But if, like the Eskimo, we have several words, all of which refer to types of snow, we will see frozen precipitation as a number of different phenomena. Similarly, roles are symbolic categories which

predispose us toward responding in certain ways to the people who fill those roles.

Roles are useful; they provide us with many categories that save us a lot of confusion. We expect certain behaviors of a bank teller. Our role expectations allow us to communicate with a person in that role with high predictability as to the outcome, even though we do not really know the person behind the role. As long as the teller's *role enactment* is consistent with his or her own and your *role expectations,* the verbal exchange between the two of you is likely to be satisfactory. In this way roles are extremely helpful in making the world more predictable for us.

Understanding roles is useful in interpersonal communication in another way as well. *Role taking* is the ability we have to step outside of ourselves and project ourselves into the role of another person. Role taking can be particularly helpful when there is interpersonal conflict. A dispute between a professor and a student is likely to reach a more satisfactory resolution if each will attempt—as fully as possible—to see the problem from the other's point of view.

There are also some problems associated with roles. For one thing, no two people see any role in precisely the same way. An employer and a receptionist may agree that the role of receptionist involves answering the telephone, making appointments, and serving as "gatekeeper" to the inner offices. But the employer may further expect that the receptionist should be efficient and businesslike, while the receptionist believes that the job involves being friendly and making visitors feel at home. This can lead to considerable conflict and even dismissal of the receptionist.

We tend—erroneously—to assume that others see roles in the same way that we do. A truly pervasive role-related problem is found in many contemporary marriages. Husband Charlie sees the role of "wife" as "the little woman who's either by my side (and one step back) or home on the range (the kitchen range)." On the basis of his expectations for the role of "wife," Charlie will communicate with wife Mildred accordingly: "When is dinner going to be ready? Will you bring me the paper? I'm out of brown socks. When are you going to do laundry?" Meanwhile Mildred sees herself as "a competent woman with professional training." She believes that in this day and age a wife should be "an equal partner with her husband in all respects." Do you see the potential problem here?

Another potential problem with roles is that they can eventually affect personality:

> Role affects behavior, and behavior often shapes personality. We are what we have done and we shall become what we will do. Action shapes being.[19]

We may change our behavior in order to fill a role. A mild-mannered business student may begin to act aggressively upon entering the corporate world because he or she believes that is what is expected of a businessperson. Others in the business do not see the mild-mannered person filling an aggressive business person role; they see an aggressive businessperson. At the interpersonal level (Level II) they treat our mild-mannered friend like an aggressive person, thus providing our friend with evidence of actually being aggressive. In this way role enactment has led to changes in Level II speech communication, which may, in turn, filter down to Level I. At the intrapersonal level, our formerly mild-mannered person not only begins to believe that he or she is aggressive, but in fact is.

A fascinating contemporary phenomenon that we shall not explore here but that deserves notice is the dramatic change taking place in female/male roles. Expectations that have been fairly rigid for a very long time are now in a state of flux. Men are more willing to cry and to change diapers; women are discovering that they, too, can be assertive. "Equal partnership" marriages are springing up all over. Meanwhile, many people still hold to more traditional female/male role expectations. These changes are not only societal; they are individual and are reflected in the speech communication of individuals at all levels.

THE MODES OF SPEECH COMMUNICATION

It should be quite clear to you by now that speech communication involves a great deal more than the act of talking. It influences our perceptions of ourselves and others and provides the basis of most of our human activities. We communicate not only through the spoken word but through all of our five senses. A gentle touch on the arm and a warm smile can convey a great deal of meaning.

CONCEPTUAL DEFINITION

Mode (Modality): The method through which one manifests speech communication. The individual operational system for the conveyance of speech communication. The means of acting or doing.[20]

Much of what we usually call "nonverbal communication" is actually verbally mediated, that is, it is symbolic. A wink, a handshake, a wave, and the L.A. Freeway Salute (known in some regions as "the Bird") are all examples of gestures which are interpreted verbally. These give testimony to the fact that speech communication takes place through a variety of *modes.*

The modes of speech communication correspond with our senses: sight, hearing, smell, touch, and taste. Verbal meaning can be derived through all of these senses. Obviously, the primary mode of speech communication is auditory. But consider how our other senses come into the picture: the sight of a lover, the sound of a voice, the smell of cologne, the touch of a hand, the taste of a kiss.

Generally we use the various modes available to us to reinforce our message. When studying public speaking, for example, we learn to use body and voice in ways which help the audience to focus on our message. A smile, a firm handshake, and a pat on the back convey a much stronger greeting than a limp handshake and a deadpan expression. We ordinarily use the modes of speech communication in concert. This is called *modal reinforcement.*

There may be times when we inadvertently engage in *modal contradiction.* We send conflicting messages through two or more modes, thus creating ambiguity in our messages. If you are concerned over a problem in your life and a friend asks, "How are you today?" and you reply, "Fine" with a scowl on your face, you have sent conflicting messages. You *say* you're fine, but you *look* as if things are not so good. Another example—that we've all seen—is the slow-moving, dull-sounding, inexpressive public speaker who announces, "I'm tremendously excited to be here with you today."

At other times, we use modal contradiction intentionally. Try saying the following: "Oh, boy, am I glad to see you today." Now say it *sarcastically*. Modal contradiction creates a whole new message structure in the case of sarcastic remarks. Another example of intentional modal contradiction is the uncanny ability some people have to say "No" and mean "Yes."

We will discuss the modes of speech communication further in Chapter 6.

A FUNCTIONAL THEORY OF SPEECH COMMUNICATION

PUTTING THEORY INTO PRACTICE

In this chapter we have discussed functions, levels, roles, and modes—the building blocks for a theory of speech communication. We have not attempted to explain the processes of speech communication as they pertain to any particular context; that is what the rest of the book is for. We have tried to present a conceptual framework that describes how speech communication functions with you, the individual communicator. If you devote yourself to a thorough understanding of this conceptual framework, you will find that it provides you with a way of looking at and understanding your own communicative behavior.

We began this chapter with the question "What can we say about speech communication that is true wherever it occurs?" The truth of what we have said in response to that question exists only as it reflects real phenomena in the real world—only insofar as it describes how speech communication really functions in our lives.

We can have no control over processes we do not understand. On the other hand, knowledge is power. Speech communication is a process so central to all facets of our lives that an understanding of that process is essential if we are to maximize our effectiveness as communicators—within ourselves, with intimate friends and associates, in small groups and organizations, and in public settings.

In this chapter we have not specifically told you *how* to do *anything*. We have, however, been describing a process which is central to *everything* you do. As you read through the remaining chapters in this book, remember that we are not describing many processes, but one—speech communication—as it interacts with a variety of settings and contexts.

SUGGESTED ACTIVITIES

1. Think of someone you have known all of your life—your mother, for example. How would you have described this person to a friend when you were 6 years old? How would such a description differ today? Can you relate the change to the three functions of speech communication described in this chapter?

2. Consider the various modalities through which speech communication is expressed (auditory, visual, etc.). Which of these modes do you associate most closely with the following messages?

"I love you."

"You're fired!"

"Come over here."

"I'm hungry."

With a friend or classmate, try saying each of the statements above in ways that would foster disbelief.

NOTES

[1]Robert J. Kibler and Larry L. Barker, eds., *Conceptual Frontiers in Speech Frontiers in Speech Communication* (New York: Speech Association of America, 1969), p. 18.

[2]William F. Eadie and John A. Kline, *Orientations to Interpersonal Communication* (Chicago: Science Research Associates, 1976). p. 2.

[3]Frank E. X. Dance and Carl E. Larson, *Speech Communication: Concepts and Behavior* (New York: Holt, Rinehart and Winston, 1972), p. 63.

[4]William Morris, ed., *The American Heritage Dictionary* (New York: American Heritage Publishing Company, Inc. 1971), p. 533.

[5]Ibid., p. 63.

[6]Ibid., p. 64.

[7]Hellen Keller, *The Story of My Life* (New York: Doubleday & Co., 1954).

[8]Walker Percy, *The Message in the Bottle* (New York: Farrar, Straus and Giroux, 1975), p. 35.

[9]Frank E. X. Dance and Carl E. Larson, *Speech Communication: Concepts and Behavior* (New York: Holt, Rinehart and Winston, 1972), p. 35.

[10]Frank E. X. Dance and Carl E. Larson, *The Functions of Human Communication* (New York: Holt, Rinehart and Winston, 1976), p. 73.

[11]Ibid, p. 93.

[12]Brice Parain, *A Metaphysics of Language* (Garden City, NY: Doubleday & Co. 1971), p. 27.

[13]Lev Vygotsky, *Thought and Language* (New York: John Wiley & Sons, 1962), p. 43.

[14]Frank E. X. Dance, "Toward a Theory of Human Communication," in F. E. X. Dance, ed., *Human Communication Theory: Original Essays* (New York: Holt, Rinehart and Winston, 1967), p. 303.

[15]A.R. Luria, *The Mentally Retarded Child* (Oxford, England: Pergamon Press, 1963), p. 152.

[16]Dance and Larson, 1972, p. 85.

[17]Gerald R. Miller and Mark Steinberg, *Between People: A New Analysis of Interpersonal Communication* (Chicago: Science Research Associates, 1975), p. 22.

[18]Dean Barnlund, *Interpersonal Communication* (Boston: Houghton Mifflin Company, 1968), p. 159.

[19]Dance and Larson, 1972, p. 111.

[20]Dance and Larson, 1976, p. 195.

UNIT II

THE INTRAPERSONAL LEVEL OF SPEECH COMMUNICATION

In Unit I we focused our attention on basic concepts, the relationship of theory to practice, and a functional theory of speech communication. Using that functional theory as a guiding principle, we now turn our attention to the intrapersonal level of speech communication—to those communicative processes that take place within you, the individual communicator. An *awareness* of yourself as a communicator (as you will recall from Chapter 1) is the important first step in gaining further *understanding, recognizing* potential *alternatives* to your communicative behavior, and *choosing.*

The chapters in this unit discuss some of the ways speech communication functions to link us with ourselves and each other. *Chapter 3* is about that peculiarly human phenomenon of self-awareness through which we become not only participants but participant-observers in our own lives. It is designed to help you become more *aware* and to *understand* the role speech communication has had and is having in the shaping of your self-concept. Conversely, it is about the effects of your self-concept on your communication with yourself and others.

Chapter 4 discusses the power of words and their relationship to perception, the development of beliefs, attitudes, and values, and human behavior. Suggestions will be made that, if followed, can help you to *recognize* more effective *alternatives* in your use of language and to *choose* from among them.

3 SELF-AWARENESS

After studying this chapter you should be able to:

Discuss the process of self-reflexiveness and its importance to the regulation of human behavior

Explain the distinctions between "self" and "self-concept"

Give examples of ways in which self-concept can affect your communication with others

Describe the role of speech communication with others in the development and maintenance of self-concept

Distinguish between "self-image" and "self-esteem" and describe how these combine to affect speech communication

Give an example that demonstrates the interaction of role enactment, speech communication and self-concept

Explain the importance of self-awareness to the improvement of communication skills

One can no more look at his mind with his mind than see the pupils of his eyes with his eyes.

—*Hakuin*

Continually, we have been reminding you that this is a book about you, the reader. Our focus throughout is on the individual communicator as he or she interacts in a variety of contexts. But who *is* that individual communicator? *Who are you?*

Pause for a moment and answer the question, "Who are you?"

Did you begin with your name? Perhaps you answered with some of your roles: student, friend, lover, son, daughter. Maybe you thought about your home and your upbringing ("I grew up in a family of four in Larchmont, New York"). Is that who you are? How about some descriptive adjectives: sensitive, assertive, caring, fat, tall, sort-of-good-looking, poor, wealthy, interesting, depressed, boring, lazy, intelligent. Are you and the words you use to describe yourself the same? Are you who you *say* you are? Or is there a "real you" underneath all of those descriptions?

WHAT IS A SELF?

This is a question that has perplexed philosophers, theologians, psychologists, and other thinkers from time immemorial. Is there one great Universal Self of which we are all a part? Are we islands of consciousness in a cosmic ocean of mind? Is the self, as Karen Horney stated it, " . . . that central inner force, common to all human beings and yet unique in each, which is the deep source of growth"?[1] Perhaps the Buddhists are correct in believing that the whole idea of "self" is an illusion.

Whatever the "true" nature of the Self may be, we know that we are conscious of something that we refer to as "I" or "Me." "I" includes all of our past experiences, our thoughts, feelings, bodies, possessions—in short, everything about us as we view it from within ourselves.

I think about myself.
I talk about myself.
I am the thinker.
I am also the thought.
I am the speaker.
I am also the speech.

Self-reflexiveness

In Chapter 2 we discussed the ways in which speech communication functions to link us with the environment. We are inextricably connected with the world simply through the fact of our existence as conscious, responding organisms. But speech communication takes us a step further and brings that linkage into conceptual awareness. To put it another way, we are not only aware, but we are aware of our awareness; we are not only conscious, we are conscious of our consciousness. This is a human phenomenon known as *self-reflexiveness*. It is our unique ability to think about what we're doing as we're doing it, to think about what we're saying while we're saying it. We respond not only to the environment, but to ourselves responding in that environment. Stepping to the lectern, we have a sudden acute awareness of ourselves and the situation. In our minds we may comment to ourselves, "Well, here I am and there they are. I sure am nervous. Hope it goes all right." Walking into a party where we know only the host, we may experience a heightened consciousness of our own appearance and actions. These situations in which we feel self-conscious heighten our self-reflexiveness. We become much more aware than usual of our own awareness. But we are self-reflexive to varying degrees. We are always monitoring our own behavior and

making decisions based on our self-observations. The conceptual linkage with ourselves made possible through our use of symbols gives rise to a kind of duality within the self. We are both "I" and "Me," subject and object. We are participant/ observers in our own lives. The subjective self—"I"—is the active agent who lives and loves and acts and feels. The objective self—"Me"—is the object of our re-flections about our actions and feelings. Our evaluations of "Me" (self-as-object) then determine, in part, the further actions of "I" (self-as-subject).

Here we can see the interrelatedness of the functions of speech communi-cation as we described them in Chapter 2: Because we are linked conceptually with ourselves through speech communication (linking function), we can evalu-ate and make judgments about our own behavior (mentation function) and ad-just our behavior accordingly (regulatory function).

SELF-CONCEPT

When you answer the question, "Who are you?" your responses comprise a sym-bolic (verbal) representation of yourself. Taken together, *all of the things you can say about yourself that you believe to be true over time and across situations con-stitute your self-concept.* Self-concept, then, is a relatively consistent set of beliefs you have about yourself. It is a *theory* that serves to explain yourself to yourself, from which you make predictions and control your actions.

Who are you?
My name is Freddy.

Who are you?
I'm a student, a friend, a lover.

Who are you?
I'm a shy and sensitive person.

Who are you?
I'm an intelligent person.

Who are you?
I'm a person who avoids competition.

Who are you?
I'm OK looking, but that's all.

Who are you?
I seem boring because I'm shy, but I can be fun once you get to know me.

Who are you?
I'm a good listener. I care about others.

For our purposes, "self-concept" is a more useful concept than "self." The nature of the "true self" is a question for philosophers, theologians, and psychoanalysts to ponder. But we are interested in communication; it is through communication that the self-concept arises and it is communication that is affected by self-concept. As Brooks and Emmert put it so well, "It is *what* and *who* a person thinks he is that is crucially important to interpersonal communication. It is not so much *what he is,* but *what he thinks he is* that is disabling or enabling; he acts and behaves according to what he thinks he is."[2]

In the terms of the theory presented in Chapter 2, self-concept involves the *linking* function of speech communication at the *intrapersonal* level. Just as the linking function is the foundation for the other functions (mentation and regulation), self-concept provides the basis for your interactions with others at all levels of speech communication (interpersonal, small group, and public).

We, ourselves, and us

At this point, we have distinguished the notion of "self" from "self-concept." But who is the *real you?* A goal for many is to be able to "be myself" in all situations. We are admonished to "just be yourself." But in fact we are not one self, but many selves. As we pass through different situations, contexts, and relationships, different components of our self-concepts come to the fore. Think about it: Does your mother see the same "you" that your professor sees? Do you feel like the same person in the classroom and on the athletic field? Do you feel the same when you're talking with your best friend as you do while a police officer is writing you a speeding ticket? The self-concept is not a single entity but is composed of many components.

One of the earliest theorists to talk about the different facets of self-concept was William James.[3] James described three components of the self: the material self, the social self, and the spiritual self.

The material self

Do you like your body? Are you too tall, short, fat, thin? Are you shaped like an hourglass? Are you broad at the shoulders and narrow at the hips? Are you pear-shaped? Do you wish that your body weight were distributed differently? Do you exercise regularly? Why or why not? Do you take good care of your body? Do you abuse it? Your body is part of your material self and an important part of your self-concept.

How do you dress? Do you have a closet full of the latest fashions? Do you wish you did? Are you glad you don't? Are nice clothes important to you, or are you proud not to be shackled to the changing tides of the fashion world? How do you like to appear to others? "Trendy"? "Preppy"? "Laid back"? Clothes are certainly a reflection of our self-concepts. They are a part of the material self.

How about your home? Does the decor reflect your personality? Does it represent a life-style that fits you? Is it formal? Informal? Is it a comfortable place to be?

Do you drive a car? What kind? Are you proud of your car? Ashamed of it? Does it matter? Perhaps you ride a motorcycle or bicycle. Do you identify with these things? To what degree?

All of these things—your body, clothes, home, car—are part of your material self. They all reflect your self-concept in that they represent choices you have made based upon who you think you are. While many of the items listed here are "just things" and may not seem like a real part of you, they are all things that communicate to others about you. They are reflections of that part of you that assigns values to these things—the material self.

The social self

... a man has as many social selves as there are people who recognize him.

—William James

The quotation suggests that each of us possesses a multiplicity of social selves, and in fact we do. You will recall that interpersonal communication is a transactional process in which the behavior of each participant is contingent on the behavior of the other. Every person is a unique individual. Interpersonal communication (as we noted in Chapter 2) is aimed at discovering the uniqueness of the other person. Through the transactional process of interpersonal discovery a unique relationship is formed. Each relationship makes different demands upon us, to which we respond with different emphases on different components of our self-concepts.

Think of any two people you know. Imagine yourself interacting with each of them. Picture the way you look in each case. How much eye contact do you maintain? What is your posture like? How much distance is there between the two of you? What are your feelings with each person? What are you talking about? School? Your love life? Politics? Your innermost feelings?

If you chose your mother and your professor to compare, you probably found dramatic differences in all of the categories. But even if you chose two close friends, you probably discovered that your mental, physical, and verbal responses to each are at least slightly different. Each relationship gives a slightly (or dramatically) different definition to "who you are."

Ironically, with as many social selves as we have, it is through social interaction that our entire self-concept is built and maintained. We make our decisions about who we are based on our relationships with others. Returning for a moment to the material self, consider why it is that you dress the way you do. Is your appearance based solely on how you feel within yourself? Or do you have others in mind when you dress in the morning?

We'll continue our discussion of self-concept and interaction with others later in the chapter. For now, let it suffice to say that the social self is the multifaceted way in which we view ourselves in relationship to all the people with whom we interact.

The spiritual self

What is left if we strip away our material self and our social selves? Even without all of our material possessions and our relationships with others, we exist; we are conscious of our being. The spiritual self has two dimensions. On one hand it is the consciousness of our being-in-the-universe; it is our "essence," our awareness. As such, it is rather like the "true self" we discussed at the beginning of the chapter. On the other hand, this spiritual self is our attempt to understand this inner essence, whether we call it consciousness, spirit, or soul. Our religious feelings and beliefs, and other attempts to understand or explain the meaning and purpose of our lives on Earth, comprise the spiritual self.

It is interesting to observe how different aspects of the self vary in importance from person to person. For some, their religious faith is the predominant force in their lives and is central in guiding their behavior and interactions with others. For others, pursuit of material things is of primary concern. But for all, social interaction—communication with others—is the basis for the overall self-concept. It is through speech communication that the self-concept is built and maintained.

SPEECH COMMUNICATION AND SELF-CONCEPT

Speech communication empowers each of us to share in the development of our own self-concept, and the fulfillment of that self-concept.[4]

The quotation suggests that self-concept is not simply something we *have,* but something we *do.* Indeed the development of self-concept is a process in which we actively participate. While we are born with a set of potentialities imprinted in our genes, self-concept is not given, it is achieved.[5] In fact, we are born with no self-concept whatsoever. It is not until we begin to manipulate the world symbolically through speech communication, at about 2 years of age, that we have a sense of self at all.

Think back. What are your earliest memories? What is the youngest age at which you actually recall being "you"? For you to recall past events it is necessary for you to *displace*—to "step outside of yourself" and the present moment. You should recall from Chapter 2 that our ability to displace is contingent upon speech communication. We obviously do not carry around with us the past events themselves, but *symbolic representations* of those events. Thus we cannot usually recall events that predate the time at which we began to relate to the world symbolically. Most people can remember back to about the age of 3. A few will claim to have memories from even earlier, but some of these memories are questionable. One of your authors has rather vivid recollections of seeing only the tops of cars over the snow banks during the "Blizzard of '47" in New York City, at which time he was 1 year old. One of our colleagues claims to remember the face of his brother peeking through the bassinet fringe. In both of these cases, though, it is freely admitted (in fact, assumed) that these memories have their roots more in hearing stories told and retold at a young age than in recollections of the actual events.

The point here is that self-awareness begins as speech communication links us symbolically with the world, which includes ourselves:

At around the second year of life we begin to name things. We begin to manipulate word/symbols in order to get what we want. We speak. Our speech comes from us and yet we hear the sound of our own voice existing outside of ourselves. We experience our speech as both an internal and external phenomenon and the duality of our consciousness is born. We are both the subject and the object of our interactions with the world. From this point forward we deal not only with the world but with our symbolic representations of it. We can deal symbolically only with those things for which we have symbols. At first we interact with the world in large chunks; perhaps with those things and events which bring us pleasure and those which do not. Gradually we become more adept at symbolic manipulations. As we pass through our lives we accrue experience and progressively refine our symbolic constructs to more accurately represent the world.[6]

Speech communication is the chief mechanism constitutive of self-hood, language is the mark of man, . . . man is literally talked into self-hood.[7]

Try to imagine yourself without the ability to use words at all. It's difficult, but try. Look around you. All of the things you see—this book, your own hands, the curtains, the window—would be essentially meaningless. The world would be a phantasmagoria of undifferentiated sight, sound, color, and sensation. You would be a point of awareness, perceiving all of these things, but you would not be aware that you were aware. You would seem to be at the center of a small world. Nothing would exist for you outside of the perceptual moment.

What we are doing here is asking you to return to infancy, to a prelinguistic state. It is a world you once inhabited. But you didn't stay there, because in addition to being born into a world of sight and sound and sensation, you were born into a symbolic world. The people around you *talked.* They talked to you and near you and about the things around you. Perhaps they said "bottle," and soon you learned to associate "bottle" with a warm, pleasurable, liquid sensation. You probably didn't associate "bottle" with a class of containers that come in various shapes and sizes, but you learned to use the sound "bottle" (or, more likely, "ba-ba") to get what you wanted. Before long you discovered that words could be put together to get what you wanted ("mama . . . baba") and soon came the realization that words were not only a means to personal pleasure but that they represented other things! And you heard your own words and realized that they came from somewhere. They came from you, and yet you could hear them. In that moment, when your power of words was turned back on yourself, your self-concept was born.

Self-concept arises out of spoken symbolic interaction with the other symbol-using humans around us. We learn to speak simply through exposure to speech communication. No one has to teach us; we do it spontaneously. It is this ability to symbolize that enables us to decenter and to see ourselves as the object of our thoughts. It allows us to ask the question "Who am I?" While we may not ask ourselves this question overtly at the age of 2 (in fact, we don't), the development of self-concept over the entire span of our lifetimes is essentially a very lengthy response to this question. And just as self-concept arises through symbolic interaction with others, it is through interaction with others that it develops and is maintained.

Self-concept and interpersonal communication

At the beginning of the previous section, we suggested that self-concept is a process in which we are actively engaged, that it is something we *do,* something we *achieve.* When we ask ourselves who we are, we make decisions about who we are based on our interactions with others. Self-concept does not arise and develop in a vacuum. Just as it is impossible to see your own face without some reflective

surface, it is impossible to view the self without using the reflected appraisals of others. We decide who we are by interpreting the responses of others toward us.

The small child behaves, the parent responds, and the child catches a glimpse of how others see her. She stumbles in the grocery store and knocks down the toilet paper display and her mother shrieks, "You clumsy little monster! Look what you've done!" Her Aunt Bonnie calls her an "adorable child." Her mother and father hug her warmly and kiss her "Good night." These are all messages from which the child will build her self-concept. Some messages will be taken more seriously than others. Messages from those she is closest to will be taken most seriously. Messages that are repeated continually are the strongest. Her self-concept will evolve through a selection process from the myriad of messages about herself she receives from others. Herein lies the centrality of the social self: Who we are is defined and redefined through our interactions with others.

Self-concept: an ongoing process

Our self-concepts tend to be fairly consistent over time and across situations, at least at basic levels. If you think of yourself as basically shy, introverted, intelligent, and sensitive, this picture of yourself is not likely to change very much overnight. But in the right environment, even these basic beliefs about the self can change.

Every message we emit says something about our self-concept. The way we sit, dress, act, speak—the things we choose to talk about and with whom—whether we are assertive, shy, or tender in our presentation—all of these behaviors are reflections of our self-perceptions, which are based on all of our previous interactions. The feedback we receive from others in an interpersonal transaction is monitored continuously by us and checked against our self-perceptions. As we discussed in Chapter 1, feedback serves a corrective function. We use it to compare our message as intended to our message as received. If there is a discrepancy, we reformulate the message in an attempt to be understood.

Usually we encode messages that are consistent with our self-concept. If you see yourself as assertive, for example, you will communicate in an assertive and forthright manner. The feedback you receive, then, will be not only to the specific content of your verbal message, but also to your assertiveness. Thus, any interpersonal transaction provides information on how others perceive us.

Ralph   I love you, Alice.
Alice   Don't be so pushy.

Speech communication is an interpretive process. In an interpersonal transaction we are interpreting others' interpretations of our interpretations of ourselves. This convoluted process can be seen more clearly by examining this diagram, proposed by Kinch.[8]

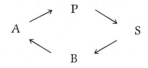

P = perception of others' responses toward self
S = self-concept
B = own behavior
A = actual responses of others toward self

Wilmot describes this cyclic process as follows:

One's self-concept influences his behavior, which of course impacts on the actual responses of the other participant. In turn, your perception of the other's responses develops your self-concept, *ad infinitum.* As Kinch states it, "The individual's concept of himself emerges from social interaction and, in turn, guides or influences the behavior of the individual."

   This is the process of interplay as sketched from the viewpoint of one participant. There are two participants engaged in the process, and as a result, a similar description should be provided for the second person. *Each person's view of himself affects his as well as his partner's behavior.* Stated another way, each self-concept influences and is influenced by the communicative transaction.[9]

Let's outline the process in yet another way:

➤ You are linked with yourself symbolically through speech communication.

➤ You possess a symbolic representation of yourself that is based on all of your previous experiences and interactions—your self-concept.

➤ In an interpersonal transaction you regulate your behavior according to the nature of your link with yourself (self-concept) and your link with the other person (how well you know him or her, his or her role, etc.).

➤ The other's responses to you (feedback) are compared with your responses to yourself. Others' responses to you will be either consistent or inconsistent with your self-concept.

➤ If responses are consistent with your self-concept, your self-concept has been reinforced. If responses are inconsistent with your self-concept, your self-concept has been called into question; the other does not see you as you see yourself.

➤ When there is inconsistency between how the other sees you and your self-concept, you may either:
   1. try to regulate the behavior of the other through attempts to alter his or her perceptions of you to be more congruous with your self-concept or
   2. try to regulate your own behavior by adjusting your self-concept to be more congruous with the feedback.

These two alternatives are very generally stated. Obviously there are many possible responses to feedback that do not reinforce your self-concept. But most of these responses would fall within either or a combination of these two. The primary exception would be the dysfunctional, neurotic resolution of restructuring your perceptions of reality to make them consistent with your self-concept.

   Self-concept, then, is an ongoing process of adaptation; we adapt ourselves to messages, and messages to ourselves. We regulate our communicative behavior—intrapersonally and interpersonally—according to our interactions with others. You probably say of some of the people you know that they "bring out the best in me." This is an example of interpersonal transaction eliciting and reinforcing certain aspects of your self-concept. We tend to seek out interpersonal relationships that confirm and reinforce our self-concepts. But interpersonal transactions, if they are persistent, can also dramatically change the self-concept, sometimes positively and sometimes negatively.

Self-concept: consistency and change

The self-concept remains relatively stable over time, because we tend to select those messages that reinforce it and to ignore those that don't. We will discuss the process of selective perception more fully in the next chapter, but for now consider this: *Most of us would rather be consistent than happy.* This may seem like a bizarre statement, but think about it for a moment. The self-concept is a very personal matter. To change the self-concept is to change your identity; it is to sacrifice what is familiar (and perceived as safe) and to move into the unknown. To take on a new identity is to give up an old one. For a new self-concept to emerge, the old one must die. This is perceived as very threatening to most people, even those whose self-concept is extremely negative and uncomfortable. Therefore, we tend to pay close attention to messages that reaffirm who it is we believe ourselves to be; and more often than not, we disregard messages that do not support our self-concepts.

At this moment, you probably know of someone who has such a low opinion of himself or herself that words of praise will "bounce off"; but a sharp criticism will be met with a cynical smile, a shrug of the shoulders, and "See? I told you so."

Self-concepts can and do change, though. On the negative side, a boy with a healthy opinion of himself in his early years frequently undergoes a negative shift in his self-concept when the other boys in the schoolyard discover that he is uncoordinated—that he consistently strikes out in baseball and can't control the ball in any sport. Receiving persistent messages that he is not wanted on the team, that he "stinks at sports" and "throws like a girl" will often effect a shift in his self-concept.

More positively, when the music teacher discovers in that same child a real gift for tuba playing, and critical acclaim and admiration begin to come his way, his self-concept may shift again toward the more positive side. In both cases, it is persistency of messages from others that can effect a change in the self-concept.

We can see that through interaction in different settings (the playground and the music room) the child's self-concept may be sometimes positive and sometimes negative. On the ball field, he probably feels insecure and somewhat worthless. In the music room he is happy and confident. This leads us to two important components of self-concept: self-image and self-esteem.

Self-image and self-esteem

Take a moment and picture yourself in the following situations. Relax and allow yourself to feel the way you'd feel in each.

- ➤ Delivering a public speech
- ➤ A job interview
- ➤ A cocktail party
- ➤ Driving a car

➤ A conference with the dean
➤ Taking an examination
➤ Introducing yourself to a stranger
➤ Participating in a group discussion
➤ An argument
➤ The athletic field

Self-image is your objective view of yourself as you relate your self-concept to various situations. Are you a good athlete? A musician? Are you a competent and capable student? What is your view of yourself as a communicator? Are you comfortable interacting with strangers? Are you a good speaker? Are you a natural leader? Or are you better at following others' leadership? Are you sociable or are you a "loner"?

Self-esteem is the degree to which we feel a sense of self-worth. Self-esteem varies from person to person and from situation to situation. Some persons have generally high self-esteem; they like themselves. Others have rather low self-esteem. No matter what your general level of self-esteem, it varies from situation to situation. We know many students who have a strong sense of their self-worth in the classroom and the professor's office. They are confident and aggressive in that situation. But on the athletic field, their confidence evaporates.

Self-image (how you view yourself in a situation) and self-esteem (the value you assign that view) combine to have a powerful effect on communication.

EFFECTS OF SELF-CONCEPT ON COMMUNICATION

It is through speech communication that self-concept arises, and it is through communication that it develops and is maintained. While self-concept is very clearly affected by communication, it also controls or regulates communication. Self-concept affects communication in essentially two ways: *self-fulfilling prophecy* and *selection of messages*.

Self-fulfilling prophecy

We have often noted in our teaching that one of the biggest obstacles to overcome in a public speaking class is the student's belief about the public speaking situation. We have known many a student who communicates dynamically and enthusiastically outside the classroom door only to enter, walk to the lectern, and deliver a hideously boring speech. What is operating here is an image of the self as "not a good speaker." To be consistent with that self-image, the student does not perform well at the lectern (remember . . . we would often prefer to be consistent than happy). This is self-fulfilling prophecy. The self-concept directs our behavior in ways that are consistent with that self-concept. Therefore, if you believe—even erroneously—that you are, for example, a poor communicator, "klutzy," but an excellent student, these beliefs tend to become true. We behave according to our beliefs about ourselves, and it is behavior to which others respond. Thus their feedback reinforces the behavior and the self-image that gen-erated it; our beliefs about ourselves literally become "who we are."

Selection of messages

We pointed out earlier that self-concept is not something that happens to us; it is something we *do.* The way in which we participate in the shaping of our own self-concepts is through *selection of messages*—both the messages we send and the messages we receive.

As *senders* of messages, we select those messages that are consistent with our self-concepts. *Intrapersonally* we engage in explaining and rationalizing our behavior to ourselves so that it will "make sense" within the context of our self-concepts. *Interpersonally* and at the other levels of speech communication, we communicate according to our view of ourselves. This phenomenon has been dis-cussed in several previous sections.

We are also actively engaged in message selection as *receivers* of messages. The selectivity we exhibit in an interpersonal transaction to maintain consistency has already been noted. On a broader level, the television shows we watch, the books we read, the magazines we buy are all indicative of this message-selection process. Those whose self-concepts do not include "intellectual" will probably not be found reading Goethe, Proust, or the *Atlantic Monthly.*

ROLES AND SELF-CONCEPT

It is always interesting, and sometimes mildly comic, to observe recent college graduates a few months after taking their first jobs. The changes in role defini-tion from "student" to "professional person" usually result in observable person-ality changes. Typically, returning former students seem more self-confident and assertive than when they left the university. Their new roles in life not only affect their workday behavior but also seem to spill over into their relationships with others and their self-concepts.

Role affects behavior, and behavior often shapes personality. We are what we have done and we shall become what we will do. Action shapes being.[10]

To a great extent you are what you do. What you do is a reflection of how you see yourself. Part of how you see yourself is how you define your *roles.* Each of us has many roles in life, beginning with "son" or "daughter." Roles, you should remember, have been defined as "patterns of expectations regarding the occu-pant of a position."[11] New roles which we take on—husband, wife, business-person, graduate student—bring with them new expectations for ourselves and new expectations of others for us. We tend to conform our behavior to these ex-pectations. Thus, if you believe that businesspersons are aggressive, and you become a businessperson, you are likely to begin to behave more aggressively in order to conform to your own expectations for that role. When you behave more aggressively as a function of your new role, people begin to respond to you as an "aggressive person." Their responses reinforce this new self-image. What began as "role playing" becomes a routine part of the self-concept.

We know a number of professors (and you probably do too) who simply cannot leave their professorial role behind in any situation; they are just as pedantic at a cocktail party as they are in the classroom. Roles and role expectations are powerful determinants of human behavior; and our behavior and others' responses to it are powerful determinants of self-concept.

SELF-AWARENESS

"... I ain't a good man," The Misfit said after a second as if he had considered her statement carefully, "but I ain't the worst in the world neither. My daddy said I was a different breed of dog from my brothers and sisters. 'You know,' Daddy said, 'it's some that can live their whole life out without asking about it and it's others has to know why it is, and this boy is one of the latters. He's going to be into everything!' "[12]

Recently, we heard a story about a man who had been tremendously successful in his professional life. He had made a lot of money at an early age and had put that money to work for him. As a result, by the time he was 40, he had accumulated great wealth, as well as power in the business community. He was admired and respected by all with whom he had contact. One evening at a cocktail party, a young admirer complimented him by saying, "Mr. ———, you must be so very intelligent to have been so successful at everything you do."

"No," he responded, "I'm not all that bright. *You don't have to be intelligent to be successful. All you have to do is pay attention.*"

We like this story (a true one, by the way) because it points to the importance of *awareness*. We know so many people who plod through their lives with a sense of resignation to the "fact" that they are who they are, the world is as it is, and there's nothing they can do about it. They are out of touch with a very real source of power they possess; and that source of power is *choice*.

The word that allows *yes,* the word that makes *no* possible.
The word that puts the free in freedom and takes the obligation out of love.
The word that throws a window open after the final door is closed.
The word upon which all adventure, all exhilaration, all meaning, all honor depends.
The word that fires evolution's motor of mud.

The word that the cocoon whispers to the caterpillar.
The word that molecules recite before bonding.
The word that separates that which is dead from that which is living.
The word no mirror can turn around.
In the beginning was the word and the word was
                              CHOICE[13]

CHOICE. A person's looking for a simple truth to live by, there it is. CHOICE. To refuse to passively accept what we've been handed by nature or society, but to choose for ourselves. CHOICE. That's the difference between emptiness and substance, between a life actually lived and a wimpy shadow cast on an office wall.[14]

To say that we are products of our environment would be only a small fraction of the truth, because much of our environment is our own creation! We do not deal directly with the world but with our symbolic representations—our *words*— for it. We live in a symbolic world, a world built up on the language habits of groups and individual human beings. Every individual holds a unique representation of that world and his or her place within it; and that representation is based upon individual interpretation and *choice.*

We hope that we have made it clear in this chapter that your self-concept is a function of your ability to use human speech communication; that it is your ability to symbolize—to interact with others, to reflect upon that interaction and yourself—that brings self-concept into being. We have stated continually throughout these first three chapters that speech communication is an *interpretive* process; it is a process of "making sense" out of the world. Interpretation involves *choice.*

Who you are, then, is who you have *chosen* to be. The problem is that we are often not *aware* of the choosing process. We choose automatically the most intense message, without reflecting on the alternatives. We select messages that are consistent with what we already believe and "tune out" those that are not. We hear and believe the third-grade teacher who tells us we aren't as smart as the others, while ignoring quiet Uncle Ben who tells us, "You can do it."

Self-awareness is a growing awareness of alternatives, of choice. It is a gradual shift from a sense of being controlled to one of being in control. It is an increasing awareness of the intentionality behind our own actions, our reasons for doing what we do. Speech communication gives us the power to reflect upon a situation and to choose our response. Self-awareness is an awareness of the one who's doing the choosing.

Wherever a process of life communicates an eagerness to him who lives it, there life becomes genuinely significant. Sometimes the eagerness is more knit up with the motor activities, sometimes with the perceptions, sometimes with the imagination, sometimes with reflective thought. But, wherever it is found, there is the zest, the tingle, the excitement of reality; and there *is* "importance" in the only real and positive sense in which importance ever anywhere can be.

—*William James*[15]

SELF-AWARENESS

PUTTING THEORY INTO PRACTICE

This chapter has focused on the role of speech communication in the development and maintenance of the self-concept. Self-concept is not something static that we simply *have,* it is something we *do,* something we *achieve.* Self-concept is inextricably entwined with our communicative behavior with ourselves and others. We behave according to our beliefs about ourselves. Through our interpretations of others' responses to us we develop and maintain our self-concepts.

If what we have said in this chapter is essentially true—and we are convinced that it is—then self-concept can change. If you are a person who is thoroughly satisfied with yourself and all aspects of your life in all situations, if you believe that you are as effective a communicator as you will ever be and there is no room for improvement, then read no more. If, on the other hand, there are some situations in which you would like to feel more comfortable and pleased with yourself (say, a job interview or a public speech, an interpersonal relationship or a group discussion), then self-awareness and understanding of the contexts of communication can help.

The one common denominator of all the situations in which you find yourself is *you.* Therefore it is important that you become more than a participant in your own life, that you become a participant-*observer.* Here are some observations and suggestions that may help you along the way:

- You will recall from Chapter 2 that speech communication functions to regulate behavior. Examine the situations in which you find yourself from day to day—the classroom, part-time jobs you may hold, parties, intimate relationships, and so forth. What are your beliefs about yourself in each of those situations? How are these beliefs reflected in your behavior? Are there beliefs and/or behaviors you would like to change? Try to identify the alternatives that are available to you.
- Analyze the messages you send to others—through dress, behavior, punctuality (or lack thereof), speaking style, choice of subjects, choice of friends, and so on. How do these behaviors relate to your self-image? Are there any inconsistencies?
- In any and all of the things you do from day to day, ask yourself why you're choosing to do them.

- Examine your beliefs about yourself, both positive and negative (for example, "I'm a good student" or "I'm not a very good conversationalist"). Explore the origins of these beliefs.
- The idea that self-concepts can change and that you can choose your behaviors is powerful and liberating. But a few words of caution are in order: Though change is possible, it is not easy. There are no shortcuts, and attempts to find them can be frustrating and bewildering. We have a friend who recently completed a series of sensitivity-training seminars after which she proclaimed that she was "liberated," that she "had learned to take responsibility for her life," and that from that point forward she was going to do "only those things that she chose for herself." She proceeded to put her newfound theory into practice by returning to her family and refusing to do any of her usual domestic chores that she felt had been oppressing her for many years. Needless to say, these new behaviors were most bewildering to her husband and children, who had not themselves attended the seminars. The result was a very negative experience for all concerned. Change does not take place overnight *intra*personally or *inter*personally. Our link with ourselves and each other is built over time and takes time to change.
- Observe yourself. Analyze your behaviors. Investigate alternatives. Experiment. And be patient with yourself. It's worth it.

SUGGESTED ACTIVITIES

1. Make a list of the various books and periodicals you read. What are the common elements found throughout this list? How do your choices of literature reflect your self-concept?
2. Ask yourself, "Who am I?" Write down a one-sentence response. Now ask the question again and write another one-sentence response. Continue the process until you have written twenty responses to the question. Review your twenty sentences. Now write three additional sentences beginning "I learned . . ."
3. In this chapter we discussed the importance of role expectations to our communicative behavior. For each of the following roles, write five adjectives that you associate with them. How do your role perceptions influence your behavior toward persons in those roles?

   Mother:
   Clergyman:
   Policeman:
   Professor:
   Friend:

   Try the same exercise with other roles of your choosing. Discuss the results of your exploration.

NOTES

[1]Karen Horney, *Neurosis and Human Growth* (New York: W. W. Norton & Co., 1950), p. 17.
[2]William D. Brooks and Philip Emmert, *Interpersonal Communication* (Dubuque, IA: William C. Brown Company, 1976), p. 41.

[3]William James, *Principles of Psychology*, Vol. I (New York: Henry Holt and Company, 1890).

[4]Frank E. X. Dance and Carl Larson, *The Functions of Human Communication* (New York: Holt, Rinehart and Winston, 1976), p. 141.

[5]Brooks and Emmert, p. 39.

[6]John T. Masterson, "Speech Communication: The Paradox of Consciousness," unpublished paper presented at the annual meeting of the Speech Communication Association, San Antonio, Texas, 1979.

[7]Paul F. Pfeutze, *Self, Society, Existence* (New York: Harper & Row, 1961), p. 302.

[8]John W. Kinch, "A Formalized Theory of the Self-Concept," in Jerome Manis and Bernard Meltzer, eds., *Symbolic Interaction*, 2nd ed. (Boston: Allyn and Bacon, 1972), pp. 245–252.

[9]William W. Wilmot, *Dyadic Communication: A Transactional Perspective* (Reading, MA: Addison-Wesley Publishing Co., 1975), p. 46.

[10]Frank E. X. Dance and Carl Larson, *Speech Communication: Concepts and Behavior* (New York: Holt, Rinehart and Winston, 1972), p. 111.

[11]Dean Barnlund, *Interpersonal Communication* (Boston: Houghton Mifflin Company, 1968), p. 159.

[12]Flannery O'Conner, "A Good Man Is Hard to Find," in *Three by Flannery O'Conner* (New York: Signet Books, 1953).

[13]Tom Robbins, *Still Life with Woodpecker* (New York: Bantam Books, 1980), p. 190.

[14]Ibid., p. 253.

[15]William James, "Blindness in Human Beings," in Edwin Van B. Knickerbocker, ed., *Present-Day Essays* (New York: Henry Holt and Company, 1923), p. 199.

4 PROCESSING INFORMATION: LANGUAGE AND PERCEPTION

After studying this chapter you should be able to:

Describe the process of intrapersonal communication and its components

Explain how beliefs-attitudes-values influence the intrapersonal communication process

Define "perception" and explain the four stages of the perception process

List and explain three sets of variables affecting the perception process

Describe four selective processes influencing the accuracy of our perceptions and some ways to overcome these barriers

Define "language" and two influences that language has on us

Identify and describe five barriers to effective language usage and several suggestions for overcoming these barriers

The trait that sets human mentality apart from every other is its preoccupation with symbols, with images and names that *mean* things, rather than with things themselves. ... (T)he human mind ... is like a great projector; for instead of merely mediating between an event in the outside world and a creature's responsive action, it transforms, or, if you will, distorts the event into an image to be looked at, retained, and contemplated. For the images of things that we remember are not exact and faithful transcriptions even of our actual sense impressions. They are made as much by what we think as by what we see.

—*Susanne K. Langer*[1]

Experience means *eundo assequi,* to obtain something along the way, to attain something by going on a way. What is it that the poet reaches? Not mere knowledge. He obtains entrance into the relation of word to thing. This relation is not, however, a connection between the thing that is on one side and the word that is on the other. The word itself is the relation which in each instance retains the thing within itself in such a manner that it "is" a thing.

—*Martin Heidegger[2]*

This is a chapter about the intrapersonal processes through which we make sense out of the world. They are processes that we often take for granted and accept without question. We assume that the world as we see it is simply the way it *is.* But *nothing could be farther from the truth.*

The perceptual processes through which we come to know ourselves and the world around us are so intricate and complex, with so many variables which influence our interpretations of our experience, that it is amazing that the perceptions of any two people coincide at all.

As we shall see in this chapter, *language* is the variable that makes human perception so different from that of any other species on earth. Otherwise, our perceptual processes are similar to those of an orangutan. Assuming no physiological dysfunction, we all have rather similar upper and lower limits on our five senses; we are capable of receiving sensory stimuli (sound, light, odors, pressure, tastes) within a similar range. We do not perceive stimuli that fall above or below this range (ultraviolet light, for example). But in the human organism language intervenes to reshape and redefine our perceptions.

To a great extent we are the creators of our own perceptions. We do not simply react to environmental stimuli. Because we are linked symbolically with the environment through speech communication, we assign *meaning* to those stimuli and respond to the meaning *we assign*.

There is great virtue in the figure of speech, "I can make nothing of it," to express a failure to understand something. Thought and memory are processes of *making* the thought content and the memory image; the pattern of our ideas is given by the symbols through which we express them. And in the course of manipulating those symbols we inevitably distort the original experience, as we abstract certain features of it, embroider and reinforce those features with other ideas, until the conception we project on the screen of memory is quite different from anything in our real history.[3]

A familiar example of this process takes place with regularity in a court of law. Witnesses to the same event frequently provide drastically different accounts of what they saw, each testifying under oath, and each believing in the verity of his or her statements.

As we pointed out in Chapter 2, even the simple experience of seeing a tree outside a window can result in dramatically different perceptions among a group of people. To one the tree represents cork, cambium, phloem, xylum; to another it is a poetic image; and so forth. In this chapter we will look at various components of the perceptual process and the interrelationships among them in an effort to help you understand the marvelous intricacy of human perception as it relates to human communication.

THE BARKER MODEL OF INTRAPERSONAL COMMUNICATION

Human perception is a communicative process. We do not perceive the world directly through our senses; rather, we enter into a dialogue with the world through our symbolic representations of it. All of this occurs at the *intrapersonal* level of speech communication. An excellent model of intrapersonal communication has been provided by Larry Barker[4]—see Figure 4.

Stimuli

Perceptions begin with sensory data, and stimuli comprise those data. Stimuli may be either *internal* or *external*. Your stomach's gurgling and growling would be an example of an internal stimulus to which you might assign meaning ("I'm hungry"). External stimuli originate outside of your body. They are the "raw

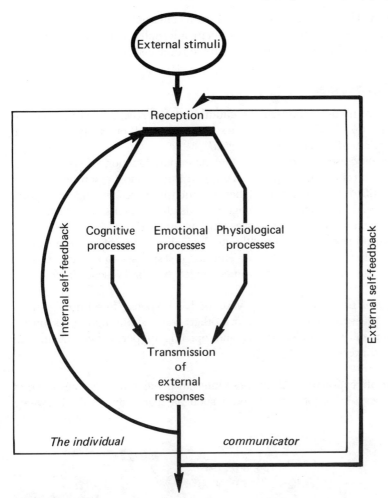

FIGURE 4 The Barker model of intrapersonal communication. (From Larry L. Barker, *Communication*, 2nd ed., ©1981, p. 33. Reprinted by permission of Prentice-Hall, Inc., Englewood Cliffs, N.J.)

data" from which we make sense of the world around us. Starting at the top of Barker's model we can see these "raw data," these external stimuli, as they strike our receptor organs (eyes, ears, etc.).

Reception

As we suggested earlier, perception is limited in part by the physiological capacity of our receptor organs and nervous system. For example, unlike the bird, which can look at the world holistically, seeing everything in its field of vision simultaneously, we can only focus on one thing at a time. Likewise our ability to hear is more limited than that of the dog, which can hear much higher frequencies than we can. Thus, many of the stimuli in the environment are screened out even before we have a chance to process them internally. Our receptor organs serve as "physiological filters" through which we receive stimuli.

Perceptual processes

Once stimuli have made it through the gauntlet of our receptor organs, our internal processes take over. Barker divides these internal processes into three areas: *cognitive, emotional,* and *physiological.*

Cognitive processes are related to the mentation function of speech communication we described in Chapter 2. To quote Dance and Larson once again, "Activities identified by the term 'higher mental processes' include memory, planning or foresight, intelligence or cognitive insight, thinking, judgment, and speech communication and its derivatives reading and writing."[5]

Emotional processes constitute "the nonlogical response of an organism to a stimulus."[6] Various factors affect your emotional responses to stimuli. Among these are your beliefs, attitudes, and values, which we shall discuss later in the chapter.

Physiological processes make up your body's response to stimuli, usually experienced as pleasure or pain. There are other, more subtle bodily responses, such as dilation of the pupils, closing and opening of pores, perspiring, and changes in blood pressure.

Transmission of responses All of these internal perceptual processes interact with one another. An emotional response such as fear may result in sweaty

palms and a rise in blood pressure. We may respond to these symptoms rationally and try to calm ourselves. *Internal self-feedback* is our response to our own internal responses. All of these perceptual processes combine to shape perceptions and *external responses* (messages) of the person to the environment.

External self-feedback is your own reception of the messages you send. When you speak, you hear the sound of your own voice, thus beginning the whole process all over again.

By now you should be beginning to understand the complexity of human perception. Human perception is an *interpretive* process. You may recall from the previous chapter that we tend to "filter out" messages about ourselves which are inconsistent with our self-concepts. This statement can be generalized to all forms of perception: We are most likely to notice and respond to those features of the environment which conform to what we *already believe to be true*.

BELIEFS, ATTITUDES, AND VALUES

Whatever one believes to be true, either is true or becomes true in one's mind within limits to be determined experimentally and experientially. These limits are beliefs to be transcended.

—John Lilly [7]

Your beliefs, attitudes, and values are primary determinants of your perceptions and your behavior. Whatever you believe to be true is true *for you* simply by virtue of the fact that you believe it to be so. We act on the basis of our beliefs, attitudes, and values.

Beliefs

A belief is whatever you accept as being true. Our beliefs structure our perceptions and our actions. The presence or absence of a strong belief in God, for example, will shape our experience of the death of a loved one. To one person the loss will be seen as "God's will." To another it will be seen as a tragic and senseless loss. Likewise a belief about types of people (stereotypes)—"nerds," for example—will affect our perceptions of individuals who fit the descriptions associated with that stereotype. This kind of belief, of course, hinders our ability to see people as they really are. We'll pursue this point further later on in the chapter.

Attitudes

Attitudes have to do with what we like and don't like. They are learned tendencies to respond positively or negatively. In some cases our attitudes are derived from our experience. Perhaps all it took was one anchovy for you to learn that you don't like them on your pizza. Other attitudes are based on beliefs. Our political beliefs, for example, can affect our attitudes toward those who do not hold the same beliefs.

Values

Values are judgments we make about the relative importance of things. Our values reflect a hierarchy of beliefs—an arrangement of our beliefs from most important to least. When we are confronted by a situation over which we have conflicting beliefs, our values help us to decide how to behave. A powerful contemporary example of this kind of situation is provided by recent court cases involving individuals who have "helped" a suffering patient to end his or her life. In these cases the defendants had decided that the positive value of ending suffering outweighed the negative value associated with ending a life.

As you can see, beliefs, attitudes, and values do not operate independently. They are interrelated and function together as a *system,* which from this point forward we shall refer to as the *B-A-V System.* Your B-A-V System—what you believe is important in life—is a primary determinant of your perceptions and your behavior.

Thus far in the chapter we have been discussing various intrapersonal processes that influence perception. But specifically what is perception? And how do language and perception interact? These questions provide the focus for the remainder of the chapter.

WHAT IS PERCEPTION?

How do we gather material from which intrapersonal and other levels of speech communication evolve? How do we know what to talk about, and whether what we talk about is worth talking about? How do we organize and use this material so that we can talk about it? The answer to these questions is "perception."

Perception: The complex process by which people select, organize, and interpret sensory stimulation into a meaningful picture of the world.[8]

As we pointed out in the previous section, "sensory stimulation" can originate from either an external or an internal source. When such stimulation occurs, the incoming sensations are transformed into electrochemical impulses and transmitted to that gray piece of meat between our ears commonly known as "the brain." Here, through some processes not yet well understood, we organize and interpret those stimuli in an attempt to categorize, interpret, and store such information as we believe is or will be useful in making sense out of our world. This process is sometimes conscious and sometimes subconscious, sometimes rapid and sometimes relatively slow. However it happens, it happens. Physiologically, cognitively, and emotionally, it happens.

Physiologically, it happens through the vehicles of our five senses: sight, hearing, touch, smell, and taste. Cognitively, it happens as we select, sort, store, and retrieve the stimuli as sensed. And emotionally, we react in various ways depending upon our beliefs, attitudes, values, mood, and personality. Although we cannot yet explain *how* this all happens, we are sure it *does* happen.

Because this process depends so strongly on us as *unique* human beings, we feel justified in speaking of perception as a "creative act":

> Each percept (that which is perceived), from the simplest to the most complex, is the product of a creative act. . . . We can never encounter a stimulus before some meaning has been assigned to it by some perceiver. . . . Therefore, each perception is the beneficiary of all previous perceptions; in turn, each new perception leaves its mark on the common pool. A percept is thus a link between the past which gives it its meaning and the future which it helps to interpret.[9]

On the basis of a variety of influences (to be discussed in the next section), we *create* meanings for our percepts. Our past experiences with identical or similar percepts allow us to organize and interpret (assign meaning to) each new percept. This, in like fashion, allows us to organize and interpret future percepts. Since each one of us is a unique individual with unique experiences and a unique system of beliefs, attitudes, and values, each of us organizes and interprets (perceives) objects, events, and people in a different way. That's why "beauty is in the eye of the beholder."

We have chosen a definition of perception which indicates that it is a "complex process." If perception is a process, it must have several stages. In fact, we say that there are four: stimulation, selection, organization, and interpretation. *Stimulation*—the first stage—occurs continually. We are bombarded by stimuli through our five senses nearly twenty-four hours a day. (The exceptions, of course, being "womb rooms" or sensory deprivation chambers or tanks as seen in the movie *Altered States.*) If we were to attempt to organize and interpret each of these billions of stimuli, our efficient but not omnipotent brains would soon overload and probably short circuit. To prevent this information overload, we consciously and subconsciously make *selections* from among the stimuli available to us. Look out a window. What do you see? People? *All* the people, or just *certain* people? All buildings, all the windows, all the doors? Probably not. Why not? Because if you were to attempt to organize and interpret (perceive) all the people, buildings, windows, doors, objects, and events that are available to you right now, out that window, information overload would strike. To prevent this from happening, we psychologically select from among available stimuli those which are most intense, useful, or important to us at any one time.

The creative aspect of the perception process intensifies during the third stage—*organization*. We relate those stimuli selected to our previous experiences and stored information. Some experiences and information are related, some are not. If they are related to these new stimuli, in what relation are they? How will these new pieces of information be integrated into our "common pool" of percepts? Exactly how this organization process occurs, no one is really sure. Once this organizational stage has taken place, in any event, we assign meaning to the new stimuli. This is the *interpretation* stage. We have, at this point, been *stimulated* by a multitude of sights, sounds, tastes, smells, and tactile stimuli, we have *selected* from among these various stimuli, and we have *organized* these percepts within our framework of beliefs, attitudes, and values, on the basis of our past experiences. Now we attempt to make sense out of that part of our world which we have received, selected, and organized. We attempt to assign some meaning to what we are currently experiencing. Let's take an example through these four stages to see what typically happens during the process of perception.

Imagine that you've finally come to that time of the week you reserve for the luxury of watching your favorite television program. It's 8:15 P.M. on a Wednesday night and—oops! Time for a commercial. You watch the 30-second spot for "Doctor Dirty" laundry detergent and convince yourself that you will never buy that product. Why? Although there is plenty to do during a commercial break other than watch the commercials, you've just finished adjusting the color on your set and want to make sure it's right. The focus of your *stimulation* at this point is the color on the set. The actress on the commercial is the typical commercial homemaker-type, and the music is nice. But that name—"Doctor Dirty." What a strange name for a laundry detergent! You have *selected* from among the stimuli produced in the commercial that stimulus which is most important to you. Then you attempt to organize the name of the product in terms of your past experiences with dirty things. Dirty apartment, dirty feet, dirty clothes, dirty anything. Well, does the detergent look dirty? Does it make your clothes dirty? Does it smell dirty? Probably not, but your *interpretation* of a laundry product with the name "Doctor Dirty" is that it doesn't sound as though it's anything that you'd want to do to your clothes. Just the thought of putting your best shirt in the washing machine with "Doctor Dirty" has resulted in an interpretation of that product as being disgusting. The marketing department for "Doctor Dirty" had better reconsider the meaning you've assigned for that product, along with thousands of other potential customers.

Now we know that perception is a complex process made up of four stages—stimulation, selection, organization, and interpretation. It is a creative act during which we attempt to relate new information to our own past experience and to assign some meaning to (interpret) those new stimuli. In the next section we will examine some physiological, contextual, and psychological influences on the perception process, as well as some limitations on perceptual accuracy.

WHAT INDIVIDUAL AND SITUATIONAL VARIABLES INFLUENCE THE PERCEPTION PROCESS?

In the television commercial example in the previous section, we suggested several influences on the perceptual process which seemed to be working in that situation—concern for the color adjustment on your set, the name "Doctor

Dirty," your past experiences with dirty things, your best shirt, and your negative reaction to the name and the product itself. The focus of this section is on these and similar variables which influence the process of perception. These variables may be categorized in terms of physiological, contextual, and psychological influences.

Physiological influences

Have you ever missed a route sign because you forgot to wear your glasses while driving? Have you ever missed an important part of a conversation because you had your "good" ear turned away? Or have you ever failed to smell that delightful odor emitted by a beautiful rose because you had a head cold? If you have ever experienced these or similar problems, you have some idea how physiological factors influence perception. If one or more of our *senses* are impaired, our perceptual process will be influenced in some way.

Our perceptual processes are also influenced by the *intensity and duration of competing stimuli.* You may have difficulty concentrating on and perceiving what you are now reading because of a neighbor's loud stereo or your roommate's lengthy telephone conversation with a friend. Initially you may be able to ignore your roommate's telephone conversation. But after a time, you may need to move to a different room or request that your roommate end the conversation, especially when a roar of tumultuous laughter breaks your train of thought for the tenth time. You may think that you've been stimulated and have selected, organized, and interpreted the last few pages effectively, but the intensity and/or duration of competing stimuli may have prevented you from gaining anything useful. Or have you ever found it impossible to watch the road at night when an oncoming motorist refuses to dim bright headlights? It's a great relief when that car passes you and you can again concentrate on your own side of the road. How intense competing stimuli are and how long they endure will influence how effectively you are stimulated by and select from the objects or events that you wish to perceive.

Contextual influences

Perception does not occur in a vacuum. There are virtually billions of competing stimuli in any situation. The nature and intensity of these competing stimuli, the setting in which we find ourselves, and the environmental conditions surrounding us at the time of perception all influence our selection, organization, and interpretation of those stimuli. For example, think of yourself lost in a forest, surrounded by tall pines. Dusk is approaching and the forest is very quiet. You begin to worry about finding your way out. There doesn't seem to be anything or anyone around but the trees and you. Survival is your primary concern. Suddenly you perceive movement in the tree twenty-five yards ahead. It startles you and you dive behind a tree. Upon closer examination, you note that the movement you have just perceived was a squirrel jumping from one tree limb to another. You pick yourself up and laugh at your insecurity. In this setting, under these uncertain circumstances, your reaction is not so surprising.

Compare this perceptual event and your reaction to the identical event—a squirrel jumping from tree to tree—in a different environment under much different circumstances. If you were walking through a city park surrounded by people, with cars buzzing by on every perimeter, your reaction to this event would probably not be the same as it was in the deep, dark forest. Setting and environmental conditions in these two situations are very different and dramatically change your perception of and reaction to the same event. In the park, you may not even see the squirrel.

You probably wouldn't interpret a student with eyes closed in front of a television set in the same way you would the same student with eyes closed in the back row of a classroom. Similarly, you might not even be aware of nor select from among various stimuli a conversation about you at a noisy cocktail party. If the conversation were taking place at the other end of a table in a small, quiet study room in the library, your ears would probably perk up and the focus of your attention would probably be that conversation. The setting and environmental conditions surrounding us as we attempt to select, organize, and interpret our world definitely do influence our perceptual processes.

Psychological influences

Our moods, internal distractions, needs, expectations, and B-A-V systems all influence our perceptions. These psychological factors influence *what* we perceive, *how* we organize and interpret stimuli, and *how we react* to those perceptions. It's difficult to concentrate on reading an economics book when you're anxious about a speech you have to give the next day. You might find that your *expectations* concerning tonight's date with that gorgeous person are *distracting* you from effectively perceiving a classroom lecture. Your lack of sleep and resulting grouchy *mood* may distort your perception of a facetious comment about your new haircut. This distortion may turn a well-intentioned joke into an argument. And your *need* to get a personal problem off your chest may turn that perfect stranger sitting next to you on the airplane into the most willing and sympathetic listener you know. Although this may not really be the case, your perceptions of that person may influence you to disclose information that, under ordinary circumstances, you would only tell to your best friend.

Our B-A-V systems, in conjunction with the physiological, contextual, and psychological factors discussed above, strongly influence four aspects of the perception process: what stimuli we expose ourselves to, what stimuli we pay attention to, how we organize and interpret stimuli, and which stimuli we are able to remember. These factors combine to form what are commonly known as four *selective processes:* selective *exposure,* selective *attention,* selective *perception,* and selective *retention.*

Selective exposure is the process of seeking out information which is consistent with our own needs, opinions, and values. We listen to or read material which throws a positive light on the political party we favor. We usually attend lectures or meetings during which ideas or information that we agree with will be discussed. We listen to our favorite newscaster or read our favorite newspaper or news magazine because we know that the approach toward the news taken in these media parallels the approach that we would take. In other words, the choices that we make concerning which stimuli we choose to expose ourselves to (if we have a choice) are largely determined by our beliefs, attitudes, and values, and by our preconceived notions of which stimuli will reinforce our personal perspectives.

We tune in certain stimuli and tune out others. On the basis of our needs, interests, and expectations, we attend to selected messages or part of messages and let the remainder "go in one ear and out the other." When attending a class, we pay little attention to certain segments of a lecture or a discussion when we feel that the information is useless, we already know the information, or we have no interest in the subject matter. Although we may use the radio as background music, we pay close attention when our favorite song is played or when the football scores are given. Thus, we *selectively attend* to stimuli we feel are important, interesting, or satisfying.

The third selective process is that of *selective perception*. We organize and interpret stimuli according to the beliefs, attitudes, and values that we have developed prior to the reception of the stimuli. Our feelings that all history classes are boring usually result in our finding the required history course boring. (This realization of expectations is known as the "self-fulfilling prophecy.") While listening to a presentation by a speaker with whom we do not agree, we will most likely perceive the speaker as dishonest, uninformed, and ineffective. The application of labels to people often results in distortions in perception. One of the authors has encountered distorted perceptions of people labeled "mentally retarded." He has observed individuals interacting with people so labeled exhibiting such inappropriate behaviors as baby talk, speaking more loudly than most people could tolerate, and calling a 35-year-old man a "kid." In these cases, it was the "normal" people's distorted expectations and perceptions of individuals labeled "mentally retarded" which caused them to act in these inappropriate ways. It was selective perception which limited and stereotyped these people in a way that influenced their interactions with them.

The final selective process—*selective retention*—results in our remembering only a part of that which we perceive. We tend to remember the good or reinforcing stimuli and forget the bad or opposing stimuli. You would probably remember more accurately those arguments favoring your point of view on draft registration than opposing arguments. The reason for the existence of this selective process is not well defined, but it is probably related to the idea of preserving our self-concept by seeking out and retaining information which reinforces an integral segment of our self—our B-A-V system.

As we have seen, these physiological, contextual, and psychological influences on the perception process often result in inaccuracies of perception. How we perceive our world determines how we talk about it. If we perceive the world inaccurately, we stand the chance of thinking and communicating about that world inaccurately. No two people perceive the world in exactly the same way.

But many potential communication problems might be eliminated if inaccuracies in perception could be resolved.

HOW CAN WE INCREASE OUR ACCURACY OF PERCEPTION?

We can increase our accuracy of perception first by checking our perceptions through *repeated observations.* Just as no two people perceive the same person or event in the same way, few of us perceive the same event or person in exactly the same way at different times. Compare your own observations with one another. New information is usually gained to aid in the organization, interpretation, and reaction to incoming stimuli each time you observe them. *Check your perceptions with others'.* Because no two people perceive the world in exactly the same way, gather as much information as possible by checking with others. This can only serve to benefit you as you attempt to make more sense out of your world. Thirdly, be *open-minded.* Resist preconceived expectations and biases. Because our B-A-V systems are, of necessity, based on limited knowledge and experiences, we need to be receptive to a wide variety of ideas, opinions, and information. This variety will increase our accuracy of perception and widen our field of experience.

Finally, when meeting and communicating with people, *treat each as a unique individual,* just as you wish to be treated. Don't give in to prejudices and preconceived expectations associated with labels and stereotypes. Gather as much information as possible, through repeated observations and by checking with others. Be open and receptive to all this information, and then make your own judgments from an informed and objective perspective. Increased accuracy of perception will lead to increased effectiveness in communicating with and about that part of our world we call "people."

PERCEPTION AND COMMUNICATION

Of what utility is all this stimulation, selection, organization, and interpretation? What can we do with it? Does making sense of information about the world sit idly in our heads? Hardly. We use it to communicate with and about others. Making sense of our world allows us to make sense when communicating with others at the interpersonal, group, and public levels of speech communication. Perception serves all three functions of speech communication. We link with others; we develop higher mental processes; we regulate the behavior of ourself and of others. We do none of these without speech communication at the intrapersonal level. We have no intrapersonal communication without some materials with which to develop it. The perception process provides the material from which intrapersonal communication is established. Perception plays a vital role in the speech communication process. In the next section we will examine the vehicle through which this speech communication process is mediated. That vehicle is language.

WHAT IS LANGUAGE?

Human language: A system of vocal-auditory communication, interacting with the experiences of its users, employing conventional signs composed of arbitrary patterned sound units and assembled according to set rules.[10]

The ability to use language means the ability to transfer something of experience into symbols and *through the symbolic medium to share experience.*[11]

Language, then, is just what we said it was at the end of the previous section—the vehicle through which we share our sense of the world. It is a medium, the users of which decide by convention or collective agreement to assign certain meanings to unique combinations of sounds. Language users determine, in addition, the sets of rules by which these sounds will be combined. These combinations of sounds and their associated conventional meanings are symbols. We use these symbols to share our experiences and our sense of the world. Sounds simple, doesn't it?

Language isn't simple—it's very complex. We have already seen how complex we language users are intrapersonally. We have also seen how complex is the perception process—the process through which we gather information and make sense out of our world. The use of language is no less complex.

Language usage is doubly complex in that we not only use language to share *our* world definition with *others,* but also to have *others* share theirs with *us.* We must attempt to perceive secondhand experiences of others accurately. To add to this complexity, others' use of language affects us. As we communicate with others, we gain more information about our world. This information, in turn, changes our sense of the world. Not only does the content of a message affect us, the message tells us something about the other person, about the other person's use of language, and about the other person's sense of her or his world.

Take, for example, the simple (?) phrase "I love you." Assuming that you barely know the person who says this to you on your first date, what does this do to your sense of the world? You know, for one thing, that you are a desirable person. But do you really know this? What were the other person's motivations for saying this on the first date? A mere compliment? An attempt at initiating a sexual encounter? Standard first-date procedure for this person? Is your sense of the world coming apart at its seams? Is "love" becoming a term for the question "Can I see you again?" without your being aware of this change in language usage as you know it? Indeed, language and its use are not simple matters. Let's examine this complex process in more detail.

THE POWER OF WORDS

In this chapter we have been talking about how language affects us. We respond to our world by talking about what we see. Recall our definition of speech communication as a human process through which we make sense out of the world and share that sense with others. It is important to realize just how powerful words are. About forty years ago Alfred Korzybski wrote a book called *Science and Sanity* in which he argued that the words we use (and misuse) have a major effect on our behavior.[12] From Korzybski's writing an area of study known as *general semantics* was developed. *General semantics is the study of how language affects our attitudes and behavior.* A general semanticist believes that our inappropriate use of words creates major problems for us, a result of the tremendous power that words have to affect our attitudes and behavior. In this section we will base our discussion primarily upon the teachings of general semantics. First, we will note how words have the power to create and affect attitudes and behavior. Second, we will identify word barriers that hinder the communication process. And finally, we will identify some suggestions for overcoming word barriers.

In 1967 Joe McGinnis was hired by Richard Nixon's campaign committee to help elect Nixon President of the United States. What Nixon's campaign committee did not know was that McGinnis was writing a book called *The Selling of the President 1968,* in which he described some of the behind-the-scenes problems with Nixon's quest for the Presidency. The following excerpt from McGinnis' book provides a good example of how words or, in this case, one word, can affect attitudes and behavior. The passage describes a problem with one of Nixon's TV commercials that included a shot of a soldier with the word "Love" written on his helmet.

> Another problem arose in the Midwest: annoyance over the word "Love" written on the soldier's helmet. "It reminds them of hippies," Harry Treleaven said. "We've gotten several calls already from congressmen complaining. They don't think it's the sort of thing soldiers should be writing on their helmets." Len Garment ordered the picture taken out of the commercial, Gene Jones inserted another at the end; this time a soldier whose helmet was plain. This was the first big case of "political" guidance, and for a full week the more sensitive members of the Gene Jones staff mourned the loss of their picture. "It was such a beautiful touch," one of them said. "And we thought, what an interesting young man it must be who would write 'Love' on his helmet even as he went into combat." Then E.S.J. Productions received a letter from the mother of the soldier. She told what a thrill it had been to see her son's picture in one of Mr. Nixon's commercials, and she asked if there were some way that she might obtain a copy of the photograph. The letter was signed: Mrs. William Love.[13]

This example illustrates how a word can lead to a misunderstanding of meaning. Words have the power to communicate beautiful images and great truths. Words can also create confusion and miscommunication. Specifically, words have the power both to create images and to affect our attitudes and behavior. Let's take a closer look at how words can affect us.

Words have power to create

A French philosopher, Georges Gusdorff, in talking about the power of words said, "To name is to call into existence—to call out of nothingness."[14] In essence, he was saying that words give us the power to create our world. When something is given a name, it is created for us. For example, we credit Sir Isaac Newton with discovering gravity. Of course we know that he did not invent it: he named it. But in a sense, he "created" it by giving the phenomenon we know as gravity a name.

You probably don't remember when you were 2 years old. But it was at this point in your life that you were learning how to talk—how to label your world. Gusdorff would say that you were calling things into existence by giving people, objects, and places a name. Captain Kangaroo was probably around before you were born, but once your parents turned on the TV, pointed to the screen, and said, "That's Captain Kangaroo," this individual with a bunny rabbit and a moose for friends came into existence for you. And since you had a word to describe him, you could call him into existence at will just by saying the words "Captain Kangaroo." Words, then, help create our world by giving us the ability to call what we see and experience into existence.

Words have power to affect attitudes and behavior

You're hungry. You have a couple of hours before your night class, so you decide to stop by a highly praised restaurant for a bite to eat. You're seated by the hostess and handed a menu. You have your heart set on a thick, juicy steak. But to your consternation, when you look at the menu you see that the restaurant does not serve steak. Instead, they serve horse meat. You decide you're not that hungry and leave.

One theory as to why horse meat has never caught on is that we have no other word for it. We don't say that we are going to eat cow meat or pig meat. We say, instead, we are going to have steak, roast beef, or pork chops. "Horse meat" just doesn't sound good, even though those who have tried it have found it quite tasty. The words we use to label our world do have a clear impact upon our attitudes (likes and dislikes) toward what we label.

In the late 1960s a sociology professor who lived in Los Angeles decided to conduct an experiment to test the assumption that words have the power to affect behavior.[15] He selected two groups of students to participate in his research. In order to participate in the study, students had to have a car, have good driving records, and drive approximately the same distance each week as other students in the study. One group of students were told to drive normally and go about their business as they usually did. The other group of students were given large orange and black bumper stickers which had the words "Black Panthers" in large letters on them. This second group of students were also told to go about their business as they normally would, the only difference being the large bumper sticker on the rear of the car.

It didn't take many days for the results of the study to become clear. Those students who had the "Black Panthers" bumper stickers were being issued traffic tickets at an alarming rate. At the end of the study, seventeen days later, this group of fifteen students with good driving records had received thirty-three traffic citations! The point the researcher wanted to make was this: words affect behavior. In this case, the words "Black Panthers" affected the behavior of traffic cops. The children's verse "Sticks and stones can break my bones, but words can never hurt me" was not supported by this study. *Words* can harm you. Language does affect behavior.

WORD BARRIERS

Clearly, words have the power to create images and affect our attitudes and behavior. And it is precisely because of this power that words can become a barrier to effective and accurate communication. The following example nicely illustrates how a word, or in this case an abbreviation for a word, can be a barrier to communication accuracy.

> An English lady, while visiting Switzerland, was looking for a room. She asked the school master if he could recommend any. He took her to see several rooms. When everything was arranged, the lady returned to her home to make final preparations for the move. When she arrived home, she suddenly realized that she had not seen a water closet (a toilet). She immediately wrote a note to the school master asking him if there was a "W.C." around the place. The school master was a poor master of English so he asked the parish priest if he could help out in this matter. Together they tried to discover the meaning of the letters "W.C." The only solution they could come up with was a "Wayside Chapel." The school master wrote the following letter to the lady.

> Dear Madam:

>   I take great pleasure in informing you that a "W.C." is situated nine miles from your house, in the center of a beautiful grove of pine trees, surrounded by lovely grounds.

>   It is capable of holding twenty-two persons and is open on Sundays and Thursdays only. As there are a great number of people expected during the summer months, I would advise you to come early. Although there is usually plenty of standing room, this is an unfortunate situation, particularly if you are in the habit of going regularly.

>   You will no doubt be glad to hear that a great number of people bring their

lunch and make a day of it, while others, who can afford to, go late and arrive just in time. I would especially advise your ladyship to go on Thursday when there is an organ accompaniment. The acoustics are excellent, and often the most delicate sounds can be heard everywhere.

It may interest you to know that my daughter was married in the "W.C." It was there she met her husband. I can remember the rush there was for seats. There were ten people to seats usually occupied by one. It was wonderful to see the expressions on their faces.

The newest attraction is the bell donated by a wealthy resident of the district. It rings every time a person enters. A bazaar is to be held to provide the plush seats for all, since the people believe it is a long-felt need.

My wife is rather delicate so she could not attend regularly. It is almost a year since she last went. Naturally, it pains her very much not to be able to go more often. I shall be delighted to reserve the best seat for you if you wish, where you will be seen by all. For the children there is a special time and place so they will not disturb the elders.

Hoping to have been of service to you.

Sincerely,

To help you overcome some of the misunderstandings that can result from words, we will identify several specific problems or barriers to effective communication and then we will suggest ways of overcoming those problems.

Barrier 1: Bypassing

Bypassing occurs when the same word is used to mean two different things. Our W.C. story is a good example of bypassing. "W.C." was used by the lady in our story to refer to a water closet or toilet. The parish priest thought "W.C." meant a wayside chapel. "Meet me at the circle drive after school," you tell your friend. After your classes you wait at the circle drive for your rendezvous. Thirty minutes pass and there is no sign of your friend. Finally, you leave disgusted and mumbling something about your ex-friend. Your friend, however, was dutifully waiting at the circle drive on the north side of the campus—you had been waiting at the south side circle drive. Your meanings for the words "circle drive" bypassed each other. One researcher estimated that the 500 most used words in the English language have more than 14,000 different dictionary definitions. The word "run," for example, can have more than 800 different meanings! And because of our different experiences and cultures, think how difficult it is to communicate with others without bypassing the intended meaning. Our guess is that most of you have experienced this problem.

Barrier 2: Polarization

Polarization occurs when we describe things in terms of extremes, such as good or bad, beautiful or ugly, hot or cold, positive or negative. What's wrong with that? What's wrong with talking about what we see in terms of how good or bad, positive or negative something is? The problem occurs when we don't consider the middle ground. When we describe something as "good" or "awful," our brief evaluation does not take into consideration the midway position, and may result in an inaccurate label of what we observe.

In early movies about the Old West, you could always tell the "good guys" from the "bad guys" by the color of their hats. The heroes wore white hats and the villains wore black ones. Unoftunately, life is not quite that simple. Categorizing everything in terms only of good or bad, black or white, does not accurately reflect what really exists. Once we pronounce something "good" or "bad," we tend to believe our self-imposed label. It becomes more difficult to realize that life is not that simple.

Barrier 3: Allness

In some ways it would be very convenient to develop simple generalizations to describe our world. All girls are smarter than boys. Men can run faster than women. Everyone who lives in Florida drinks orange juice every day. Perhaps it would be convenient, but certainly it would not be very accurate. Because of the power of language to create, when we state an all-encompassing generalization, we begin to believe what we state. And the problem is that we simply cannot know everything about any one topic. Think how many times we use statements that really sound as it we do know everything about a subject. Statements like "This class is going to be hard" or "This person is not a very good conversationalist" sound as if we know all there is to know on the subject. The barrier here is not the fact that we say these things, but the fact that we believe them once we say them. An allness statement implies that we know everything about a subject, and we judge or prejudge what we experience because we believe our own allness generalizations.

Barrier 4: Static evaluation

We remind you of the ancient philosopher who noted, "You can never step in the same river twice." His point was that our world is constantly changing. For example, since you started reading this chapter you have changed. You are older now. You may be more tired than when you began. Your hair has grown. Your fingernails may have grown. Granted, you have not changed so much that you or anyone else will notice. But you have changed. Similarly, our whole world changes, but our labels to describe the world do not always reflect this change. And, again, because we tend to believe what we say, the fact that our words do not often reflect change can be a barrier to communication.

If you've ever used an old road map for a vacation trip, you know some of the problems it can cause. New highways are not shown on your map. Old roads that are on your map may have been closed. Because you believe what you see on your map, you may miss opportunities to save some time. Your map simply does not accurately reflect the current, changed highway system. This situation is similar to what happens when our words do not accurately refect the changes that have occurred in our world. Today, for example, many of us still refer to a modern electric refrigerator as an "ice box." Our world changes, but language does not always reflect that change.

Barrier 5: Fact-inference confusion

What's a fact? Most people respond by saying that a fact is something that has been proven. Or a fact is something that everyone agrees is true. Then the questions arises, "How has it been proven?" At one time it was thought to be a "proven" fact that the world was flat. Did that make it a fact? No, not necessarily. Perhaps a better definition is that a fact is something you observe to be true. If you haven't observed it, you can't state with certainty that something is a fact or not. Of course, as noted earlier in the chapter, perception plays a part in determining what we observe to be true. In a court of law the judge and jury are interested primarily in facts, in the form of testimonies of those who have observed certain things to have occurred. Statements of inference are permitted only by experts.

The barrier created by fact-inference confusion occurs when we respond to something as if it were a fact—something we have observed—when, in reality, it is an inference we have made. While statements of fact can be made only after we have observed something, inferences can be made before, during, or after an occurrence, and no observation is necessary. The key distinction is that a statement of inference can speculate about and interpret what we *think* occurred.

Perhaps you have heard someone say, "It's a fact that men are better at solving mathematical problems than women." To say that this statement presents a fact would mean that *all* men and women were tested and the results indicated that men are superior to women in solving mathematical problems. The statement is, in reality, an inference, perhaps drawn from research that has attempted to investigate the issue. Rather than to say, "It's a fact that . . . ," it would be more appropriate to say, "Some studies have found that men are better at solving mathematical problems than women." This statement more accurately describes reality than the claim that these differences are "a fact." Confusing fact for inference, then, can lead to misunderstandings and inaccuracies.

OVERCOMING WORD BARRIERS

Thus far we have focused on the problems words create for us. Meaning can *bypass* us because we are not sure what another person is referring to when he uses a word to describe something. *Polarization* is a problem that results from looking at the world in absolutes—black or white, good or bad—and failing to consider the middle ground. *Allness* is a word barrier when our language implies that we know all there is to know about a subject. *Static evaluations* can result in our not being sensitive to the way our world is constantly changing. Finally, *fact-inference confusion* is a problem that occurs when we mistake an inference for an observable fact. Because words have both the power to create and the power to affect attitudes and behavior, word barriers will continue to plague us.

There are, however, some suggestions for trying to overcome these barriers. Advocates of general semantics endorse the following suggestions as useful ways of coping with problems that occur when we use words inappropriately.

Avoid signal response to symbols

To understand what a signal response is, you first must know what we mean by a signal. A signal (or sign) is something that has a fixed single meaning, regardless of the context. The same response is made, regardless of any other factors. Nonhuman animals use signs to communicate. When the bell rang, Pavlov's dog salivated, regardless of whether he saw food or not. The bell served as a signal, and thus the dog responded.

In coping with word barriers, the challenge is for humans to avoid responding to something as if it had a fixed meaning. Don't treat a word as if it had only one fixed interpretation. Before responding to what someone is saying, determine whether you are responding out of habit or have tried to understand what the person really meant when using a word or phrase.

Avoid rigid, nonprocess orientations

Word barriers such as polarization, allness, and static evaluation occur when we fail to realize that our world is constantly changing. A nonprocess orientation is likely to evoke a response that does not consider change. But if we remind ourselves that a word or label may not always reflect our personal meaning for a concept because of change, we can avoid the problem of making a static evaluation.

Try to clarify fact-inference confusion

We noted that we often make the mistake of acting upon information as if it were a fact, something that we have observed, rather than treating it as an inference. If you make the effort to determine whether you are responding to a fact or inference, you will be in a better position to evaluate the validity of the conclusion you reach.

For example, imagine that you are a detective investigating a death. You are given the following information: (1) Tom and Mary are lying together on the floor; (2) Tom and Mary are dead; (3) they are surrounded by water and broken glass; (4) on the sofa near Tom and Mary is a cat with his back arched, apparently ready to defend himself. Given these sketchy details, do you, the detective assigned to the case, have any hypotheses about the cause of Tom and Mary's deaths? Perhaps they slipped on the water, crashed into a table, broke a vase, and died (that would explain the water and broken glass). Or maybe their attacker recently left the scene, and the cat is somewhat disturbed by the commotion. Clearly, several inferences could be made as to the probable cause of death. Oh yes, there is one detail we forgot to mention: Tom and Mary are fish. Does that help?

Perhaps you responded to the names "Tom" and "Mary" as if they were people, not fish. If so, you made an inference based upon previous response patterns.

We need to make inferences. Without them it would be difficult to make any decisions in life. The problem occurs when we take too much for granted. If we respond to words and information as if they are facts and not inferences, we may create communication problems that are difficult to correct.

Realize that meanings are in people, not in words

This last suggestion summarizes the other three that we have made. Words don't have meanings. People give words meanings. If you can keep this in mind, you can save yourself several problems that result from word barriers. Each individual assigns meaning to a word based upon that person's culture, education, and experiences. We assign meaning to a word or phrase as we try to understand what another person is saying. Have you ever said, "I'd like to send a message to so-and-so"? We often think of communication as transmitting a message to another. But in actuality, a message is not "transmitted" or "sent," it is *created* in the mind of the listener. The meaning is assigned, not directly transported between speaker and listener. The meaning for a word, then, is in people, not in the word or phrase used to communicate meaning.

PROCESSING INFORMATION: LANGUAGE AND PERCEPTION

PUTTING THEORY INTO PRACTICE

In this chapter we have discussed a broad range of topics related to language and perception. Both are complex in terms of understanding them and effectively using them in our dealings with others. The best advice that we can give at this point is for you to become more aware of your perceptual limitations, biases, and reactions. Try to become more sensitive to when your B-A-V systems, moods, and personality are influencing you in a way that decreases the accuracy of what you are perceiving. Verify your perceptions by repeated observations and by checking with others.

Increasing your effectiveness in using language imposes similar needs for increased awareness and sensitivity. Become more aware of the powers that words have over all of us, both intrapersonally and in our dealings with others. Identify language barriers whenever and wherever they occur, and work toward overcoming those barriers.

As we have stated so often previously, being aware of and understanding these inaccuracies and barriers is not enough. You need to recognize that there are ways of improving your perceptual and language usage skills, as suggested in the guidelines in this chapter. Once this has become apparent to you, the choice is yours.

At this point, we hope that the steps in the learning process—awareness, understanding, recognition of alternatives, and choice—have begun to materialize in your intrapersonal communication. You should now be able to translate these steps into choices that will result in improvements in your speech communication behavior. Intrapersonal communication serves as the basis for all other levels. Observe. Think. Evaluate. React. Communicate. Improve your own intrapersonal communication toward the objective of increasing the effectiveness of your speech communication behavior at the interpersonal, group, and public levels.

As you move into the rest of the book, keep in mind that all of the processes described in this chapter are operating within you during every conscious moment of your life. As you read on, and in all of your interactions with others, remember that you are actively participating in the creation of your perceptions, that you are selecting certain features of what is going on and excluding others, that your beliefs, attitudes, and values are shaping your perceptions and your behavior. Be mindful of the power of words, for it is with words that you build your image of reality and affect the images of others.

SUGGESTED ACTIVITIES

1. List three beliefs, three attitudes, and three values you have concerning a college education. What are the sources of these? How are they related to form a B-A-V subsystem? How does this subsystem affect your intrapersonal communication about your college experience? What effect(s) does this subsystem have on your behavior as a college student?

2. Using the B-A-V subsystem you developed in Activity 1, describe how your perceptions of your college experience are influenced by these B-A-V's. Outline these influences using the four stages of the perception process as a framework. For instance, how does each belief, attitude, and value influence the stimulation stage of perception? How do these B-A-V's influence what, how, and when you allow yourself to be affected by various stimuli (courses, instructors, extracurricular activities)?

3. Write a brief essay describing perception and language usage as "creative" acts. Include some personal experiences to illustrate differences in several individuals' perceiving and talking about the same event or object. What influences can you identify which may have contributed to these individual differences in perception and language usage? How might these differences be overcome?

NOTES

[1]Susanne K. Langer, "The Lord of Creation," retitled "Signs and Symbols," in Kenneth G. Johnson, et al., *Nothing Never Happens* (Beverly Hills: Glencoe Press, 1974), p. 206.
[2]Martin Heidegger, *On the Way to Language* (New York: Harper & Row, 1971), p. 206.
[3]Langer, p. 208.
[4]Larry L. Barker, *Communication* (Englewood Cliffs, NJ: Prentice-Hall, 1978), p. 120.

[5]Frank E. X. Dance and Carl Larson, *The Functions of Human Communication: A Theoretical Perspective* (New York: Holt, Rinehart and Winston, 1976), p. 93.

[6]Barker, p. 124.

[7]John C. Illy, *The Center of the Cyclone* (New York: Julian Press, 1972), p. 9.

[8]Bernard Berelson and Gary A. Steiner, *Human Behavior,* Shorter Edition (New York: Harcourt Brace Jovanovich, 1967), p. 141.

[9]Hans Toch and Malcolm S. MacLean, Jr., "Perception and Communication: A Transactional View," *Audio Visual Communication Review,* 10 (1967): 55–77.

[10]Dwight Bolinger, *Aspects of Language,* 2nd ed. (New York: Harcourt Brace Jovanovich, 1975), p. 14.

[11]John C. Condon, Jr., *Semantics and Communication,* 2nd ed. (New York: Macmillan Publishing Co., 1975), p. 9.

[12]Alfred Korzybski, *Science and Sanity,* 2nd ed. (Lancaster, PA: Science Press, 1941).

[13]Joe McGinnis, *The Selling of the President, 1968* (New York: Trident Press, 1969), pp. 91–92.

[14]Georges Gusdorff, *Speaking* (Evanston, IL: Northwestern University Press, 1965), p. 9.

[15]F. K. Heussenstann, "Bumper Stickers and Cops," *Transaction,* 35 (1971): 32–33.

UNIT III

THE INTERPERSONAL LEVEL OF SPEECH COMMUNICATION

This unit is an exploration of the functions of speech communication within interpersonal relationships. Our relationships with others are defined, built, maintained, and sometimes destroyed through communicative behavior.

Again our aim is to provide you with a balance of theory and skills—one that will help you to understand the dynamics of interpersonal relationships as well as enhance your effectiveness as a communicator.

Chapter 5 contains a variety of perspectives and suggestions to help you understand why speech communication is effective or ineffective in various interpersonal situations. "Why are we attracted to some people and not others?" and "What forms of communication arouse defensiveness?" are a sample of the questions addressed in this chapter.

Chapter 6 discusses the fascinating realm of nonverbal communication. This is an important topic, as a majority of the social meaning we assign to situations is based on nonverbal variables.

Chapter 7 focuses on the improvement of two of the most important skills you can possess: listening and feedback. In many respects, effective listening and feedback skills are the keys to satisfactory interpersonal relationships.

Chapter 8 suggests ways to enhance your effectiveness in one of the most important interpersonal situations you will encounter: the interview. The ability to conduct yourself properly in interviews can be an important factor in business and professional success.

5 INTERPERSONAL COMMUNICATION: RELATING TO OTHERS

After studying this chapter you should be able to:

Describe the relationship between silence and reciprocal identification

Relate "competence and performance" to "theory and practice"

Explain the importance of shared field of experience to interpersonal communication

Distinguish between inter-role relationships and interpersonal relationships

Describe the relationships among risk, trust, intimacy, and self-disclosure in interpersonal relationships

Observe and define relational stages based on interpersonal interaction

Communicate in ways that are more supportive and confirming

Every man is a potential adversary, even those whom we love. Only through dialogue are we saved from this enmity toward one another. Dialogue is to love, what blood is to the body. When the flow of blood stops, the body dies. When dialogue stops, love dies and resentment and hate are born. But dialogue can restore a dead relationship. Indeed, this is the miracle of dialogue: it can bring relationship into being, and it can bring into being once again a relationship that has died.[1]

The interpersonal relationship is the fundamental human relationship. It is the basis for the development and maintenance of our self-concepts; it can be the most intense, intimate, and pleasurable or painful human relationship; in it our needs for love, acceptance, and understanding can be gratified. Interpersonal communication is the process through which relationships are initiated, built, maintained, and sometimes destroyed.

This chapter is about the ways in which we link ourselves with others

through speech communication. It is about how we discover the uniqueness of another human being and how we make ourselves known to that person. It is about messages that bring people closer together and messages that push them apart. Our goal is to help you to understand the dynamics of interpersonal transaction and to evaluate and improve your own use of speech communication at the interpersonal level.

To help you focus on the process of interpersonal communication we'll begin with a discussion of two models that effectively define some of the major components of an interpersonal transaction.

THE BAKER MODEL

How comfortable are you when sitting with another person in absolute silence? Does your comfort (or discomfort) vary from person to person? Are there some people with whom you can be happy just being together, without saying anything? Is silence with another person sometimes painful? Have you experienced "awkward silence"?

A fairly good test of friendship is the ability to be with someone without feeling a need to speak. It seems to reflect comfort, acceptance, and what Baker calls "reciprocal identification."[2] Reciprocal identification is the degree of commonality between two people. Once we truly "get to know" someone, the person becomes more predictable for us; we know how he or she is responding to a situation. For example, one of the authors can sit on a mountainside in Montana

92

with his wife, both silent as they watch the sun sink below the horizon while a flock of pine siskins chirps its salute to another day completed. Neither needs to say, "Gee, honey, isn't it a nice sunset and aren't the mountains beautiful, and isn't it lovely that the birds are singing?" In fact, it would be an interruption of a very beautiful, warm, intimate moment. In such a situation, each of us knows how the other is feeling and there is a strong sense of sharing in the beauty of the moment—with no words whatsoever passing between us. This is "reciprocal identification."

Unlike most models of communication, the heart of the Baker model is *silence*. Silence, claims Baker, is the aim of communication; we need to talk until there is no more that needs to be said. Let's look at the components of his model—see Figure 5.

Reciprocal identification

Across the bottom of the model are represented various degrees of reciprocal identification. On the left we can see that person A and person B have virtually nothing in common in this particular situation. It could be that they are having a terrible misunderstanding and that neither is able to see the situation as the other is seeing it. Another example would be two people from vastly different backgrounds, perhaps different cultures and different languages. They have little or nothing in common.

At the bottom center we can see an overlap—an area that is shared by both person A and person B. To an extent, each can identify with the other; there is some degree of understanding between them. This could be as basic as a common language and some shared meaning within that language. Within established relationships it would represent an element of *empathy*—ability to understand what the other is feeling and thinking.

At the bottom right is represented complete reciprocal identification. Here persons A and B are as one; there is complete understanding between them—a state rarely experienced, but certainly to be desired.

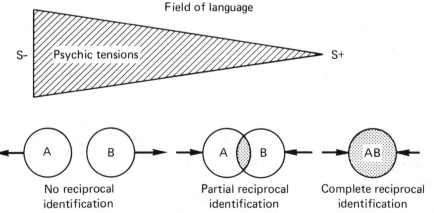

FIGURE 5 The Baker model. (From Sidney J. Baker, "The Theory of Silence," *Journal of General Psychology*, 53 (1955):145–167. Reprinted by permission.)

Psychic tension and silence

At the center of the model is an inclined plane labeled "Psychic tensions." To the left is "S −", to the right "S +." The S's here refer to silence. To the left is negative silence, to the right positive. Putting this figure together with reciprocal identification, we can see that when there is little or no reciprocal identification, psychic tension tends to be high; we are uncomfortable with the situation and have nothing to say. There is negative silence. On the right, where there is total reciprocal identification, there is little or no psychological discomfort; we understand and feel understood. We are quiet and content. The silence is positive.

Field of language

Language, expressed through speech communication, is the key to reciprocal identification. You will recall that speech communication makes *decentering* possible; because we can symbolically "step outside" ourselves, we are able to take the point of view of another person. Through speech communication we share our "interiority" with others. It is only through speech communication that reciprocal identification is possible.

THE DEVITO MODEL

The DeVito model[3] draws on a number of earlier models to provide one of the most comprehensive yet clear models of interpersonal communication.

To orient yourself, look first at the center of the model—see Figure 6. Do you recall the components of the communication process we discussed in Chapter 1? In DeVito's model we can see some of the same components and processes—source, receiver, encoding, decoding, messages, feedback, and noise. We discussed these components in Chapter 1 and so we will not elaborate on them here. If you need a "refresher," take a few minutes to review that discussion before proceeding.

Now let's look at the components of the DeVito model that we have not covered. They include *competence, performance, field of experience, effect,* and *communication context.*

Competence and performance

Communication competence refers to our knowledge of the "rules" of effective communication. On one level this means that each of us has some degree of *linguistic competence*—a knowledge of the rules and structures of a language. At another and more important level, we have varying knowledge of the relation of speech communication to its social context. This involves "knowing how to act" in a variety of situations. Clearly some messages (both verbal and nonverbal) that are perfectly appropriate on the construction site are inappropriate at a Georgetown soiree or a debutante ball. Communication competence, then, is your repertoire of social rules and your understanding of communicative behavior as it relates to those rules.

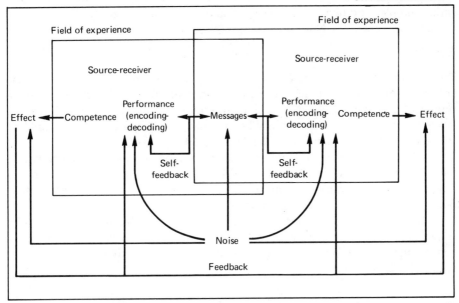

FIGURE 6 The DeVito model. (From Joseph A. DeVito, *The Interpersonal Communication Book,* 2nd ed., p. 6. Copyright © 1980 by Joseph A. DeVito. Reprinted by permission of Harper & Row, Publishers, Inc.)

Performance is related to competence and refers to your actual behavior as you speak and listen, and adjust to a variety of situations and contexts. Our favorite example of a competent communicator, which was proposed to us by one of our colleagues,[4] is James T. Kirk, captain of the Starship *Enterprise* on the long-running television series, *Star Trek.* Captain Kirk continually exhibits considerable knowledge and skill (competence and performance) in adapting his behavior to the situation. He has a vast communicative repertoire; he can be dominant or tender, authoritarian or democratic, formal or informal, aggressive or conciliatory—as the situation demands it. In short, this fictitious character is the epitome of the competent communicator.

Field of experience

DeVito asserts that "effective communication can only take place to the extent that the participants share the same experiences."[5] Note the similarity between this concept and the notion of "reciprocal identification" from Baker's model. In order for us to communicate effectively with another person, we need to share not only a common language but a similar frame of reference for that language. You probably know from your own experience that it is much easier to communicate with people who are "like us"—people who share similar attitudes, values, and experiences. It is difficult, at best, to understand fully the feelings of someone who has had drastically different experiences than we have. To use a rather extreme example to make the point, even if the two shared the same language, a Harvard physicist would have difficulty in getting an aborigine from the Australian outback to understand the subtle but exquisite pleasure to be derived from an elegant theory. Likewise, the aborigine would have trouble communicating the pleasure he receives from eating a freshly killed lizard.

Effect

Every communicative act results in some effect. Sometimes the effect is observable and sometimes it is not. The most prevalent effect in interpersonal communication is the effect on further communication. Every communicative act limits the possible responses to it. When we say, "Hi, how are you?" it is unlikely that the other will respond with "My sister got a new car."

Many of the effects of interpersonal communication are *intrapersonal* effects. We discussed at length in Chapter 3 how self-concept is shaped and maintained through interpersonal communication. The words of other persons affect our feelings about ourselves and others.

Effects may also be external to the communicators themselves, as when interpersonal communication is used to plan a meeting or a date. The effects of communication are many and varied. In fact, most of this book is devoted to the study of effects of communication.

Communication context

Communication always occurs in a context. Context—the temporal, social, psychological, and physical environment—has a powerful effect on our communicative behavior. Everything from the time of day to the shape of a table to the number of people in a group can influence our perceptions of a situation and thus effect our communication with others and ourselves.

Much of the remainder of this book is a discussion of the effects of context on speech communication.

INTERPERSONAL ATTRACTION

A starting point in viewing the interpersonal relationship is to consider those things that bring people together in the first place. Why do we choose certain people to be our friends and not others? What makes another person attractive to us? There are many answers to these questions. A discussion of some of the most common factors in interpersonal attraction follows.

Physical attraction

Particularly at the initial stages of attraction, physical attractiveness plays an important role. Luckily, individual perceptions of what is attractive vary widely enough so that virtually everyone appears attractive to someone. This factor becomes much less important as we get to know a person. You probably know of people who appeared strikingly handsome or beautiful to you until you got to know them, after which you hardly noticed their physical attributes. Likewise we tend to overlook "unattractive" physical traits once we get to know a person's "inner beauty."

Similarity

One of the strongest influences on interpersonal attraction is similarity. Remember your first day on campus? That feeling of newness, strangeness, and aloneness? You needed a friend, and you probably found one. Who did you look for to be your friend? Did you seek out someone whom you perceived to be very different from you? Probably not. If the principle of similarity in interpersonal attraction applies here, you probably looked for someone to talk to who appeared to be in the same boat—another lonely freshman, perhaps someone who was dressed in a similar manner to the way you dress.

Who are your closest friends? Do you share many of the same attitudes, beliefs, and values? Do you enjoy the same activities? More than likely, you do. We are often attracted to people whom we consider to be like ourselves. A probable explanation for this phenomenon is that similar backgrounds, beliefs, attitudes, and values make it easier to understand one another—and we all like to feel as if we are understood.

Complementarity

As you read the previous section on similarity, you may have been shaking your head and saying to yourself, "No, that's not the way it is at all. My best friend and I are about as similar as an orchid and a fire hydrant!" As the saying goes, "No generalization is true . . . including the present one," and so it is with the principle of similarity. While there is some truth to the statement that "birds of a feather flock together," it is also true that "opposites attract." Thibaut and Kelley suggest that some interpersonal relationships are based primarily on similarity while others are based on complementarity.[6] At times we may be attracted to others who exhibit qualities which we do not possess but which we admire. While the principle of similarity seems to be the more pervasive phenomenon, we can all cite instances of complementarity. For at least a partial explanation of attraction through complementarity we can look to Schutz's theory of interpersonal needs. According to Schutz's theory, a person with a high need to express control would be most compatible with a person who has a high need to be on the receiving end of controlling behavior. The same would be true in terms of needs to express and receive inclusion and affection.[7] Needs in these instances are complementary rather than similar. Our final (and most dramatic) example of the complementarity principle of attraction is the masochist, who, in order to find satisfaction in life, will probably be attracted to a sadist.

Proximity, contact, and interaction

We tend to be attracted to people who are physically close to us—people with whom we live and work, people we see and talk with often. If we know that we have to live or work close to another person, we may tend to ignore or overlook

that person's less desirable traits in order to minimize potential conflict and keep things running smoothly. Furthermore, proximity, contact, and interaction breed familiarity; and familiarity has a positive influence on interpersonal attraction.[8] Interaction with another person helps us begin to "get to know" that other person, and through this process we may uncover similarities and discover ways in which we can satisfy one another's interpersonal needs. It is not, then, the actual physical distance between people which influences attraction, but the interpersonal possibilities which are illuminated by proximity, contact, and interaction.

INTERPERSONAL COMMUNICATION: "GETTING TO KNOW YOU"

In Chapter 2 we pointed out that speech communication at the interpersonal level is aimed at discovering the uniqueness of another human being. When we say that we are "getting to know" someone, it means that we are discovering what it is that sets that person apart from others who are similar. Someone we have learned to know *well* becomes relatively predictable for us. Our knowledge of people's beliefs, attitudes, values, experiences, and self-concepts allows us to judge with some accuracy how they are likely to respond in a given situation. To know people well, then, is to have a good *theory* about them—not a formal theory, of course, but an *explanation* of "who they are" that allows you to make *predictions* about their probable behavior and to *control* or regulate your own behavior and, to an extent, theirs.

Keep in mind our definition of speech communication as "making sense" out of the world. We use speech communication to make sense out of the behavior of another person. We call this "getting to know" someone.

What isn't *interpersonal communication?*

By "interpersonal communication" we do *not* mean the whole range of events that take place between two people. To do so would be to include events such as a simple request for a pack of chewing gum at a drugstore counter. Such an encounter is really an *inter-role* relationship rather than an *interpersonal* one. We relate to the position (in this case, "clerk") more than to the person who fills the position. The customer and clerk do not relate to the "personhood" of one another.

We have adopted the distinction made by Miller and Steinberg between *interpersonal* communication and *non*interpersonal communication.

> (W)hen predictions about communication outcomes are based primarily on a cultural or sociological level of analysis, the communicators are engaged in noninterpersonal communication; when predictions are based primarily on a psychological level of analysis, the communicators are engaged in interpersonal communication.[9]

What is *interpersonal communication?*

Interpersonal communication, then, is *dyadic* (two-person) communication based on the individuality of each person and aimed toward further discovery of the uniqueness of the other. We move now to a discussion of the process through which we reveal our uniqueness to another, self-disclosure.

SELF-DISCLOSURE

To self-disclose is to share information about yourself which could not otherwise be known. It is a revealing of your *interiority* to another, a sharing of your self-concept.

He *(contritely)*   Honey, I'm sorry. I didn't know it meant so much to you.
She *(emotionally)*   If you really *loved* me, you'd *know* what I need.

The brief dialogue above is an example of a common myth many of us hold about interpersonal relationships; that caring and affection bring knowledge. You cannot be truly known to another unless you choose to reveal yourself. *Others cannot know who you are and what you need unless you tell them!*

> Self-disclosure, my communication of my private world to you, in language which you clearly understand, is truly an important bit of behavior for us to learn something about. You can know me truly only if I let you, only if I *want* you to know me. Your misunderstanding of me is only partly your fault. If I want you to know me, I shall find a means of communicating myself to you. If you want me to reveal myself, just demonstrate your good will—your will to employ your powers for my good, and not for my destruction.[10]

Self-disclosure is a matter of *choice*. We can choose to allow others into our private worlds, or we can choose to exclude them. It is very easy to talk about ourselves for hours without engaging in authentic self-disclosure. For example, I (one of us) could go to great lengths, telling you about the somewhat circuitous route that brought me to where I am today. I could tell you about my parents and my childhood, my various interests, jobs, skills. I could show you my curriculum vitae on which are listed my educational background, committee service, awards and honors, books, papers, and so forth. At the end of all of this you would know a great deal *about* me. But would you really *know* me? What I would have given you was what Gerard Egan calls *History*.[11] My history is something that you could find from other sources. It deals with my *exteriority*. But my *interiority* is another story. And *Story* is precisely what Egan calls authentic self-disclosure: information about me that you will never find out unless I tell you—the fact that I often cry in the movies, my frustrations in dealing with university bureaucracies, my feelings about my family, my career, my students. It is a sharing of our *interiority* that comprises authentic self-disclosure, *and it is through speech communication and our ability to decenter that it is possible to see the world as another sees it.*

The dyadic effect

Through mutual self-disclosure, we progressively reveal ourselves to one another. Self-disclosure is the foundation of an interpersonal relationship. Without it, we can deal only with superficialities—with roles, appearances, and stereotypes. But self-disclosure does not happen all at once; it tends to come in small increments.

Sally   Hi, David, how's it going?
David *(dejected)*   My cat died this morning.

Consider the brief dialogue above. Imagine yourself in David's situation. If Sally were a close friend, the news about the recent demise of your cat would be an appropriate response to her query. She would understand your sadness, because of knowing you and the affection you felt for your pet. If, on the other hand, Sally were only a casual acquaintance, (1) you would probably not reveal your feelings about your loss in the first place, and (2) if you did, it would probably make her uncomfortable. The reason for her discomfort would be that self-disclosure tends to be reciprocal and symmetrical; both partners in a dyad tend to disclose at about the same level of intimacy. If you disclose very personal information to one who does not know you well, it will cause that person psychological discomfort. Remember that interpersonal messages have both a content and a relationship dimension. High levels of disclosure state that there is a high level of trust in the relationship, and it takes time to develop trust and intimacy in a friendship.

Through self-disclosure we build trust and intimacy. Trust and intimacy allow us to disclose further. When disclosure by one person leads to disclosure by the other, this is the dyadic effect. When developing an interpersonal relationship, the dyadic effect serves us as follows:

1. I disclose a small part of myself to you.
2. The relationship dimension of my message says that I trust you enough to tell you what I told you.
3. Because I trusted you, it is easier for you to trust me.
4. You disclose an equivalent part of yourself to me.
5. Now we have both made a statement about the relationship: we trust each other. The presence of trust allows me to risk a little more and disclose more of myself to you.
6. This, in turn, makes it easier for you to disclose more of yourself, and the pattern repeats itself.

Risk, trust, self-disclosure, and intimacy

We can see here a spiraling process through which relationships develop. Self-disclosure is perceived as very risky by most people.

Why am I afraid to tell you who I am? Because if I tell you who I am you may not like who I am and that's all I have.[12]

To reveal who we really are makes us vulnerable. This is one of the greatest barriers to self-disclosure. But without risk, there can be no trust; and without trust there can be no intimacy; and without an intimate relationship with at least one other human being, we are alone.

Self-disclosure and self-awareness

As we discussed in Chapter 3, interpersonal communication plays a central role in the development of our self-concepts. One of the benefits of self-disclosure—and, ironically, one of the barriers as well—is increased self-knowledge. Sidney Jourard wrote:

> Through my self-disclosure, I let others know my soul. They can know it, really know it, only as I make it known. In fact, I am beginning to suspect that I can't even know *my own soul* except as I disclose it. I suspect that I will know myself "for real" at the exact moment that I have succeeded in making it known through my disclosure to another person.[13]

He also said:

> . . . it seems to be another empirical fact that no man can come to know himself except as an outcome of disclosing himself to another person.[14]

In an interpersonal transaction we are communicating simultaneously with ourselves and the other person. Open, honest self-disclosure brings intrapersonal communication and interpersonal into harmonious relationship. Putting our inner feelings—our interiority—into words to share with another externalizes and objectifies those feelings. Other people serve as "mirrors" for us; through their feedback they reflect "who we are" back to us. If we truly self-disclose to another, the reflection we see is an accurate image of who we are. Through others, we learn to know ourselves.

The fact that self-disclosure brings self-knowledge actually prevents many people from self-disclosing. People with negative self-concepts and low self-esteem frequently fall into this category. If you believe that, beneath it all, you are not a very acceptable person, you are not likely to put it to the test and find out for sure. Continuing our "mirror" analogy, if you don't want to see yourself, you'll avoid mirrors.

Remember, though, that self-concepts can, and do, change. But they do not change in a vacuum. Your best hope if you do not disclose yourself because of a negative self-concept is that you will find someone—a friend or counselor—whom you can trust enough to reveal your inner fears. You will, no doubt, find that you are not so unacceptable after all.

RELATIONAL STAGES AND INTERPERSONAL COMMUNICATION

We remind you once again that there are both *content* and *relationship* dimensions to our speech communication with others. If you arrive at your professor's office door and she says to you, "Hi. Come in, close the door, and sit down," both of these dimensions are clearly reflected. The content dimension is clear; she has given you a greeting and a series of directives. But she has also said something about your relationship, namely, that she has the *right* to give you directives. She is clearly in the more powerful position, at least in her office.

A current body of research is attempting to identify and analyze characteristics of speech communication at various stages in the development of interpersonal relationships. Rather than examining individual behaviors, studies in relational communication focus on the relationships between individual behaviors. The goal of such studies is to determine if there are common rules or message strategies that we use in building and maintaining interpersonal relationships. Mark Knapp has suggested the following questions as central to the study of relational communication:

> (1) Are there regular and systematic patterns of communication that suggest stages on the road to an intimate relationship? Are there similar patterns and stages that characterize the deterioration of relationships? (2) Can we identify communication strategies that attract and repel us at various stages in a relationship? Specifically, how do people talk to each other when they are building, maintaining, or tearing down a relationship? (3) What are these mysterious forces that propel us in and out of relationships? And what determines how fast or slow a relationship progresses or dissolves?[15]

A growing body of theory and research in speech communication is attempting to answer these questions.[16] At this point it appears that there are, indeed, sys-

AN OVERVIEW OF INTERACTION STAGES[17]

Process	Stage	Representative dialogue
Coming Together	Initiating	"Hi, how ya doin?" "Fine. You?"
	Experimenting	"Oh, so you like to ski . . . so do I." "You do?! Great. Where do you go?"
	Intensifying	"I . . . I think I love you." "I love you too."
	Integrating	"I feel so much a part of you." "Yeah, we are like one person. What happens to you happens to me."
	Bonding	"I want to be with you always." "Let's get married."
Coming Apart	Differentiating	"I just don't like big social gatherings." "Sometimes I don't understand you. This is one area where I'm certainly not like you at all."
	Circumscribing	"Did you have a good time on your trip?" "What time will dinner be ready?"
	Stagnating	"What's there to talk about?" "Right. I know what you're going to say and you know what I'm going to say."
	Avoiding	"I'm so busy, I just don't know when I'll be able to see you." "If I'm not around when you try, you'll understand."
	Terminating	"I'm leaving you . . . and don't bother trying to contact me." "Don't worry."

tematic patterns of communication that are associated with different relational stages. Just as individuals pass through developmental stages (infancy, preschool period, elementary years, adolescence, etc.), relationships pass through stages that are identifiable by the interpersonal communication that characterizes them. Knapp has proposed the model shown in the table. This model represents the types of interaction that seem to characterize various stages in the growth and decay of interpersonal relationships. The model and the discussion of it that follows are not intended to give you the skills to diagnose problems in interpersonal relationships; a great deal more information than is presented here would be required for that. Rather, it is intended to help you increase your sensitivity to and awareness of the nature and importance of dialogue in interpersonal relationships.

Initiating

The purpose of our messages in the initiating stage is to open channels of communication. With a stranger whom we are trying to get to know—perhaps an attractive member of the opposite sex—we are usually very cautious at this stage. We tend to be hypersensitive to verbal and nonverbal cues. Choosing an opening line is often difficult. But once we find that line and initate interaction, this stage passes very quickly, often in less than fifteen seconds.

Experimenting

At this stage, we are "testing the water"—checking out our initial impressions to see if this is indeed a person we want to get to know. We usually search for similarities between us: "Are you a student here? What's your major? Where are you from? Do you like to party?" In short, the experimenting stage is characterized by "small talk." The importance of small talk should not be underestimated. Even though there is little or no real self-disclosure and no real commitment to the other person in such casual conversation, it provides the foundation on which deeper relationships can be formed.

Intensifying

If the experimenting stage results in continuing interest in the other person, we become aware not only of the other person but of the relationship itself. We become less superficial in our interaction and begin to share more personal information. Self-disclosure increases trust and intimacy in the relationship. Our verbal behavior tends to become more personal. We begin to talk about "us" instead of "you and me." Expressions of feelings about the other person appear at this stage.

Integrating

Perhaps one of the best outward signs of the integrating stage we've noticed are matched "his and hers" T-shirts. At this stage in the relationship the participants begin to think alike, act alike, sometimes even look alike. We have noticed with some of our closest friends a tendency for us to say the same thing at the same time. There is an emphasis on the similarity of the interactants and on that which sets them apart from others. It is a stage reached only by extremely close friends and/or lovers.

Bonding

Bonding involves a public statement of a couple's commitment to one another. It is an institutionalization of the relationship and is included as a separate stage because of the powerful impact that such a formal contract—whether it be "going steady," "getting pinned," engagement, marriage, or becoming "blood brothers"—can have on a relationship. Such public commitments bring with them new role expectations that can literally change a relationship overnight.

Differentiating

Unfortunately, not all deep interpersonal relationships live "happily ever after." The decline of the relationship is also characterized by interactional stages, and the first of these is *differentiating*. Whereas similarity and connectedness were the hallmarks of the previous two stages, differences come into focus at this stage. However, it should be noted that while most, if not all, love relationships reach this stage, it does not *necessarily* mean the beginning of the end for such relationships. Most couples who are in love and at the integrating and bonding stages have difficulty seeing each other as they really are!

But love is blind, and lovers cannot see the pretty folly that themselves commit.

—*Shakespeare,* Merchant of Venice, *II, 2*

Many lovers describe their emotional state as one of "ecstasy" (from the Greek *ekstasis,* which means "deranged"). Lederer and Jackson note:

> . . . when an emotional courtship starts, the man and woman appear to relinquish whatever sense of balance and reality they ordinarily possess. Courtship, the time of ecstatic paralysis, has been cleverly designed by Nature to lure members of the species into reproducing themselves.[18]

In a way, people who are in love are more in love with love itself than with each other. Their intense emotional state associated with their togetherness prevents them from seeing that they are still unique human beings who have their natural differences.

While in many cases the process of differentiating forecasts the end of the relationship, in others it marks a period of adjustment, a greater sense of reality, a truer acknowledgment of each other's personhood, and a renewed commitment to the relationship. Indeed, as people grow and change together their relationship may pass in and out of this stage repeatedly.

Circumscribing

In the circumscribing stage there has been deterioration of the relationship to the point that many topics are seen as too touchy or painful to discuss.

> Familiar phrases at this stage include: "Don't ask me about that anymore"; "It's none of your business"; "Just stick to the kind of work I'm doing and leave my religion out of it"; "You don't own me and you can't tell me what to think"; or "Can't we just be friends?" The last example is a suggestion that prescribes a whole new set of ground rules for permissible topics in the interaction.[19]

Stagnating

During this stage, each person feels that he or she "knows" what the other is thinking and sees efforts at breaking down the barriers to communication as futile. The relationship is going nowhere and any discussion of the relationship itself is nearly nonexistent. Messages that pass between the two are unspontaneous, hesitant, and awkward. Nonverbal messages are frequently negative. This stage is painful, of course, but for many it is prolonged, because they believe that it is less painful than complete termination of the relationship is likely to be.

Avoiding

When this stage is reached, physical separation is the aim of communication. "The overriding message seems to be: 'I am not interested in building a relationship; and I would like to close the communication channels between us.' "[20]

Terminating

Termination is the end of the relationship. It may come abruptly or gradually. Depending on a variety of factors such as the history of the relationship, the relative status of the people involved, their personalities, and a host of other variables, communication at this point can vary widely. It may be explosive or quiet, hostile or amicable. In any event, messages at the termination point are likely to convey a desire for distance, both physical and psychological.

Speech communication is at the heart of the building—and the demise—of intimate relationships. An increased knowledge of your own communicative processes can help you to be more self-aware. Understanding how you use communication in interpersonal relationships can give you the power to regulate your own behavior more effectively, with awareness of the likely consequences of your actions. We move now to an area of speech communication behavior that affects your relationships with everyone you contact: *defensive and supportive communication.*

DEFENSIVE AND SUPPORTIVE SPEECH COMMUNICATION

Most of us know what it is like to feel defensive. We feel as if we are under attack, as if we need to protect ourselves, and the self—self-concept, self-image, self-esteem—is precisely what we are trying to protect when we feel defensive.

The arousal of defensiveness is the antithesis of effective interpersonal communication. If we make someone defensive, his or her subsequent intrapersonal and interpersonal messages are likely to be aimed at self-protection rather than remaining open to the ideas and feelings of the other person. But what do we do that makes others defensive? *What kinds of behaviors should we avoid,* and, conversely, *how can we communicate in ways that facilitate free and open dialogue?*

After several years of research in this area, Jack Gibb[21] identified certain types of communicative behaviors that tend to arouse defensiveness in others, and a paired set of behaviors that are perceived as supportive. It is possible to communicate the same message at the content level in ways that are either defense-inducing or supportive at the relationship level. Clearly, we can be more effective communicators if we construct our messages in a supportive manner.

Evaluation vs. description

"Look what you made me do!"
"Listen, Bozo, can't you do anything right?"
"Wow, is that ever a stupid idea."

None of us enjoys being evaluated, criticized, and judged. It makes us feel defensive. In a nutshell, *evaluation* is "you" language. It directs itself to the *other person's* worth or the worth of that person's idea. As a result, it can provoke much defensiveness. *Description,* on the other hand is "I" language. It describes the *speaker's* thoughts and feelings about the person or idea. For example, you might say, "If I understand you correctly, I disagree." This type of response leads to greater interpersonal trust and facilitates further communication rather than impeding it.

Control vs. problem orientation

Communicative behavior that aims at controlling the behavior of others can produce much defensiveness. This pattern characterizes many aggressive sales people who, quite intentionally, manipulate us into agreeing to a series of trivial questions by limiting our alternatives and thereby lead up to the final question of buying the product. Various persuasive tactics aim at controlling behavior (as any student of television commercials can observe). Implicit in attempts to control lies the assumption that the controller is more knowledgeable or knows better what is good for the controllee. It's the "I know what's good for you" assumption. When we become aware of this attitude, we frequently get defensive.

A more effective approach is *problem orientation.* Rather than trying to get others to do what *you* want them to, strive to find an alternative that is equally beneficial to *both* of you. When others perceive that you are genuinely striving for mutually satisfying solutions to problems, it can lead to more open communication, less defensiveness, and more effective solutions to interpersonal problems.

Strategy vs. spontaneity

Like controlling behavior, strategy suggests manipulation. Strategy implies preplanned communication. If others detect that you are following a script rather than being open and honest with them, they can become defensive.

On the other hand, if others perceive you as a person who acts *spontaneously* (that is, not from hidden motivations and agendas) and as a person who immediately and honestly responds to the present situation, they will feel more supported and more free in their own communication.

Neutrality vs. empathy

Almost any emotion another may feel toward us is easier to deal with than neutrality or apathy. If another is angry with me, at least I know I matter enough to them to arouse their anger. Neutrality is lack of emotional involvement with the other person. It conveys the message "You're simply not worth getting excited about." As such, it can bring on considerable defensiveness. Verbal and nonverbal expression of involvement and concern for the other—empathy—is much more supportive.

Superiority vs. equality

You probably know of people who approach others in the class after tests have been returned and always ask: "What'd ya get?" Frequently this question is merely a preface to their showing you their superior grade. Sound familiar? Most of us label this behavior as obnoxious. It makes us feel defensive. Some people preface their remarks with words such as "obviously" or point out their greater knowledge of the facts or their greater experience, or use some such strategy to make themselves appear to be in a position superior to others'. This behavior is usually met with defensiveness and resistance. The more supportive behavior is to approach others with a sense of equality and mutual respect.

Certainty vs. provisionalism

Do you know people who always have all the answers, whose ideas are "truths" to be defended, who are intolerant of those with the "wrong" (that is, different) attitudes? These highly dogmatic people are well known for the defensiveness they can arouse in others. Our usual response is to want to prove them wrong. Again, this kind of behavior is counterproductive. We are likely to be more effective if our attitudes appear to be held *provisionally*; that is, if we appear flexible and genuinely committed to solving problems rather than simply taking sides on issues. If we leave ourselves open to new information and if we can admit that, from time to time, we may be wrong about something, we will be much more effective in our communication with others.[22]

You are the regulator of your own actions. Your knowledge of defensive and supportive behaviors can guide you toward greater effectiveness as a communicator.

Another important area of theory and research deals with interpersonal confirmation and disconfirmation. This body of research deals not with those communicative behaviors which you initiate, but with the ways in which you respond to others.

CONFIRMING AND DISCONFIRMING RESPONSES

In an investigation of communication in effective and ineffective groups, Evelyn Sieburg examined the ways in which group members responded to the communicative acts of others. In this seminal study and in later work with Carl Larson,

Sieburg identified several types of responses, which she classified as *confirming* or *disconfirming*. Simply stated, *confirming responses* are those which cause people to value themselves more, while *disconfirming responses* are those which cause people to value themselves less.[23] Sieburg's identification of confirming and disconfirming responses has been one of the most salient contributions to our understanding of interpersonal and small group communication.

Some forms of interpersonal responses are obvious examples of confirmation and disconfirmation, such as when a person responds to another with overt praise or sharp criticism. But there are more subtle ways in which we confirm and disconfirm one another. Sieburg and Larson identify some of those behaviors as follows:

DISCONFIRMING RESPONSES

1. *Impervious response.* When one speaker fails to acknowledge, even minimally, the other speaker's communicative attempt, or when one ignores or disregards the other by not giving any ostensible acknowledgment of the other's communication, his response may be called impervious.

2. *Interrupting response.* When one speaker cuts the other speaker short or begins while the other is still speaking, his response may be called interrupting.

3. *Irrelevant response.* When one speaker responds in a way that seems unrelated to what the other has been saying, or when one speaker introduces a new topic without warning or returns to his earlier topic, apparently disregarding the intervening conversation, his response may be called irrelevant.

4. *Tangential response.* When one speaker acknowledges the other person's communication but immediately takes the conversation in another direction, his response may be called tangential. Occasionally, individuals exhibit what may appear to be direct responses to the other, such as "Yes, but . . ." or "Well, you may be right, but . . ." but then may proceed to respond with communicative content very different from or unrelated to that which preceded. Such responses may still be called tangential.

5. *Impersonal response.* When a speaker conducts a monologue, when his speech communication behavior appears intellectualized and impersonal, contains few first-person statements and many generalized "you" or "one" statements, and is heavily loaded with euphemisms or clichés, the response may be called impersonal.

6. *Incoherent response.* When the speaker responds with sentences that are incomplete, or with rambling statements difficult to follow, or with sentences containing much retracing or rephrasing, or interjections such as "you know" or "I mean," his response may be called incoherent.

7. *Incongruous response.* When the speaker engages in nonvocal behavior that seems inconsistent with the vocal content, his response may be called incongruous. For example, "Who's angry? I'm not angry!" (said in a tone and volume that strongly suggests anger). Or, "I'm really concerned about you" (said in a tone that suggests lack of interest or disdain).

CONFIRMING RESPONSES

1. *Direct acknowledgment.* One speaker acknowledges the other's communication and reacts to it directly and verbally.

2. *Agreement about content.* One speaker reinforces or supports information or opinions expressed by the other.

3. *Supportive response.* One speaker expresses understanding of the other, reassures him, or tries to make him feel better.

4. *Clarifying response.* One speaker tries to clarify the content of the other's message or attempts to clarify the other's present or past feelings. The usual form of a clarifying response is to elicit more information, to encourage the other to say more, or to repeat in an inquiring way what was understood.

5. *Expression of positive feeling.* One speaker describes his own positive feelings related to prior utterances of the other: for example, "Okay, now I understand what you are saying."[24]

The ways in which we respond to others on both the content and relationship levels structure further communications, reflect upon the self-concepts of both interactants, and influence the building up or tearing down of the relationship. An awareness of your own interpersonal responses can help you to be more confirming and constructive as a communicator with others.

INTERPERSONAL COMMUNICATION: RELATING TO OTHERS

PUTTING THEORY INTO PRACTICE

Speech communication at the interpersonal level is based on the uniqueness of the individual communicators. We regulate our behavior according to our view of ourselves, the other person, and the relationship itself. This chapter began with an overview of the components of an interpersonal transaction provided by two models of interpersonal communication. Discussions of various functions and processes of interpersonal communication comprised the rest of the chapter.

There are a number of reasons that people are attracted to one another. The primary factors in attraction discussed in this chapter were *physical attractiveness, similarity, complementarity, proximity, contact, and interaction.*

Self-disclosure is the process of revealing information about ourselves which would otherwise be unknown. It is essential to the development of trust and intimacy in interpersonal relationships. Through self-disclosure we make ourselves known to others. We can also achieve greater self-knowledge through self-disclosure.

Systematic patterns of communication characterize relationships at different stages of their development. Using the model proposed by Mark Knapp, we examined some of these relational stages.

Many messages can be phrased in ways that either arouse *defensiveness* in others or are perceived as *supportive.* When defenses are aroused, interpersonal communication suffers. In this chapter we looked at six sets of paired behaviors that are perceived as defensive or supportive. We also examined patterns of communication in which we respond to others in ways which are *confirming* or *disconfirming.*

The goal of interpersonal communication is the building and maintenance of satisfying interpersonal relationships. If we can learn to be confirming and supportive in our communication with others, and if we understand the need for self-disclosure, trust, and free and open dialogue, that goal will be better served.

Examine your relationships with others. Look for ways in which your communicative behavior is facilitating or impeding the healthy growth of the relationship. You should now be more aware of alternative interpersonal behaviors and their likely consequences. The rest is up to you; the choice is yours.

SUGGESTED ACTIVITIES

1. Think about a relationship in which you are now involved. Applying Knapp's classification of relational stages, how does your interaction with the other person reveal the nature of the relationship?

2. With a friend or classmate, stage a conversation in which you attempt to use all of the behaviors associated with disconfirmation. Note the feelings you experience as you do this. Now repeat your conversation, covering as many of the same topics as possible, but this time be as totally confirming as possible. Again, note your feelings. Discuss the differences.

3. What beliefs, feelings, and other things about yourself do you freely disclose to others? What parts of yourself do you keep hidden from others? What would be the consequences of revealing these hidden parts to your most intimate friends?

NOTES

[1]Reuel Howe, *The Miracle of Dialogue* (New York: The Seabury Press, 1963), p. 3.

[2]Sidney J. Baker, "The Theory of Silence," *Journal of General Psychology,* 53 (1955):145–167.

[3]Joseph A. DeVito, *The Interpersonal Communication Book,* 2nd ed. (New York: Harper & Row, 1980), p. 6.

[4]Thanks for this example go to our friend and colleague Phillip Backlund.

[5]DeVito, p. 12.

[6]John Thibaut and Harold Kelley, *The Social Psychology of Groups* (New York: John Wiley & Sons, 1959).

[7]William Schutz, *The Interpersonal Underworld* (Palo Alto: Science & Behavior Books, 1958).

[8]Robert B. Zajonc, "Attitudinal Effects of Mere Exposure," *Journal of Personality and Social Psychology,* 9 (1968):1–29.

[9]Gerald R. Miller and Mark Steinberg, *Between People* (Palo Alto: Science Research Associates, 1975), p. 22.

[10]Sideny M. Jourard, *The Transparent Self* (New York: D. Van Nostrand Co., 1964), pp. 5–6.

[11]Gerard Egan, *Encounter: Group Processes for Interpersonal Growth* (Belmont, CA: Brooks/Cole Publishing Company, 1970).

[12]John Powell, *Why Am I Afraid to Tell You Who I Am?* (Niles, IL: Argus Communications, 1969), p. 12.

[13]Jourard, p. 10.

[14]Ibid., p. 5.

[15]Mark L. Knapp, *Social Intercourse* (Boston: Allyn and Bacon, 1978), p. 4.

[16]See, for example, Ben W. Morse and Lynn A. Phelps, *Interpersonal Communication: A Relational Perspective* (Minneapolis: Burgess Publishing Company, 1980) for an excellent overview of research in this area.

[17]Knapp, p. 13.

[18]W. J. Lederer and Don Jackson, *The Mirages of Marriage* (New York: W. W. Norton & Co., 1968), pp. 42–43.

[19]Knapp, p. 24.

[20]Ibid., p. 26.

[21]Jack R. Gibb, "Defensive Communication," *Journal of Communication,* 11 (1961):141–148.

[22]Much of the preceding discussion of Gibb's work was taken from Steven A. Beebe and John T. Masterson, *Communicating in Small Groups: Principles and Practice* (Glenview, IL: Scott, Foresman and Co., 1982).

[23]Evelyn Sieburg and Carl Larson, "Dimensions of Interpersonal Response," paper delivered at the annual conference of the International Communication Association, Phoenix, April 1971, p. 1.

[24]Alvin Goldberg and Carl Larson, *Group Communication: Discussion Processes and Applications* (Englewood Cliffs, NJ: Prentice-Hall, 1975).

6 NONVERBAL COMMUNICATION

After studying this chapter you should be able to:

Define nonverbal communication

Identify three reasons for studying nonverbal communication

Describe the functions of nonverbal communication

Be able to distinguish sign, action, and object language

More effectively interpret the nonverbal behavior of others

Discuss applications of nonverbal communication research to the impression formation process, public speaking, small groups, and classroom communication

"Do you love me?" asks Patty.

"Of course I love you! Haven't I told you enough times that I love you?" shouts Kenneth. Patty would like to believe her boyfriend, yet she detects he is less than sincere in his declaration of affection for her.

Aggie and Nephi are attending a lecture at the University. After the speaker is about half finished, Aggie nudges Nephi and says, "Boy, this guy seems to know what he's talking about, but I wish he wouldn't read his speech. No eye contact, little vocal variation—he really doesn't seem to be very interested in the topic."

Both of these examples have something in common. The nonverbal elements of the message are having a major effect on how the message is interpreted. It is clear that the nonverbal factors of communication, whether between two people, in a small group, between speaker and audience, or broadcast on radio or television, have a major impact upon how we interpret the messages we receive.

In this chapter we are going to examine the ways that nonverbal communication influences your communication with others. First, we will define nonverbal communication and stress why it should be of interest to you. Then we will note the various ways scholars have studied nonverbal communication in a variety of disciplines. And, finally, we will discuss applications of nonverbal communication research to your communication with others.

WHAT IS NONVERBAL COMMUNICATION?

When you are talking to your friend on the telephone, are nonverbal communication variables affecting how your message is being interpreted? Do you have to see someone to claim that the nonverbal message is having an impact upon the total message communicated? As you may suspect, although not all communication scholars agree on a definition of nonverbal communication, most feel that your phone conversation does involve elements of nonverbal communication. The tone, pitch, rate, and volume of your speech are nonverbal elements that have an important effect upon how your message is interpreted by your friend.

To help you understand what nonverbal communication is, we offer the following definition: Nonverbal communication consists of *communicative behavior that does not rely upon a written or spoken linguistic code, but that creates meaning intrapersonally, or between two or more individuals.* This definition includes not only vocal cues, but body posture and movement, eye contact, facial expression, use of personal space and territory, personal appearance, and the communication environment.

APPROACHES TO THE STUDY OF NONVERBAL COMMUNICATION

This book is about speech communication, but speech communication scholars are by no means the only people who have been interested in studying nonverbal communication. Researchers from several disciplines have examined how nonverbal behavior affects us.

A discipline that has a long tradition of studying nonverbal communication is anthropology, which in a general sense is the study of human beings across cultures. Since as much as 65 percent of human communication is nonverbal, anthropologists are interested in learning about human use of nonverbal symbols by studying the nonverbal evidence of our culture.

Sociology is another academic discipline that has an interest in nonverbal behavior. Sociologists are interested in the study of humankind's social behavior—such as how groups are formed and how we react toward people in social situations.

Psychologists, too, are much interested in studying nonverbal behavior, since they are concerned with how individuals behave and respond to their environment. Researchers following the psychological tradition may devise controlled laboratory experiments to determine the impact of nonverbal behavior on individuals.

This book adopts a communication approach to studying nonverbal communication. Communication researchers combine the methods of the anthropologists, sociologists, and psychologists. They are interested in both how to describe and how to improve the process of communicating a message to others. Communication researchers are also interested in applying theory and principles of human behavior to specific contexts, such as public speaking settings, small groups, business, organizations, and the classroom. As authors of a communication text, we want you to be able to identify principles of nonverbal behavior. But we also want you to be able to apply communication theory to your own interactions with others so that you can improve your communication skills. To help you do that, we will discuss some principles that can help you better interpret nonverbal messages and then we will identify applications of nonverbal communication research to such situations as meeting people, speaking in public, working in groups, and communicating in the classroom.

WHY LEARN ABOUT NONVERBAL COMMUNICATION?

Anyone you ask for advice about how best to prepare for a job interview will most likely mention the importance of presenting a neat appearance to your prospective employer. Talking loudly enough to be heard, maintaining good eye contact with your interviewer, and dressing on the conservative side will probably also be mentioned as important things to consider.

In public speaking, how the message is delivered has a major effect upon how your audience responds to you and your message. Your eye contact, posture, and vocal cues combine to affect how your message is received by your audience.

If you were taking a tour of the offices of a large organization, you could probably identify, without being told, the people who had greater power and status in the company. Undoubtedly each of their offices would be larger than average and more expensively decorated, would have more windows and might also be located in a corner of the floor, with at least one and possibly several secretaries' desks outside the door.

In a variety of communication contexts, then, nonverbal message variables play an important role. There are at least three reasons why you should be interested in learning more about nonverbal communication. (1) Nonverbal communication plays a major role in our overall communication with others. (2) Nonverbal communication is the primary way we communicate our feelings and attitudes toward others. (3) Nonverbal communication cues are usually more believable than verbal messages. Let's consider this rationale in greater detail.

1. Nonverbal communication plays a major role in our overall communication with others

It has been estimated that we rely upon the nonverbal variables of a communication message for up to 65 percent of its social meaning. In a variety of communication situations you will spend more of your time communicating nonverbally than verbally. Most communication teachers agree with the statement, "You *cannot* not communicate." This adage views nonverbal communication from the broadest perspective. Can you think of a time when you are not potentially communicating something to someone else? Even when you are asleep, others make inferences about your need for rest. Your facial expression, appearance, clothing, eye contact or lack of it, all contribute to others' perceptions of you.

Even though the inferences others make about you may be inaccurate, you are nonetheless, even though unintentionally, providing cues that others interpret.

2. Nonverbal communication is the primary way we communicate our feelings and attitudes toward others

In many cases, if a wife is upset with something her husband has said or done, the husband knows before any words are spoken. We can often detect feelings of frustration, anger, resentment, or anxiety, before such feelings are verbalized. Mehrabian and some of his colleagues devised an experiment to indicate how much of the total feeling of a message is based upon verbal and nonverbal components. His research indicates that as little as 7 percent of the emotional impact of a message is communicated by the words that we use.[1] About 38 percent is communicated by our vocal expression. But our facial expression accounts for 55 percent. Therefore, generalizing from this formula, approximately 93 percent of emotional meaning is communicated nonverbally. Even though there are some scholars who question applying this formula to all communication settings, Mehrabian's research does suggest that nonverbal variables provide important information about interpersonal relationships.

3. Nonverbal cues are usually more believable than verbal messages

"Are you listening to me?" shouts a mother to her son, trying to get his attention so that she can explain his household chores for the weekend. "Yes, Mother," her son replies, his eyes intent upon a *Star Trek* rerun. She is probably not convinced that he hears her. The reason is that nonverbal cues are so important to the communication process that when our nonverbal behavior contradicts our verbal statements, our listeners believe the nonverbal message rather than what is said.

Just how do our nonverbal messages betray our verbally encoded messages? Research suggests that when attempting to deceive another, a person may have a vocal quality with higher pitch, slower rate, and more pronunciation mistakes than normal. Ekman and Friesen's research indicates that the face, hands, and feet are important sources of information when one is attempting to determine whether someone is trying to hide the true meaning of the message being communicated.[2] Hess has discovered that the pupils of our eyes dilate when we become emotionally aroused.[3] Blushing, sweating, and changing breathing patterns also may betray our intended meaning. The polygraph (lie detector) test monitors the nonverbal responses accompanying statements that we offer as truth.

Several researchers have concluded that nonverbal messages are often more difficult to fake. Although we can monitor certain parts of our nonverbal behavior, it is difficult to consciously control all of our nonverbal behavior.

The previous discussion emphasized the importance of nonverbal communication in our communication efforts with others. Understanding the general functions of nonverbal communication will help you be more observant of both your own communication behavior and the communication patterns of others. First we will identify the relationships between nonverbal communication and the verbal communication code as they affect the meaning of messages. Then we will review three dimensions of nonverbal communication that should also assist you in understanding how nonverbal cues affect meaning.

FUNCTIONS OF NONVERBAL COMMUNICATION

Relationships between nonverbal communication and verbal communication

You may have gotten the impression that nonverbal communication is separate and distinct from verbal communication. But the truth is that verbal and nonverbal communication work together to create meaning. To help us understand how these communication codes work together, one researcher has identified six general purposes of nonverbal communication: (1) repeating, (2) contradicting, (3) substituting, (4) complementing, (5) accenting, and (6) regulating.[4]

Repeating Nonverbal communication may repeat a verbal message. When asked how to get to the personnel department, a security guard said, "Just go up those stairs and to the right," while pointing toward the stairway. His nonverbal message simply repeated his verbal direction.

Contradicting A professor who says, "Sure, I've got time to talk to you. What's on your mind?" while he is nervously looking at his watch, reaching for his hat, and grabbing his attache case, illustrates verbal/nonverbal contradictory messages. His nonverbal communication is providing *meta-communicative* information about his desire to sit and chat. "Meta-communication" means "communication about communication." In this case, the professor's nonverbal signals are providing communication about the validity of his verbal message. As previously noted, when there is a contradiction between the verbal and nonverbal messages, the nonverbal message will more than likely affect the meaning of the communication more than will the verbal message.

Substituting Nonverbal messages may be used as a substitute for the verbal message. As Edgar, a usually cheerful father and husband, comes to the breakfast table with a stern facial expression and suspiciously stares at each family member, his family need not be told that Edgar is upset and disturbed about something. No words were spoken, yet the message was communicated. Because our nonverbal cues are often more subtle and ambiguous than verbal messages, we may intentionally rely upon nonverbal behavior to communicate a message.

Complementing Nonverbal communication may also add additional meaning to the verbal message. Again, the nonverbal information may meta-communicatively assist in providing an appropriate interpretation of a message. A secretary who took a too leisurely lunch break, resulting in failure to complete an important assignment on time, may provide "complementary" nonverbal cues when apologizing to a superior; reduction in eye contact and vocal volume provides additional information about the sincerity of the apology.

Accenting Nonverbal communication may emphasize or accent a verbal message. By using more volume and shaking a fist, a public speaker can underscore the climax of a speech. Or you may often shake your head when you say "no" or nod your head when you say "yes," to accent your rejection or affirmation.

Regulating Nonverbal communication also performs the extremely important function of regulating the flow and interaction of communication between communicators. In a formal communication situation, such as a large conference, an individual may nonverbally signal a desire to communicate by raising a hand. In a less formal situation, making eye contact, leaning forward, and raising eyebrows serve as a regulatory cues to signal a desire to make a point.

Dimensions of nonverbal communication

How do you interpret the nonverbal messages that you receive? Mehrabian has developed a three-factor approach to identify how we respond to nonverbal messages. His model is useful because it can be used to understand better how we interpret nonverbal messages in a variety of contexts, and to help us assign meaning to specific nonverbal behaviors. Mehrabian's research suggests that we assign meaning to nonverbal behavior along three dimensions: (1) immediacy, (2) potency, and (3) responsiveness.

Immediacy   After being introduced to someone for the first time, you decide that you find the person attractive. You like this person, but you may not be able to identify specifically why you are attracted to him or her. It may be the individual's display of nonverbal immediacy cues. We are often not impressed by someone who does not look at us and requires a greater area of personal space. As defined by Mehrabian, immediacy refers to such nonverbal behaviors as those just identified—ones that affect whether we like or dislike another. The immediacy principle states, "People are drawn toward persons and things they like, evaluate highly, and prefer; and they avoid or move away from things they dislike, evaluate negatively, or do not prefer."[5] What are those specific nonverbal cues that contribute to perceptions of liking? Touch is one of the most important and powerful cues which indicate liking. A forward lean, eye contact, and close distances between people also can communicate liking. We may have more fa-

vorable impressions of people who sit closer to us, establish eye contact with us, and orient their bodies toward us.

Potency Mehrabian's second dimension of meaning refers to the communication of status or power. Persons of higher status generally determine the degree of closeness permitted in their interactions with others. A person of high status, for example, generally has a more relaxed body posture when interacting with a person of lower status. During a job interview, the personnel director may feel quite comfortable leaning back and relaxing, but the applicant (with considerably less status) is more likely to maintain a formal posture.

An individual's use of personal space provides another indication of his status; high status individuals generally maintain greater personal distance from others. And it is usually the higher status individual who determines what constitutes appropriate personal distances. The dean of a college probably has a larger desk than a newly hired secretary. The larger desk not only signifies status, but also serves as a barrier to keep others at a greater personal distance. When talking with someone of equal status, the dean will, more than likely, come from behind the desk and converse at a closer personal distance.

Responsiveness The third dimension of Mehrabian's three-factor model refers to our perceptions of others as active or passive, energetic or dull, fast or slow. The speed of a person's movement, the expression of emotion on her face, or her variation of the pitch, rate, volume, and quality of her voice all contribute to our perceptions of her as responsive or unresponsive. Some people with whom we talk just seem to be more responsive to our conversation with them. They usually have a more immediate posture, occasionally shake their head in agreement or disagreement with a point we have made, maintain an animated vocal quality, and generally express interest in our conversation.

DESCRIBING NONVERBAL BEHAVIOR

To help you understand how to be a better observer of nonverbal communication, it will be useful for you to learn how to classify nonverbal behavior. Several scholars have devised approaches to labeling different categories or types of nonverbal behavior. One of the easiest to understand is also one of the earliest developed. Reusch and Kees divided nonverbal behavior into three categories: (1) sign language, (2) action language, and (3) object language.[6] Let's take a closer look at these three types so that you can be more observant and accurate in your descriptions of the nonverbal behavior that you observe.

Sign language

Sign language consists of nonverbal behavior that takes the place of spoken words. A hitchhiker's thumbing for a ride is a good example. Similarly, rather than shouting "Hello" at friends we see at a distance, we may wave an arm or hand to indicate that we are glad to see them.

Action language

This category of nonverbal communication includes all facial expressions, postures, and movements that are not designed to signal a specific word or number. As you ride home from work on the bus, you may notice which of your fellow passengers have had a hard day at work because they look tired as they sit slumped over in their seats. The way a person walks, stands, or sits and uses facial expressions constitutes nonverbal action language.

Object language

Object language includes both intentional and unintentional displays of material things, such as architecture, works of art, and clothes and jewelry. The size of your office, number and size of rooms in your house, your designer jeans or three-piece suit, and the color and kind of car that you drive may not have been selected to make an intentional statement about you, but even though the inferences others make about you from such objects may not be totally accurate, they provide clues about your personality, attitudes, and feelings.

INTERPRETING NONVERBAL MESSAGES

Despite articles in magazines, newspapers, and paperback books, we cannot really "read a person like a book." The state of nonverbal communication theory and research does not permit us to make conclusive statements about a person's personality and personal habits, based solely upon nonverbal information. We do know, as we discussed earlier, that nonverbal communication is important in determining the way we respond to others and the way others respond to us. But we should be careful when trying to determine what a specific nonverbal cue means.

1. Context can affect the meaning of the nonverbal communication

Do you remember your English teacher's counseling you not to take quoted material out of context? Quoting a sentence or phrase out of context can distort its meaning. The same principle holds true for nonverbal communication. Simply looking at someone's posture without taking the contect into consideration can result in a misinterpretation of the behavior. For example, the fact that a woman is sitting with crossed legs and folded arms does not necessarily mean that she doesn't want to communicate to others, or that she is a "closed person." Other variables may be operating in the communication system to affect her posture and position.

It has been noted that the 500 most-used words in the English language have over 14,000 different dictionary definitions. It is thus very easy to misinterpret the word-usage of another. Even with comprehensive dictionaries we often have problems clearly understanding what other people mean. Nonverbal communication is even more ambiguous. And because it is, there is an even greater potential for misunderstanding the meaning of someone else's nonverbal cues. We do not have a comprehensive dictionary of nonverbal communication behavior. Therefore, we must be extra cautious not to think that we know what someone else is saying or feeling just by looking at nonverbal cues, without taking the context into consideration.

2. People respond differently to a common experience

Besides keeping the context in mind when trying to interpret the nonverbal communication of others, you should also remember that people respond differently to the same stimuli. For example, not all people express emotions in the same way. Usually, the longer you know people, the more accurate you can be in interpreting their nonverbal behavior. But it may take considerable time before you can begin to understand the unique, idiosyncratic meanings underlying specific nonverbal behaviors exhibited by another person. Family members are probably more accurate in judging the nonverbal communication of other family members than is someone from outside the family group. A wife may learn that when her husband comes home from work and turns on the television without offering a greeting, he has probably had a rough day. Children may also learn specific non-verbal cues that signal that their parents are in a silly mood, or may sense when to be on their best behavior because their parents are in no mood for foolishness.

3. What is appropriate in one culture may not be appropriate in another

A third principle to keep in mind is that each individual nonverbally responds in a manner appropriate for the culture in which the behavior was learned. Several researchers have documented cultural differences in posture, movement, personal space, territorial claims, facial expression, and uses of time. Not only your culture, but each group to which you belong may adopt certain normative non-verbal behaviors. Behavior acceptable in one group may not be appropriate in another. For example, in one class your instructor may expect you to raise your hand if you want to speak. Another instructor may encourage you to speak without raising your hand. Learning the nonverbal norms of the group can help you better interpret the messages communicated.

APPLICATIONS OF NONVERBAL COMMUNICATION RESEARCH

Thus far in this chapter we have primarily talked about theory and general principles of nonverbal communication. You may still be wondering, "Can these principles help me with my communication with others?" Since an important goal of this text is to help make theory practical, we will apply nonverbal communication research to several communication contexts. Specifically, we will discuss the implications of nonverbal communication research to the impression-formation process, public speaking, small groups, and communication in the classroom.

As we do so, we will be discussing the following sources of nonverbal communication: body posture and movement, eye contact, facial expressions, vocal cues, use of personal space and territory, personal appearance, and the communication environment.

Meeting people: nonverbal communication and impression formation

Have you found yourself with some time on your hands while waiting for someone at a shopping center or an airport and decided to do some "people watching"? Probably so. And most of us, when we are only casually observing people from a distance, or when we are formally introduced to them, make judgments about their status, personality, and intelligence, based upon our brief observation of them. Some researchers claim that in as little as three to five seconds after meeting people for the first time, we begin to form an impression of them. Others feel the first four minutes are critical to the impression-formation process. Of course, many of our first impressions may be erroneous—but we make the inferences, just the same. As we watch people at an airport or are fleetingly introduced at a party, we often do not spend much time in detailed conversation, so we base our judgments upon nonverbal information, rather than upon information that is self-disclosed.

Personal appearance   What are the nonverbal factors that influence how we perceive and are perceived by others? One of the most important variables is personal appearance. Several studies suggest that personal appearance influences a variety of factors. For example, females rated as more attractive were more effective in changing attitudes than were females rated as less attractive. More attractive individuals are often perceived as having more credibility than less attractive ones. They are also judged to be happier, more popular, more sociable, and more successful than those who are rated as being less attractive.[7]

Wells and Siegel have found that body shape affects our stereotypical perceptions of others.[8] Fat and round silhouette figures (also called endomorph body types) were rated as older, more old-fashioned, less good-looking, more talkative, and more good-natured. Athletic, muscular figures (mesomorph body types) were rated as more mature, better looking, taller, and more adventurous. Tall and thin silhouette drawings (ectomorph body type) were rated as more ambitious, more suspicious of others, more tense and nervous, more pessimistic, and quieter.

In addition to general physical attractiveness and the size and shape of the body, what a person wears affects the perceptions others develop of him or her. Two recent books by John T. Malloy, *Dress for Success* and *Dress for Success for Women,* prescribe the types of apparel that elicit perceptions of competency, power, and status. Though research to support Malloy's claims is scant, the success of his popular advice books suggests that the American public accepts his premise that clothing helps achieve the power look. For example, a study by Lefkowitz, Blake, and Mouton found that a well-dressed man who violated a "Don't walk" sign at a busy street corner was able to attract more followers than a violator who was not well-dressed.[9] Personal appearance then, has an important influence on our overall perceptions of others.

Eye contact   Eye contact is another variable that affects how we are perceived when we meet someone. One important function of eye contact is to signal when the communication channel is open or closed. Establishing eye contact with someone often signals that you want to communicate with him or her. Have you ever been caught people watching? Have you found yourself staring at someone, only to have that person catch you staring? If so, probably you either quickly looked away to indicate that you did not want to communicate, or flashed a brief smile and said, "Hello."

When we establish eye contact with another, the amount of time we spend looking at the other person depends on whether we are speaking or listening. We have more eye contact with someone while we are listening than while we are speaking. Research also reveals that mutual eye contact between two people does not last long at all—only from three to seven seconds at a time.

Greeting others   Several researchers have studied the combinations of nonverbal signals that occur when we greet someone. Kendon and Ferber have identified six stages that we typically pass through when greeting a person.[10] First is the *sighting*—we spot someone coming from a distance. Stage two is called the *distant salutation*—here we may smile, toss our head, or wave to signal that we recognize our friend. Third stage is the *head dip*—we lower our head to provide a transition from sighting them from a distance to seeing them at closer range. Stage four is the *approach*—characterized by increased eye contact to signal that the communication channel is open. The fifth stage, called the *final approach,* occurs when we are less than 10 feet apart. This stage is illustrated by mutual eye contact and smiling, and the palms of our hands may be open toward the other person. The final stage is called the *close salutation.* This includes close physical contact (handshake, hugs) and cliché verbal communication, such as "Nice to see you."

Another team of researchers reported about the same results as Kendon and Ferber. They found that a smile is the facial expression that usually sets the emotional tone for a greeting.[11] Most greeters also engage in the eyebrow flash. This is a sudden raising of the eyebrows, which gives a wide-eyed look. Typical gestures such as handshakes are also involved.

Another researcher was interested more specifically in American courtship behavior.[12] After making films in a variety of situations involving people meeting one another and establishing interpersonal relationships, he identified four general stages of developing a courtship relationship with another. He called his categories "quasi-courtship behaviors" to indicate that these nonverbal displays do not just occur when two individuals of the opposite sex are establishing a relationship, but can apply to a wide variety of interpersonal interactions involving people meeting.

His first stage is called *courtship readiness.* During this phase, people exhibit an increase in muscle tone and a more erect posture. For example, when we are getting ready to meet someone, we may pull in our stomachs, stand up straighter, and generally prepare to provide the best possible physical impression.

The second stage involves *preening behavior.* A preen is something that we do to optimize our personal appearance, such as a last-minute combing of our hair, touching-up of makeup, smoothing of clothes, or tightening of our tie knot. We expend every effort to prepare to make the best impression possible.

The third stage is called *positional cues.* After making sure that we look our best, we put ourselves into position to meet the other person. We select a seat close to him or her or we move into position to signal that this is really the only person with whom we are interested in communicating at the moment. Our body posture provides an important cue as to how interested we are in interaction.

The final stage in this quasi-courtship behavior pattern involves *actions of appeal or invitation.* This phase includes more overt signals, such as long-held eye contact, that indicate we are very much interested in establishing a longer, more involved interpersonal relationship. Certainly not everyone engages in quasi-courtship behavior in exactly the same way. The research does suggest, however, that some predictable patterns of appearance, posture, eye contact, gestures, and facial expression are involved in our attempt to establish favorable impressions.

Speaking to an audience: nonverbal communication and speaker effectiveness

Do you have a favorite news announcer whom you like to watch on television? Perhaps there is one anchor person, either on national news or your local TV station, whom you find comfortable to listen to. Most anchor persons report approximately the same stories. The big difference is in the way they present their stories to the viewers—the way they deliver the news. When we talk about delivery we are really talking about nonverbal communication. Later on we will talk about speech delivery as an important aspect of preparing and presenting a public speech. But as we talk about nonverbal communication in this chapter, it is important to recognize the effect a speaker's eye contact, posture, vocal inflection, and facial expression has upon an audience.

Eye contact   We mentioned that one important function of eye contact is to signal when the communication channel is open—to indicate when we want to talk to someone. Eye contact performs this same function when a speaker talks to an audience. If the speaker refuses to maintain eye contact with the audience, the audience may think the speaker is not really interested in communicating the message to them. Studies also indicate that eye contact is one of the most important variables to help establish a speaker as competent, honest, sincere, and dynamic. There is also evidence that speaker eye contact can help improve listener comprehension of a spoken message.

Vocal inflection   Another important nonverbal cue is the pitch, rate, and quality of your voice. Several studies indicate that others make judgments about your personality and emotional state based upon your vocal cues.[13] Even though research indicates that listeners often inaccurately judge *personality* characteristics, judgments of speakers' *emotional states* are more accurate. Recall the estimate that as much as 38 percent of the communication of our emotional stress is achieved through vocal cues.

Variation in vocal inflection has been found by some scholars to increase the likelihood that your message will be comprehended and remembered by an audience.[14] Other researchers, however, have not found significant increases in comprehension and retention because of increased vocal variation.[15]

The analysis of several studies attempting to determine whether one can accurately identify personality characteristics from vocal cues, results in the conclusion that (1) there is usually considerable *agreement* among judges regarding certain personality characteristics communicated by the voice, and yet (2) in many cases (not all), judges *cannot accurately determine* the personality of a speaker, based solely on vocal cues.

Posture and movement   Does the posture of a speaker have an impact on the perceived effectiveness of the speaker? Evidence suggests that some feelings and attitudes can be communicated by an individual's posture, but that speaker posture and movement communicate the intensity of the particular emotion being expressed, rather than the specific emotion itself. In the context of public speaking settings, how a speaker's posture will be perceived may depend upon what the audience expects from the speaker. For example, if the audience expects the speaker to deliver a formal public address and the speaker's posture suggests a casual, informal style, the lack of a more formal posture may distract the audience. While research suggests that a speaker's posture and use of movement and gestures can have either a positive or a negative influence on perceived effectiveness, it is difficult to prescribe some best posture or set of gestures for public speaking. As will be further discussed in Chapter 11, it is better to strive for a posture and use of gestures that fits your style and is appropriate to your topic and the expectations of your audience.

Working in groups: nonverbal communication and group decision making

Seating arrangement   A fascinating place to look for the effects of nonverbal communication variables is in a small-group setting. The study of *small-group ecology*—the consistent ways in which people arrange themselves in small groups—can provide insights into leadership, status, and communication interaction patterns. Stenzor found that when group members were seated in a circle, they were more likely to talk to the person across from them than to those on either side of them.[16] At least two teams of researchers have discovered that the more dominant group members tend to select a seat at the head of a rectangular table or a seat which will maximize their opportunity to communicate with others.[17] In addition, people who sit at the corner seats of a rectangular table generally contribute the least amount of information to a discussion. If you find yourself in a position to prepare the seating arrangement for a group discussion on conference, armed with this information, you should be able to make more informed choices regarding who should sit where and the probable effect of the seating arrangement upon verbal interaction.

Did you realize that the seat you select when working with others in a small group may effect the probability of your emerging as the leader of the group? In one research study, five people sat around a table, three on one side and two on the other. The researcher discovered that there was a greater probability of the discussants' becoming leaders if they sat on the side of the table *facing* the other three discussion members.[18] More direct eye contact with more group members, which can subsequently result in a greater control of the verbal communication, may explain why the two individuals who faced the other three group members emerged as leaders beyond chance expectations.

Other researchers have discovered that such variables as stress, sex, and personality characteristics also may affect how we arrange ourselves in small groups. Dosey and Meisels concluded that people prefer greater personal space when they are under stress.[19] If you know, for example, that an upcoming discussion will probably be anxiety-producing, Dosey and Meisel's study indicates it would be preferable to hold the meeting in a room which would permit the group members to have a bit more freedom of movement. This would assist them in finding their preferred personal distance from fellow group members.

Collectively, these studies suggest that there is some consistency in the way we choose to arrange ourselves in small-group discussions. A chairperson of a group or committee who understands general group member seating preferences should be able to assist in providing a more comfortable climate for conferences and group discussions.

Earlier in this chapter we noted that object language, the physical environment, and artifacts (such as clothing and jewelry) are nonverbal variables that can affect human communication. The environment and room decor can affect a group's ability to work together. Studies by Maslow and Mintz examined whether room decor has an effect upon the occupants of the room.[20] These researchers "decorated" three rooms. One was refurbished to fit the label of an ugly room. It resembled a drab, cluttered janitor's storeroom, and was rated as horrible and repulsive by observers assigned to examine it. The second room was decorated to look like an average room, described as looking similar to a professor's office. The third room was adorned with carpeting, drapes, tasteful furniture, and room decorations, and was labeled a beautiful room. After the rooms were decorated, individuals were assigned to each of the three rooms and were given the task of rating several facial photographs. The results of the experiment indicated that the environment had a significant effect upon how the subjects rated the faces. Facial photographs were rated higher in the beautiful room than in the ugly room. Subjects in the ugly room also reported that the task was more unpleasant and monotonous than did subjects who were assigned to the beautiful room. Subjects assigned to the ugly room attempted to leave sooner than did subjects assigned to the beautiful room.

Additional research suggests that the environment can also affect your ability to solve problems in a group. People can generally do a better job of comprehending information and solving problems in a more aesthetically attractive environment. But research does not suggest that there is one best environmental condition for all group communication situations. The optimal environment is dependent upon the specific task, as well as upon the needs and expectations of group members.

Eye contact   In addition to group member seating arrangement and environment, group members' eye contact is a very important variable affecting verbal interaction. We have already noted how eye contact is important when we form impressions of people and when we speak in public. In the small group, eye contact serves an important regulatory function, helping to control the back-and-forth flow of communication. We can invite interaction simply by looking at others. For example, imagine that the chairperson of a committee of which you are a member asks for volunteers for an assignment. If you don't want to be "volunteered" for the task, you will probably not establish eye contact with the chairman, just as students do not establish eye contact when the teacher of a class asks a question and students don't know the answer. Direct eye contact may be interpreted to mean that the communication channel is open and the students would not mind being called upon for the response.

Teachers and students: nonverbal communication in the classroom

A bell rings, you enter a classroom, and a teacher begins a lecture. How important are nonverbal communication variables to the effectiveness of the teacher presenting information to you? Does the amount of teacher eye contact, movement, and gesture affect your attitudes about learning? Can the teacher's vocal inflection and appearance affect the amount of information you will remember from a lecture? From recent research, we are now convinced that nonverbal communication plays a major role in affecting how much you learn in the classroom. Let's examine some specific conclusions about the impact of nonverbal cues in the educational setting.

Posture and movement   In most classes, at the end of the semester students are asked to evaluate the teaching effectiveness of their instructor. Instructor evaluations are designed to determine whether the instructor is competent, prepared, and interested in teaching. Recent studies suggest that one important variable that influences student evaluations of teachers is the amount of activity—movement and gesture—exhibited by the teacher.[21] Studies have consistently found that teachers who are more active, use several gestures, and move around the class are rated as more effective teachers by their students. This does not necessarily mean that they are "better teachers," only that they have been evaluated more positively than teachers who move and gesture less frequently.

Eye contact   One of the authors remembers having taken a history course in which the instructor would always look just above the heads of the students. She would not look at her students. To this day what he remembers about that class is not the amount of history that he learned, but the impact of the lack of teacher eye contact with her students. As we have already discussed when we talked about public speaking, eye contact is important in affecting both amount of information recalled and the attitude that we have toward a speaker. Research conducted in the classroom yields similar results regarding communication between teachers and students. Teacher eye contact also can improve student attention and enhance class participation. Thus, eye contact is linked to many valuable educational outcomes. It can enhance learning, attitudes toward the teacher, student attentiveness, and class participation.

Vocal inflection   All of us have had the experience of listening to a teacher give a lecture in a monotone. Does this monotonous vocal inflection affect our attitudes toward the teacher and how much we are learning in the class? While the research results are not consistent, it does appear that a lack of vocal inflection will have some effect on a teacher's credibility. In other words, we may feel a teacher who uses greater vocal variation is more competent than one who uses a monotonous vocal quality. As noted earlier, however, vocal inflection does not necessarily enhance the comprehension of the information presented. As long as the teacher talks loudly enough for us to understand, we may be fairly adaptable to vocal cues and be able to comprehend information, regardless of the vocal quality. So if you find you have a teacher with an unexciting or monotonous vocal quality, don't blame your poor test performance on the teacher's voice.

Classroom environment   We have already noted how the environment of a room can affect group communication. The size, shape, and color of a classroom also have an effect upon the learning that occurs there. For example, the design of a school has been shown to affect where students will gather before and after class. After conducting a series of observations of the classroom environment, Sommer observed: "The present rectangular classroom with its straight rows of chairs and wide windows was intended to provide for ventilation, light, quick departure, ease of surveillance, and a host of other legitimate needs as they existed in the early 1900's."[22]

Sommer went on to note that in spite of technical advancements in classroom environments, "Most schools are still boxes filled with cubes, each containing a specified number of chairs in straight rows."[23] Another team of researchers noted that when students are seated in straight rows, most student participation comes from those seated in the front and center of the room—an area that allows more student and instructor eye contact than do other areas.

Did you realize that the color of the classroom you sit in can also affect your attitudes about learning and how well you learn? One study found that students who attended a school with colorful walls, as opposed to students who attended schools whose walls were in need of a coat of paint, or whose walls were painted off-white with white ceilings, showed more improvement in several academic areas after a two-year period than did students who attended the less colorful schools.[24] It is clear that the classroom environment does have an impact upon students' attitudes and achievement.

NONVERBAL COMMUNICATION

PUTTING THEORY INTO PRACTICE

In this chapter we noted how important nonverbal communication is to the total communication process. We defined nonverbal communication as communicative behavior which does not rely upon a written or spoken linguistic code, but which creates meaning within oneself or between two or more individuals.

There are several reasons you should study nonverbal communication. First, nonverbal communication plays a major role in your overall communication with others. Second, nonverbal communication is the primary way in which you communicate feelings and attitudes toward others. And third, nonverbal cues are believed more than the verbal content of a message.

Nonverbal cues operate together with verbal communication to serve several important communication functions. Nonverbal cues can repeat verbal information, contradict what is spoken, substitute for verbal communication, complement words, accent a point, and regulate the flow of communication. Mehrabian identified three dimensions of nonverbal communication—immediacy, potency, and responsiveness—that explain how we assign meaning to the nonverbal behavior we observe. We also noted three general categories for describing nonverbal communication: sign language, action language, and object language.

As we have noted in this chapter, be cautious in your efforts to "read" specific meanings into the body language of others. But this is not to suggest that you should refrain from trying to enhance your own sensitivity to the nonverbal behaviors that surround you. Look, observe, and listen. Become more aware of the unspoken messages around you. To help improve your sensitivity to nonverbal cues, consider the following key suggestions that we have made in this chapter.

Improving your skill in interpreting nonverbal messages

- Consider the context of the nonverbal communication.
- Realize that people respond differently to common experiences.
- Keep in mind that people use nonverbal behavior that is appropriate for a given culture.

Meeting people: nonverbal communication and impression formation

- Your personal appearance (clothing, body size, etc.) plays a major role in influencing how others make impressions of you.
- Eye contact often signals that you want to communicate with the person you are looking at.

Speaking to an audience: nonverbal communication and speaker effectiveness

- Establish direct eye contact with your audience to indicate that you are interested in them and that you are a competent speaker.
- When speaking to an audience, use appropriately varied vocal inflection, pitch, and rate to communicate interest and to improve listener comprehension of your message.
- Pay attention to your posture and gestures while speaking, so that you do not distract your listeners with inappropriate movement and body position.

Working in groups: nonverbal communication and group decision making

- You are more likely to emerge as the leader of a small group if you establish eye contact and direct body orientation with most of the group members.
- You can sometimes draw a person into conversation just by establishing eye contact.
- Since people prefer greater personal space when they are under stress, you should make sure that the various group members are afforded plenty of territory if you know that a group meeting is going to be stressful.

Teachers and students: nonverbal communication in the classroom

- Students generally prefer teachers who are more active to those who do not move around while teaching.
- Eye contact between teacher and student can enhance class participation.
- The size, shape, and color of a classroom can affect teacher-student interaction and learning.

SUGGESTED ACTIVITIES

1. Watch a broadcast of the evening news. Analyze the anchor person's use of nonverbal communication. Note vocal cues, physical appearance, movement and gesture, and facial expressions. How do the nonverbal cues affect your impression of the anchor person? What makes the person credible? Can you tell how the anchor person felt about the story, from the way he or she read the story? Take notes of your observations and compare your notes with those of other students in the class.

2. On the basis of the discussion of nonverbal communication and classroom communication, analyze the environment of your classroom. Do the colors make the room conducive to learning? Is the physical arrangement of the room useful or distracting? Does the style of the furniture affect your attitude about learning? Based upon the reading in the chapter and your observations as a student, design what you consider to be the ideal classroom environment.

3. Imagine that you have been invited to an interview for a top management position with an important large corporation. Taking into consideration the clothes you currently own, what would you wear to the interview? Why would you wear what you selected? Share your choices with other students. What type of image would you like to project?

NOTES

[1]Albert Mehrabian, *Nonverbal Communication* (Chicago: Aldine Publishing Company, 1972), p. 108.

[2]Paul Ekman and Wallace V. Friesen, "Hand Movements," *Journal of Communication,* 22 (1972):353–374.

[3]Eckhard Hess, *The Tell-Tale Eye* (New York: Van Nostrand Reinhold Company, 1975).

[4]Paul Ekman, "Communication Through Nonverbal Behavior: A Source of Information About an Interpersonal Relationship," in S. S. Tomkins and C. E. Izard, eds., *Affect, Cognition and Personality* (New York: Springer Publishing Co., 1965).

[5]Albert Mehrabian, *Silent Messages* (Belmont, CA: Wadsworth Publishing Co., 1971), p. 1.

[6]Jurgen Reusch and Welldon Kees, *Nonverbal Communication: Notes on the Visual Perception of Human Relations* (Berkeley and Los Angeles: University of California Press, 1956), p. 189.

[7]See, for example, Judson Mills and Elliot Aronson, "Opinion Change as a Function of the Communicator's Attractiveness and Desire to Influence," *Journal of Personality and Social Psychology*, 1 (1965):75–77.

[8]William Wells and B. Siegel, "Stereotyped Somatypes," *Psychological Reports*, 8 (1961):77–78.

[9]M. Lefkowitz, Robert Blake, and Jane Mouton, "Status Factors in Pedestrian Violation of Traffic Signals," *Journal of Abnormal and Social Psychology*, 51 (1955):704–706.

[10]Adam Kendon and A. Ferber, "A Description of Some Human Greetings," in R. P. Michael and J. H. Cook, eds., *Comparative Ecology and Behaviour of Primates* (London: Academic Press, 1973).

[11]Mark L. Knapp, Rod P. Hart, Gustav W. Fredrich, and G. M. Schulman, "The Rhetoric of Goodbye: Verbal and Nonverbal Correlates of Human Leave-Taking," *Speech Monographs*, 40 (1973): 182–198.

[12]Albert E. Scheflen, "Quasi-Courtship Behavior in Psychotherapy," *Psychiatry*, 28 (1965):245–257.

[13]See, for example: Joel R. Davitz, *The Communication of Emotional Meaning* (New York: McGraw-Hill Book Company, 1964); T. H. Pear, *Voice and Personality* (London: Chapman and Hall, 1931).

[14]Charles Woolbert, "The Effects of Various Modes of Public Reading," *Journal of Applied Psychology*, 4 (1920):162–185; G. M. Glasgow, "A Semantic Index of Vocal Pitch," *Speech Monographs*, 19 (1952):64–68.

[15]Charles F. Diehl, R. C. White, and P. H. Satz, "Pitch Change and Comprehension," *Speech Monographs*, 28 (1961):65–68.

[16]Bernard Stenzor, "The Spatial Factor in Face to Face Discussion Groups," *Journal of Abnormal and Social Psychology*, 45 (1950):552–555.

[17]A. Hare and Robert Bales, "Seating Position and Small Group Interaction," *Sociometry*, 26 (1963): 480–486.

[18]Lloyd T. Howells and Selwyn W. Becker, "Seating Arrangement and Leadership Emergence," *Journal of Abnormal and Social Psychology*, 64 (1962):148–150.

[19]Michael Dosey and Murry Meisels, "Personal Space and Self Protection," *Journal of Personality and Social Psychology*, 11 (1969):93–97.

[20]Abraham H. Maslow and N. L. Mintz, "Effects of Esthetic Surroundings: I. Initial Effects of Three Esthetic Conditions upon Perceiving 'Energy' and 'Wellbeing' in Faces," *Journal of Psychology*, 41 (1956):247–254.

[21]Thomas H. Willett, "A Descriptive Analysis of Nonverbal Behaviors of College Teachers," unpublished doctoral dissertation, University of Missouri-Columbia, 1976.

[22]Robert Sommer, *Personal Space: The Behavioral Basis of Design* (Englewood Cliffs, New Jersey: Prentice-Hall, 1969), p. 98.

[23]Ibid., p. 99.

[24]H. Ketcham, *Color Planning for Business and Industry* (New York: Harper & Brothers, 1958).

7 IMPROVING LISTENING AND FEEDBACK SKILLS

After studying this chapter you should be able to:

Identify the steps in the listening process

Describe four types of listening

List three suggestions for improving your note-taking ability

Identify reasons you have problems in listening

Identify suggestions for improving your listening ability

Describe the functions of feedback

Improve your ability to provide feedback to others

Use the active listening technique

"I'm sorry, I wasn't listening."
"What did you say?"
"How's that again?"
"Would you say that again?"

How many times a day do you use these phrases? If you're typical of many people, you probably find that these statements are sprinkled throughout your conversations. It has been estimated that we spend about 70 percent of our time engaged in communication with others. Of that communication time, we spend about 11 percent writing, 15 percent reading, 32 percent speaking, and 42 percent listening.[1] These statistics suggest that listening is a very important skill to be cultivated.

Yet most people have never had formal listening training. We spend the least amount of our communication time writing, yet we start learning how to write in pre-school and continue to improve our writing skills through graduate school. Obviously, since you are reading this book, you know how to read. We have reading specialists in most elementary schools and in many high schools and colleges. While fewer students receive formal training in speaking, chances are certainly greater that you have had a public speaking course than a listening course. Many colleges and universities require students to develop oral communication skills. Yet, despite the amount of time we spend listening to others, a relatively small number of universities offer a course in listening. Certainly we would not argue that writing, reading, and speaking are unimportant skills that should not receive considerable emphasis in educational curriculums. But it is evident that listening is a skill that needs to be taught, as well.

ARE YOU A GOOD LISTENER?

Do you really need to improve your listening skills? Do you think most people are good listeners? A study examining the listening ability of husbands and wives suggests that they could do a better job of listening to each other. Researchers studying husband-and-wife communication, using couples who had been married for several years, put husbands in one room and wives in another. Researchers asked each group, "During the past three months have you and your spouse talked about who is responsible for taking out the garbage and doing other chores around the house?" The result: 71 percent of the wives reported that they had had such conversations with their husbands, but only 19 percent of the husbands remembered hearing such a discussion. Researchers also asked each group, "During the past three months have you and your spouse talked about having children?" The result: 91 percent of the wives reported that they had had such a discussion, but only 15 percent of the husbands recalled talking about starting a family or increasing family size. While the results of a single study do

not suggest that all couples listen and recall with the same degree of ineffectiveness, this study does suggest that, at least in some families, listening could be improved.

Forty-eight hours after listening to a 10-minute presentation, most people can recall about half of the information presented. Eventually, we retain less than 25 percent of what we hear. One educator has noted, "We hear half of what is said to us, understand only half of that, believe only half of that, and remember only half of that."

A study by two communication researchers suggests that in a grammar school classroom situation you were probably a more *attentive* listener than you are today.[2] It seems that younger children, despite shorter attention spans, listen with greater intensity and attentiveness than do older children. And by the time we become adolescents, our listening attentiveness is drastically reduced. The researchers were interested in how attentively children listen in a classroom environment. While a teacher was delivering a presentation to first-graders, she was instructed to stop the lecture periodically and ask the students what she was talking about. Ninety percent of the first-grade children could repeat what the teacher was saying. The researchers conducted the same experiment with second-grade children. Eighty percent of second graders could repeat what the teacher was talking about. When the study was conducted with junior high school students, only 44 percent of them could repeat what their teacher was saying. And senior high school students were even less attentive. Only 28 percent of them could repeat what their teacher had said.

A college professor, interested in how well his students were listening to him, conducted a similar experiment.[3] While he was delivering a lecture to his students, he would, without warning, fire a blank handgun; he would then ask his students to record the thoughts that the noise had interrupted. His findings are worth noting. Twenty percent of his students were pursuing erotic thoughts or sexual fantasies. Another 20 percent were reminiscing about something. Another 20 percent were worrying or thinking about lunch. Eight percent, surprisingly enough, reported that they were thinking about religion. Twenty percent were listening to the professor—or at least that's what they reported. But only 12 percent were actively listening to the lecture and able to recall with a moderate degree of accuracy what the professor was talking about.

The evidence is clear. Most people need to improve their listening skills. In a recent survey, only 5 percent of the people polled felt that they were really good listeners. Eighty-five percent felt that they were no better than average.[4]

WHAT IS LISTENING?

It would seem that a word like "listening" would not need a formal textbook definition. Doesn't everybody know what listening is? The listening process, however, is a bit trickier than you might think. Listening involves the processes of *selecting, attending, understanding,* and *remembering.*

Selecting

Stop reading this book for just a moment. What do you hear? What sounds surround you? Did you realize that someone was playing a stereo? Or did you hear the sound of birds or rain or wind? Maybe you weren't really aware of the furnace, air conditioner, TV, voices, clock, a car, a plane, or a train. Sounds surround you. They are there to be heard if we only select the ones we want to hear, the ones that are important to us.

Attending

"Attention is a great deal like electricity: We don't know what it is, but we do know what it does and what conditions bring it about."[5] Attention is the sequel to selecting. After we select a sound from our environment, we attend to it; we focus on it. We may only attend to it for a fraction of a second, changing our focus of attention for a variety of reasons. But, however fleeting, attention must be focused for listening to occur.

Understanding

After you have selected and attended to a sound stimulus, you then attempt to understand it. Understanding is the process of assigning meaning to the stimuli that we attend to. There are several theories that attempt to describe the process of assigning meaning to what we see and hear, but as yet there is no one commonly accepted explanation of understanding. We do know that we understand what we hear by relating it to something we have already heard. If you have never had an algebra class before, your instructor would probably not be very successful in helping you to understand your calculus lesson. You would be able to *hear* what your teacher said, but you probably would not understand it. You would have no experience or concepts to help you assign meaning to what you heard.

Remembering

Most listening experts feel that the best way to describe whether listening really occurs is to determine whether the person can remember what was heard. Some definitions of listening include the notion that it involves acting in response to the information that we hear. Remembering information is a way of responding to what we hear. While it is true that we may not remember the information for a long period of time, we can determine if listening occurs by noting whether an individual can recall what was said.

Psychologists who study the memory process believe that we have both a *short-term memory* and a *long-term memory* system. Short-term memory is activated for most of the information to which we assign meaning. But unless the information is really important or we make an effort to learn it, we may forget what goes into our short-term memory system. Do you remember the phone numbers you dialed yesterday? How about the names of several people that were in your history class last year? You knew them during the semester you took history, as you came in contact with them frequently, but after you lost contact with them, it became more difficult to recall their names. On the other hand, you certainly remember your address, the names of your family members, and where you work or go to school. Long-term memory is activated by repeated exposure to information. It is also activated when information is important to us.

TYPES OF LISTENING

We noted earlier that you spend the largest share of your communication time listening. Did you ever stop to wonder why this is so? There are at least four different types of listening: (1) listening to enjoy, (2) listening to evaluate, (3) listening to empathize, and (4) listening to gain information. Let's take a closer look at each.

Listening to enjoy

Did you listen to your stereo today? Or did you recently attend a concert, watch a comedian on TV, or go to a movie? In each of these situations your prime purpose was to listen because you wanted to be entertained. You were not necessarily concerned about learning, nor were you trying to be critical or to listen for therapeutic reasons (also called empathetic listening). You just wanted to enjoy yourself. We spend a considerable portion of our time listening just because we want to hear good music, laugh, or hear a good story.

Listening to evaluate

Did you watch the presidential debates that preceded the last national election? If you did, you were probably trying to determine which of the candidates would be a better President of the United States. Your main objective was to judge the wisdom of the policies they advocated and determine who had a better command of domestic and world issues. You were evaluating their qualifications. When we listen to evaluate, we try to determine whether the information we hear is valid, reliable, believable, or useful.

One problem many of us have when we listen to evaluate a message is that we become so preoccupied with criticizing the message that we often do not completely understand the information presented. Your authors have found that when we evaluate and grade student speeches, it is difficult to recall in great detail the information presented. Often the very process of evaluation—making judgments and decisions about information—interferes with the capacity to understand and recall that information. So it is important to make certain that you understand what the speaker is saying before you make a judgment as to how effective or believable the information presented is.

Listening to empathize

Your best friend tells you that it's been one of those days. Everything just seemed to go wrong. His car didn't start. He overslept. And, worst of all, he found out he may get laid off from his job. After a day like this, he needed to talk to someone—someone who would listen. He didn't need advice, just a person who would try to understand some of his troubles. For it seems that when someone understands our frustrations, coping becomes a little easier. So you listen. You are an empathetic listener when you serve as a sounding board for someone else.

Your empathetic listening serves an important therapeutic function. You're not there to judge or necessarily to learn about all of the troubles that someone may have had. You listen because the process of sharing and listening is a soothing one that can often restore a sense of perspective about the problem.

Humorist Erma Bombeck describes a poignant example of listening to empathize. Read her story and discover the value of empathetic listening.

ARE YOU LISTENING?

It was one of those days when I wanted my own apartment . . . unlisted.

My son was telling me in complete detail about a movie he had just seen, punctuated by three thousand "You know's?" My teeth were falling asleep.

There were three phone calls—strike that—three monologues that could have been answered by a recording. I fought the urge to say, "It's been nice listening to you."

In the cab from home to the airport, I got another assault on my ear, this time by a cab driver who was rambling on about his son whom he supported in college, and was in his last year, who put a P. S. on his letter saying, "I got married. Her name is Diane." He asked me, "What do you think of that?" and proceeded to answer the question himself.

There were thirty whole beautiful minutes before my plane took off . . . time for me to be alone with my own thoughts, to open a book and let my mind wander. A voice next to me belonging to an elderly woman said, "I'll bet it's cold in Chicago."

Stone-faced, I answered, "It's likely."

"I haven't been to Chicago in nearly three years," she persisted. "My son lives there."

"That's nice," I said, my eyes intent on the printed page of the book.

"My husband's body is on this plane. We've been married for fifty-three years. I don't drive, you know, and when he died a nun drove me from the hospital. We aren't even Catholic. The funeral director let me come to the airport with him."

I don't think I have ever detested myself more than I did at that moment. Another human being was screaming to be heard and in desperation had turned to a cold stranger who was more interested in a novel than the real-life drama at her elbow.

All she needed was a listener . . . no advice, wisdom, experience, money, assistance, expertise or even compassion . . . but just a minute or two to listen.

It seemed rather incongruous that in a society of supersophisticated communication, we often suffer from a shortage of listeners.

She talked numbly and steadily until we boarded the plane, then found her seat in another section. As I hung up my coat, I heard her plaintive voice say to her seat companion, "I'll bet it's cold in Chicago."

I prayed, "Please God, let her listen."

Why am I telling you this? To make me feel better. It won't help, though.[6]

Listening to gain information

As a student, think about how much time you spend each week listening to people talk because they want you to learn something. How much time did you spend today listening to a lecture or class discussion? Your taking a phone message or receiving instructions from your boss to complete an assigned task are other examples of listening for information. Undoubtedly, you spend quite a bit of time listening when your prime objective is to be able to recall what the speaker said.

It is usually fairly difficult to remember the details of a lengthy speech or discussion without having taken notes. An individual who has mastered the art of listening for information has also probably perfected a note-taking system. When your job is to listen for information, consider the following suggestions about trying to take notes:

1. Come prepared to take notes, even if you're not sure you need to. Bring a pencil or pen and some paper with you.
2. After the presentation has started, determine whether you need to take notes or not. If you are going to receive a handout outlining the presentation after the lecture, don't waste time trying to take notes.
3. If you do decide to take notes, decide whether you need to outline the speech, identify facts and principles, jot down key words, or just record major ideas. If the speaker is not following an outline pattern, it will be tricky to outline the message. If you are going to take an objective examination on the material, maybe you just need to note facts (like names, dates, etc.) and principles that are presented. If you are going to prepare a report for someone else to read, just noting key words may be sufficient to help you remember what is said. Or you may just want to write down major ideas to help you recall the key points of the speech.
4. Don't take too many notes. Determine how important the information is to you and why you should remember what is being said. If you're going to report the essence of the presentation to someone else on the same day, you probably do not need to scribble down almost everything that is said. In addition, the less time you spend writing notes,

the more time you have to concentrate on listening to what is being said.

LISTENING BARRICADES: WHY WE DON'T LISTEN WELL

A barricade is something that keeps you from achieving your goal. It slows your progress, efficiency, and accuracy. Let's identify several listening barricades so that you can spot and try to eliminate them.

Suffering from information overload

As noted earlier, we spend the greatest proportion of our communication time listening to others. Did you realize that you listen to over a billion words a year? It may be because we have to listen to such a volume of information that we suffer from information overload.

Have you ever noticed how most medical doctors' handwriting is illegible? One reason may be that during their study for the medical profession and the execution of their duties, they have had to write such a great deal that they developed the habit of using shortcuts in writing. These may result in sloppy, illegible handwriting. The same principle may be operating in our listening ability. If we spend up to five hours a day listening to people speak, we may tune out what others say because we become fatigued and take listening shortcuts.

What's the solution to this problem? If you are speaking to someone who may be tired and suffering from information overload or listening fatigue, try, if possible, to pick a time to communicate important information when the listener is rested. Don't assume that just because you are ready to talk, the other person is going to be ready to listen to you.

On the other hand, if someone wants to talk to you and you really don't want to listen, you may have to recognize your fatigue and try a little harder to focus upon what the other person is saying. If you are really unable to concentrate and you sense that the person has very important information to discuss, perhaps you could say that you are very tired, but could set aside some time later to listen intelligently.

Deciding that the topic is not interesting

Most of us have been guilty of tuning a speaker out because we felt that the presentation was going to be boring or unimportant to us. Granted, some of the presentations we are forced or expected to sit through are dull and of little value. But we often miss out if we reach this conclusion too early. In the opening moments of a speech, the speaker should convince the audience of the relevance of the topic to them and try to rouse their interest. Unfortunately, not all (or even most) speakers follow this principle. When they don't, the listener reaches a quick conclusion that the speech is not going to be relevant, and so listening effectiveness is diminished—and perhaps something important is missed.

Don't decide too quickly that the presentation is not going to be of interest to you. The fact that a speech is not entertaining or immediately interesting does not give you a good excuse to try any less hard to listen. Yes, it is more difficult to listen to a presentation that does not immediately catch your attention and speak to your needs. But you will miss out on much useful information if you prematurely label a speech uninteresting without really giving the speaker a chance to develop the message.

Becoming wrapped up in our personal concerns

Have you ever been guilty of thinking about what you were going to say next, instead of listening to what another person was saying to you? Unflattering as it may sound, most listeners give priority to their own thoughts (intrapersonal communication) over the message of someone talking to them. Audiologists believe that we can really only concentrate on one thing at a time. If we are thinking about what we want to say, or thinking about personal problems, we will not be able to give full attention to the messages of others.

The solution? First, realize that this barricade exists—that you have a natural tendency to be more interested in your concerns or in what you want to contribute than in the messages of others. Second, try to turn off those internal concerns by concentrating on the message of the speaker. It is going to be difficult to totally block out your internal messages, but with sustained effort and self-motivation, you can accomplish it.

Outside distractions

Another barrier to effective listening is the outside distractions that reduce our ability to listen. Have you noticed that while the TV is on or other people are talking noisily within earshot, it is difficult to concentrate on the message of another? Or have you tried to listen to a speech or lecture while someone behind you provided a play-by-play description of it? No matter how interesting or important a message is to you, if you can't hear it or if there are other messages competing for your attention, your listening efficiency will decrease.

The best environment for listening is one in which there are as few noises and distractions as possible. When you want to talk to someone, try to pick a quiet time and place. In the context of a family, for instance, it may be tricky to find a quiet time to converse. With one family member going to school, another going shopping, a spouse getting ready for work or coming home from a taxing day and wanting time to relax, it is difficult to find moments when family members are available for conversation and undivided attention. But try to find times during which as few as possible of these interferences are present.

Someday, perhaps a listening text will be entitled *How to Turn Off the TV*.

It is difficult to listen with the ever-present chatter of cartoons, situation comedies, news programs, or dramas droning in the background. Listening is an activity that takes all of the powers of concentration that we can muster. Distractions interfere with the process.

Speech-rate and thought-rate differences

Dr. Ralph Nichols, a pioneer in listening research and training, has identified a barrier to effective listening that has to do with the way we process the words we hear.[7] Usually we talk at about 100 to 125 words a minute. However, we have the capacity to listen at a rate up to 400 words a minute; some suggest it could be as high as 1200 words a minute. What this means is that we can listen much faster than we normally do. Why is the differential a barrier to effective listening? Being able to process information quickly seems like an asset, not a liability. The reason it becomes a listening problem is that we do not always use the extra time effectively while listening to others. The difference between hearing words at about 100 words per minute and thinking at over 400 words per minute gives us time to daydream and permits us to tune in and tune out the speaker, giving us the illusion that we are concentrating better than we actually are.

But this extra time does not need to be a liability to our listening effectiveness. We can use it to enhance our listening effectiveness if we try periodically to make a mental summary of what the speaker is saying. Reviewing the key ideas and messages of the speaker can significantly increase listening effectiveness and help us retain additional information.

Criticizing the way the message is delivered

Most of us gain an impression of a speaker from the person's appearance and delivery. Studies suggest that more attractive people are more persuasive than those who are judged less attractive. A person's appearance also can affect our ability to listen and comprehend information presented.

Imagine that you and a friend have decided to hear a lecture about improving your business communication skills. Since you are taking a communication class this semester, you thought it would be a good idea. It's time for the speech to begin. The speaker is introduced and begins her remarks. The speaker's presentation, however, is not what you expected at all. She begins to read her speech from a manuscript. She has virtually no eye contact with the audience. Her voice drones on in a monotone. And to make matters worse, she has the annoying habit of constantly adjusting her glasses. "I certainly expected a better presentation from a speaker talking about communication," you mumble. Your friend is aware of the speaker's distracting style, but still tries to take down the major ideas presented. You, on the other hand, have become irritated because you have wasted an evening on a boring presentation. "This is terrible," you whisper.

Your friend replies, "Yes, but I'm picking up some good ideas for my term paper."

You're puzzled by that remark, because you have found it difficult to gain much of anything from the presentation. The problem here is that you have let the speaker's delivery style affect your ability to listen. If this has happened to you, don't feel too bad. It happens to most people. Several studies suggest that a speaker's delivery can significantly affect listener comprehension. The challenge is to realize that it may happen and try to concentrate a bit harder, rather than letting the delivery problems affect what you hear.

After having taken a communication course in which principles of delivery and nonverbal communication have been stressed, you may find this problem looms even larger, because you now pay more attention to nonverbal delivery variables. Try not to let this distract you from being a good listener. Refuse to allow these ineffectively executed presentations rob you of your ability to comprehend the message.

SUGGESTIONS FOR IMPROVING YOUR LISTENING

We have identified several problems that can reduce your listening effectiveness. Even though we also have indicated how those listening problems can be overcome, we would like to suggest several additional things you can do to improve your listening ability.[8] Since you spend 42 percent of your communication time listening, you should find these suggestions relatively easy to apply.

1. Look for information you can use

In every listening situation ask yourself, "What's in this for me?" "What can I use from this presentation?" "How can what this person is saying help me?" Good listeners constantly try to relate the material they are hearing to themselves. That's how we learn—by relating what we hear to our own needs and experiences. Try to find areas of interest between you and the speaker.

Of course, when you are listening to empathize with someone, the suggestion to be a selfish listener does not completely apply. You can, however, listen empathetically, noting how what you hear can help the person who is talking.

2. Listen for ideas, not just facts

Facts are just one type of information. In many cases, principles and major ideas will be more useful to you than just facts (such as a name, date, or place). Most speakers have a point they are trying to make. A fact, statistic, or specific example is often used as supporting material to make the point. Try to identify what point a speaker is trying to make when using facts, statistics, and specific examples. If you make a point of listening for major ideas, you should be able to sustain your attention for a longer period of time.

3. Try not to be distracted by an emotion-arousing word or phrase

When you begin to respond emotionally, your listening effectiveness decreases. Certain words or phrases can arouse emotions very quickly. Of course, the same word may arouse different emotions in different people. We respond differently because of our different cultural backgrounds, religious convictions, political philosophies, and so on. What words often evoke a strong negative reaction from you? Words that connote negative feelings about your nationality, ethnic origin, or religion can trigger knee-jerk emotional reactions. For some people, cursing and obscene language reduce listening efficiency.

As a listener, realize that you are going to hear words and phrases that will distract you from the message of the speaker. Try to keep your emotions under control. If you don't, be prepared to pay the consequences: reduced listening effectiveness.

4. Adapt to the speaker

We noted that a speaker's delivery and appearance can distract you from what the speaker is trying to say. Clearly, not everyone to whom we listen is an eloquent speaker or a fascinating conversationalist. To be a good listener you are going to have to adjust to the speaker's idiosyncracies and distracting mannerisms. If appearance, gestures, voice, or posture detract from the speaker's credibility, try a bit harder to concentrate on the message.

5. Be an aggressive listener by adapting to the speaking situation

Despite an obligation to control the speaking environment for maximum communication effectiveness, many times the speaker is so concerned or nervous about speaking that distractions do exist. The aggressive listener should make an effort to adapt the speaking environment for maximum listening effectiveness. If the room is too stuffy, you may need to open a window or ask that the air conditioning system be adjusted. If you can't hear the speaker, move closer. If people are talking unnecessarily, politely ask them to be quiet. If a door needs closing, don't wait for someone else to do it. The effective listener does whatever is appropriate to ensure the best possible speaking environment.

6. Practice your listening skills

You learn how to write by writing, not by just reading the rules of grammar and spelling. Nor do you learn about public speaking by just reading how to deliver a speech. You learn by doing. And so it is with listening. Listening experts report that poor listeners are also inexperienced listeners. When they listen, it is usually to easy, entertaining information. Some critics of TV point to the situation comedies and superficial entertainment programs as culprits that promote listening ineffectiveness. Good listening skills result from listening to more difficult material. Do you listen to news, documentaries, or interview programs like *Face the Nation, Meet the Press,* and *Issues and Answers?* Good listeners make a point of stretching their listening talents by listening to more difficult material.

7. Decide what your listening objective is

We noted earlier that we listen for a variety of reasons: to be amused, to evaluate, to empathize, and to gain information. One of your first tasks should be to determine your reasons for listening. If you're having a conversation with a friend, should you try to remember everything being said, or is your real purpose to serve as a sounding board? If you know that your objective is to evaluate, then you should make sure that you first understand what the speaker is saying, before you critique what you hear. If you are listening for enjoyment, you need not worry about taking notes or trying to identify the pattern of organization the speaker is using. When you listen for information, a whole host of listening principles come into play, such as listening for content instead of delivery, and trying to concentrate on the information that is most useful to you. Thus, determining your listening objective also plays a major role in determining your listening strategy.

8. Try to anticipate the speaker's next major idea

Ralph Nichols, a pioneer in listening research, suggests that trying to determine which point a speaker is going to make next can help you improve your listening ability, for at least two reasons. First, it helps to make the problem of speech speed versus thought speed less distracting, because you are using your extra thought time to concentrate on the speaker, the message, and the objective of the presentation. Second, it can help you remember the idea because you have, in essence, "heard" it once when you guessed it and again when it was stated by the speaker. Even if you guess wrong, you can compare the point you thought the speaker was going to make with the point the speaker actually made and thus learn by comparison and contrast. Comparing where the speaker ended with where you thought the speaker was heading can increase your listening comprehension.

9. Try to identify how the speaker is supporting the major ideas in the speech

Most public speakers whose objective is to inform will use facts, examples, statistics, or testimony to support the major points being presented. Try to determine how the speaker is supporting the major ideas. This process, too, helps to lessen that speech-speed/thought-speed problem. When listening to evaluate, it is vital that you try to determine how the speaker is documenting the conclusions that are offered. In Chapter 12 we will identify several specific criteria you can apply to help you evaluate a speaker's evidence.

10. Mentally summarize the key ideas

If you are trying to improve your ability to concentrate on a speech and to recall the ideas presented, mentally summarizing major ideas can help significantly. Even in listening situations in which your objective is to empathize with the listener or to critically evaluate the information discussed, mentally recapping points presented can help keep you alert and can help you follow the speaker's organization. Spoken communication should be more redundant than written communication. Repetition helps improve learning. In a public speaking situation, effective speakers provide transition phrases and internal summaries in their speeches to help the listener follow their train of thought. Many speakers, however, don't provide these services to their listeners. The listeners must then be ready to provide these summaries and transition statements for themselves. Through trying to study and retain the information while the speech is still in progress, the listener can get a head start on improving retention.

FEEDBACK: RESPONDING TO WHAT YOU HEAR

As a student, you realize that most of your teachers are going to give you examinations. They want to determine how well you listened to the material presented to the class and how well you understood what you read in the textbook. Your effectiveness as a student is based upon your ability to provide accurate feedback to your teachers about the things that you have learned.

In simplest terms, feedback is a response to another's behavior or communication. To find out how well you understood the lesson presented, your teacher asks you to respond to the lesson. If your score on the test is not as high as the teacher (or you) would like, the teacher's evaluation or grade tells you how hard you need to study to be able to master the information for future examinations.

We provide feedback to others for several reasons. First, it can tell another how much we understand the message presented. Second, it can make another aware of whether we agree or disagree with the points made. And finally, it can help the speaker correct any vague or confusing statements that may have led to misunderstanding. In essence, feedback is communication that gives people information about how they affect others. As it does in a guided missile system, feedback helps an individual keep communication "on target" and thus better achieve communication objectives.

Can you imagine what it would be like to live in a world without feedback? You would not be able to tell who was listening to you. You would not know whether the point you wanted to make was understood by your listener. Nor would you be able to determine who agreed with you and who was opposed to your ideas and behavior.

Earlier in the book we stressed the process nature of communication—communication is an ongoing activity. We feedback to one another simultaneously. During a job interview, for example, the employer is interested in your response—your feedback—to the questions asked. But in addition, if you can remember the times you have been interviewed for a job, you will probably recall that you were trying to determine how effectively you were coming across to the interviewer by noticing whether the interviewer was agreeing with you, smiling or frowning, or generally seeming interested in what you had to say. Both you and the interviewer were providing feedback to each other.

Researchers have been interested in how the amount of feedback affects communication accuracy, the amount of time it takes to communicate information, and the feelings of both the speaker and listener. In a classic study by Leavitt and Mueller, a speaker was asked to describe a diagram to another person.[9] The speaker was told not to show the diagram to the listener, only to describe the drawing. Four different feedback conditions were employed. In the first condition, as in TV and radio, the listener was not able to provide any feedback, either verbal or nonverbal, to the speaker. In the second condition the speaker and listener could see each other, but were not allowed to speak. In other words, there was nonverbal feedback, but no verbal feedback. In the third condition, the receiver could respond only by answering "yes" or "no" to questions asked by the speaker. In the fourth condition, called the free feedback condition, the sender and the receiver were encouraged to provide verbal and nonverbal feedback to each other.

The results of the study document both the advantages and disadvantages of feedback as we communicate with others. First, let's examine the advantages. The more feedback between speaker and listener, the more accurately the message was communicated to the listener. This conclusion suggests that you will more accurately learn the information presented in a class in which you can ask questions, than in a class in which no questions are permitted, such as a TV lecture class. A second advantage is that as feedback increased, both the listener and speaker became more confident that the message was being communicated accurately. A third advantage was that both speaker and listener were more satisfied with their communication when greater amounts of feedback were permitted. There was, however, one disadvantage to the increased feedback conditions. It took more time for communication to occur when more feedback was allowed. In other words, feedback results in greater accuracy, confidence, and satisfaction, but also slows down the communication process. Some efficiency must be sacrificed for accuracy and improved speaker-listener relations.

While we usually think of feedback as it occurs between people, feedback can also be intrapersonal. Intrapersonal feedback occurs when we monitor our own behavior, which we do almost all the time we communicate with others. Most of us don't want to say or do anything stupid.

As indicated in connection with the Leavitt and Mueller study, feedback can also be classified as either verbal or nonverbal. Your boss may not have to tell you that you have made a major mistake. A quick glance at her, and you can determine that she is less than pleased with your work. But certainly there are also occasions when you are told you've made a mistake—or you are given praise for a job well done.

Besides being intrapersonal or interpersonal, verbal or nonverbal, feedback can be intentional or unintentional. There are times when you intentionally let people know what you think of them. Applause, tips, and rejection letters are all examples of intentional feedback. There are also instances, however, when we don't intend to provide feedback, but do anyway. Someone at a party may overhear you admiring or ridiculing how he or she is dressed. You also may not always be aware of your nonverbal behavior as you communicate with others. A boss may not intentionally criticize a secretary for unsatisfactory work, but the boss's facial expression and tone of voice may relay displeasure with its quality. Unintentional feedback clearly can affect communication accuracy and interpersonal relationships, just as intentional feedback does.

SUGGESTIONS FOR IMPROVING FEEDBACK

We have talked about what feedback is, why it is important to you, and how it affects your communication with others. The following specific suggestions should enhance your ability to provide useful feedback to others.

1. Effective feedback should be descriptive rather than evaluative

"I see that differently" sounds better than "You're dead wrong." By avoiding evaluative language as much as possible, you reduce the need for an individual to react defensively. Of course, there are times when you will need to evaluate the appropriateness or inappropriateness of what you hear. If you are not in agreement with the speaker, say so tactfully, describing your reaction.

2. Effective feedback should be specific rather than general

To be told that you are "dominating" will probably not be as helpful as to be told that "Just now when we were deciding the issue, you did not listen to what others said, and I felt forced to accept your arguments or face attack from you."

3. Effective feedback should take into account the needs of both the receiver and the sender

Feedback can be destructive when it serves only our needs and fails to consider the needs of the person on the receiving end.

4. Effective feedback should be directed toward behavior that the receiver can do something about

Frustration is only increased by citing some shortcoming over which a person has no control. To mention someone's speech defect, when the person is obviously aware of the deficiency but has no way of correcting the problem, will only make the individual feel worse.

5. Feedback is most effective when it has been solicited, rather than imposed on the listener

Feedback is most useful when the receiver has formulated questions for the person providing the feedback to answer.

6. Feedback should be well-timed

In general, feedback is most effective at the earliest opportunity after the given behavior (depending, of course, on the person's readiness to hear the feedback and on the support available from others).

7. Effective feedback should be constructive rather than destructive

Your goal in providing feedback to someone should not be to make the person feel worse, but to provide specific suggestions as to how he or she can improve.

8. Effective feedback should not overwhelm the receiver

Feedback should be selective. Hit the high points. Too much information fed back to an individual can result in information overload.

ACTIVE LISTENING: COMBINING THE BEST OF EFFECTIVE LISTENING AND FEEDBACK SKILLS

A technique called active listening involves both feedback and listening skills. One requirement of active listening is to repeat what you understood a speaker to say, just after he or she has finished speaking. The challenge is to listen effectively and to restate the message as accurately as possible, without adding to, deleting from, or reinterpreting what the speaker has said. The active listening technique does not mean that you must repeat the speaker's exact words, playing the message back like a tape recorder. Rather, you should try to paraphrase the major ideas of the speaker, putting them in your own words, but not altering the overall meaning of the message. For example, if a husband and wife are having a disagreement about which set of parents to visit for Thanksgiving this year, the husband might say, "I think we should go to my parents' this year because they have been particularly lonely the past few months."

His wife, utilizing the active listening technique, should respond, "So you want to go to your parents' because you think they need companionship?"

"Yes, that's right," he answers. "I think they need a visit from us again this year."

"But," responds the wife, "we went to their house for the Fourth of July and Labor Day; I think my parents deserve some attention, too."

"Oh, you think we need to see your folks because we haven't been there for a few months. Is that right?" he asks.

"Yes."

"Well, I guess to be fair we should go visit your folks."

This example illustrates how active listening works. It can help improve communication accuracy and also help both sender and receiver develop improved listening and feedback skills. It can be used to defuse arguments or to make sure that communication takes place accurately. When you order a pizza, the waitress may say, "Now, let me see if I got this right. You want a large pepperoni, extra cheese; a small Canadian bacon; and four large Cokes. Right?" That kind of active listening can ensure that problems don't develop when the food is served.

The advantages of active listening, then, are that it can help improve communication accuracy and also help you pay attention and follow the points the speaker is making. Active listening can be particularly useful when someone needs a sounding board—when your job as a listener is to empathize, not just provide advice to the speaker.

Even though we have made great claims for active listening as a communication technique, you should be aware of some problems with it. First, it may seem awkward and unnatural. Second, you may become irritating if you parrot everything the speaker says. Active listening is a technique, and sometimes can become too obvious to the other individual if you have not developed the skill to use it effectively and unobtrusively. It takes times and genuine commitment to the needs of the other individual. It should not be employed without genuine sensitivity to the problem or issues affecting both you and the other person. And finally, it takes skill in both listening and feedback to use active listening effectively—skills which many people need to work on.

IMPROVING LISTENING AND FEEDBACK SKILLS

PUTTING THEORY INTO PRACTICE

We began this chapter by noting how important listening is to the total communication process. You spend approximately 11 percent of your communication time writing, 15 percent reading, 32 percent speaking and 42 percent listening. Research suggests that most people do not listen as well as they should.

We defined listening as the process of *selecting, attending, understanding,* and *remembering.* We also discussed four different types of listening: (1) listening to enjoy, (2) listening to evaluate, (3) listening to empathize, and (4) listening to gain information.

We hope the material in this chapter motivates you to be a better listener by helping you identify barriers to effective listening and providing some suggestions to improve your listening skill. Because listening is a communication activity in which you are frequently engaged, you may be tempted to take good listening skills for granted. Our advice is, don't. The ability to listen can be a powerful asset. Now it's up to you to incorporate some of the suggestions that we have recommended.

Improving note-taking skills

- Decide whether you need to outline the speech, jot down key words, or record major ideas.

Improving your listening skills

- Listen for information that you can use.
- Listen for ideas, not just facts.
- Try not to be distracted by emotion-arousing words or phrases.
- Adapt to the speaker's delivery style.
- Be an aggressive listener by adapting to the speaking situation; close a door, move up closer to the speaker, etc.
- Practice your listening skills.
- Decide what your listening objective is.
- Try to anticipate the speaker's next major idea.

- Try to identify how the speaker is supporting the major ideas in the speech.
- Mentally summarize key ideas.

Improving feedback skills

- Provide descriptive, specific, and constructive feedback.
- Effective feedback should be directed toward behavior that the receiver can do something about.
- Feedback should be provided at the earliest opportunity after a given behavior.
- Don't overwhelm the receiver when providing feedback.

Improving active listening skills

- Paraphrase what you understood a speaker to say, right after the speaker has finished.
- Don't just parrot everything a speaker says. This may alienate the speaker.
- Practice the active listening technique to improve your skill.

SUGGESTED ACTIVITIES

1. To give you a better perspective about your listening habits, keep a journal in which you record your thoughts, objectives, and various listening barriers you encounter in your listening experiences. Your journal may include:
   a. goals for improving your listening skills.
   b. daily entries which
      (1) identify the types of listening you engage in
      (2) describe each listening experience (situation, who else was present, etc.)
      (3) identify what you learn
   c. a one-day listening log which describes every listening experience you had that day.
   d. a summary of how well you achieved the goals you established for yourself.[10]
2. Make a list of the emotion-arousing words that affect your listening ability. Utilizing the discussion of language and meaning in Chapter 4, how can you try to overcome some of the listening problems these words create for you?
3. Try this listening exercise with a class that is giving you difficulty because of a listening problem you have. Make a special effort to concentrate on what is being said in this class. Keep a log of those instances in which you find it difficult to pay attention. Identify, for example, when you found yourself tuning the speaker out. What was the speaker saying? How was the delivery of the message? Try to determine why you are having difficulty concentrating on the message. Use the suggestions in this chapter for overcoming listening barriers to help you improve your listening skills.[11]

NOTES

[1]Paul Rankin, "Listening Ability: Its Importance, Measurement and Development," *Chicago Schools Journal,* 12 (January 1930):177–79.

[2]As cited by Ralph G. Nichols and Leonard A. Stevens, "Listening to People," in *Harvard Business Review,* 35 (September-October 1957):85–92.

[2]Ibid.

[3]Study conducted by Paul Cameron, as cited by Ronald B. Adler and Neil Towne, *Looking Out/ Looking In: Interpersonal Communication* (New York: Holt, Rinehart and Winston, 1981), p. 218.

[4]Survey conducted by Lyman Steil, University of Minnesota.

[5]Douglas Ehninger, Alan H. Monroe, and Bruce E. Gronbeck, *Principles and Types of Speech Communication* (Glenview, IL: Scott, Foresman and Company, 1978), p. 128.

[6]From *If Life Is a Bowl of Cherries—What Am I Doing in the Pits?* by Erma Bombeck (New York: McGraw-Hill Book Company, 1978).

[7]Ralph G. Nichols and Leonard A. Stevens, "Six Bad Listening Habits," in *Are You Listening?* (New York: McGraw-Hill Book Company, 1957).

[8]Ibid.

[9]Harold J. Leavitt and Ronald A. H. Mueller, "Some Effects of Feedback on Communication," in Dean Barnlund, ed., *Interpersonal Communication: Survey and Studies* (Boston: Houghton Mifflin Company, 1968), pp. 251–259.

[10]Adapted from Andrew D. Woluin and Carolyn Gwynn Coakley, *Listening Instruction* (Urbana, IL: Eric Clearinghouse on Reading and Communication Skills, 1979).

[11]Ibid.

8 INTERVIEWING

After studying this chapter you should be able to:

Define an "interview"

Identify the major differences between an interview and other forms of interpersonal communication

List and briefly explain four purposes of an interview

List and briefly explain fourteen types of interviews

Identify five responsibilities of an interviewer and explain what speech communication behaviors are appropriate for each responsibility

Identify three responsibilities of an interviewee and explain what speech communication behaviors are appropriate for each responsibility

Imagine that! You've passed the initial screening. They've called you in for an interview. You may actually *get* that job you were training for in college. They want to talk to *you*! An interview? Oh no!

An interview is one of the most exciting, yet often most anxiety-producing, forms of interpersonal communication. It's also a common interpersonal situation. Whether it's a job interview, a counseling interview, or a sales pitch by an encyclopedia salesman, interviews are a frequent yet disturbing occurrence for many people. We believe that the importance of this interpersonal encounter merits further discussion, especially in a book about speech communication.

In the previous three chapters, we have discussed relating to others at the interpersonal level, focusing on verbal and nonverbal communication, and the specialized skill of listening. In no interpersonal setting are these skills so important as in the interview. In no interpersonal communication setting are we required to prepare and utilize our verbal and nonverbal communication skills so effectively as we are in an interview. In no interpersonal communication setting are we so dependent upon our effective development and practice of our listening skills as we are in the interview. This chapter is intended to aid you in your development of interviewing skills, whether you find yourself in the role of the interviewer or the interviewee.

As a form of speech communication at the interpersonal level, interviews serve all three functions of speech communication. Interviews link individuals with their environment. Individuals gathering and sharing information are linked with that part of their environment which is uniquely human—one person

with another. All interviews exhibit this functional aspect. Second, in interviewing, we also develop our "higher mental processes." Through gathering and sharing information in the interviewing situation or by participating in various interview processes, we gain insight in decision making and problem solving, as well as simply increasing our intellectual capacities. Finally, we regulate and are regulated by others as a consequence of the interviewing process. We learn what others expect of us and how to meet these expectations. We acquire an increased understanding of how to make effective choices concerning what communication behaviors are productive in which situations.

WHAT IS AN INTERVIEW?

An interview is a specialized and formally structured form of interpersonal communication. Regardless of the type of interview and your role in the interviewing situation, considerable amounts and specific types of information need to be shared, usually within a limited period of time. For this reason, it is important for all parties involved to develop and practice effective interviewing communication in order to increase the likelihood that the interview will be a success for both parties.

Interview: A form of oral communication involving two parties, at least one of whom has a preconceived and serious purpose and both of whom speak and listen from time to time.[1]

Several elements of this definition deserve further discussion. First, we are concerned with face-to-face interview situations. This should *not* imply that interviews *cannot* take place over the telephone, as time, financial, or physical constraints may prohibit two parties from meeting personally. In most instances, however, an interview is conducted when the two parties are in face-to-face proximity. This characteristic reinforces the importance of nonverbal communication in the interview.

A second major element of this definition is that it always involves two parties. Not always just two *people*, but certainly two parties. "Two parties" means that you may be interviewed by a group of people, or you may choose to interview several people at one time. A common practice in college and university settings is for a committee of faculty members to conduct a group selection interview with a prospective addition to their faculty.

"A preconceived and serious purpose" is the element which sets the interview situation apart from other forms of interpersonal communication. Both parties are aware of the type and purpose of the interview before the event, and this notion of purpose and goals usually brings more formality into the interview conversation than characterizes other interpersonal encounters. An informal conversation among friends, a discussion over lunch, or a romantic *tête-à-tête* in front of the fireplace is seldom as structured and purposive as the interview.

A final important element in this definition is the sharing of speaking and listening roles. As we shall soon see, an interview is generally a series of questions and answers, thus making it necessary for both parties to listen carefully and respond accordingly. Although this reciprocity of listening/speaking roles is representative of other *interpersonal* communication events, it is not representative of many public and mass communication situations. Have you ever tried talking back to your radio or television? More importantly, did *it* respond to *your* comment?

As you can see, the interview is a specialized form of interpersonal communication. It is more structured and formal than many interpersonal encounters, it involves two parties, it has specific goals, and it requires effective speaking and listening skills. Before discussing what these skills are and how to develop them, let's look at some purposes and types of interviews.

WHY INTERVIEW?

Purposes of an interview

Medical doctors need to find out "what's ailing you." Personnel managers need to decide if you're the right person for the job. Organizational managers need to know why you don't get along with your supervisor. Candidates for public office need to encourage you to vote for them in the upcoming election. These four situations exemplify the four main purposes of an interview: information gathering, information sharing, problem solving, and persuading. Although we will discuss interviews in terms of these four purposes, remember that most interviews are conducted with more than one of these purposes in mind. For example, an employment interview is primarily *information sharing*, but both parties will attempt to *gather information*, too, and each will attempt to *persuade* the other on certain points. The interviewer will attempt to *solve the problem* of "Who is right for the job?" and the interviewee will try to answer the question, "Would I want to work for this organization?" Thus, an employment interview generally contains elements of all four purposes. We have chosen to discuss several types of interviews according to the *primary* purpose of each type.

Information-gathering interviews

In information gathering, interviewers seek specific types and forms of information to aid them in making a decision for implementing an action. *Exit interviews* provide information concerning a departing employee's reasons for leaving. Very often such information is useful to an organization in learning what improvements in benefits, working conditions, salary, promotion policy, or other factors would reduce employee turnover. *Opinion polls* gather information for a variety of purposes. Through the use of interviews, marketing researchers test new or current products, the broadcast industry assesses programming, and private pollsters determine the popularity of political candidates and government policies. All these polls provide information which is useful in developing plans of action.

Physicians, nurses, and other medical personnel use *medical interviews* for diagnosis. Treatment is prescribed as a result of your visit to a doctor's office when you are ill, but not until sufficient information is gathered through an interview. *Legal interviews* are used by police officers and lawyers to collect facts on the collision that crumpled the left rear fender of your new Maserati, and by lawyers in attempting to learn your side of the story concerning your neighbor's rake, which just happened to crumple your nose as a result of your stepping on it. And finally, reporters use *journalistic interviews* to gather names, places, facts, and dates to ensure accurate reporting in your morning newspaper.

Information-sharing interviews

In information-sharing interviews, both interviewer and interviewee provide *and* gather information. Often the amount of information shared is nearly equal; at other times one party shares more information than the other.

Information-sharing interviews are common in business and industry. In the *selection or employment* type of interview, the interviewer gathers information concerning the interviewee's qualifications and motivation. The interviewee shares this information, and gathers information concerning the organization's background, benefits, and salary and promotion procedures. Perhaps you have been in a selection interview in the past. You know that it's quite an experience, and one you'll probably never forget.

Other types of information-sharing interviews abound. At one time or another in your life, you will probably be a party to a *work-appraisal interview*. The purpose of this type of interview is to share information concerning job performance, supervisor/subordinate relations, work deadlines, production quotas, or other information connected with assigned duties. *Orientation sessions* are frequently carried out in an interview setting. These sessions are intended to explain certain procedures in employment or education. You may have been a participant in an orientation session with your academic advisor upon your acceptance or enrollment in college. The purpose of a *briefing* is to share information on the implementation of or change in a procedure, technique, or policy. Engineers hold briefings on new construction or architectural advances, and production superintendents are called upon to describe the performance of newly acquired equipment. *Instructional interviews* serve the purpose of teaching procedures or skills. Mastery of a musical instrument or of your school's registration procedures commonly necessitates instructional interviews.

Problem-solving interviews

As the name implies, problem-solving interviews are conducted to discuss and resolve a problem of some importance to both parties. The interviewer and the interviewee share information in an attempt to resolve the difficulty.

Psychiatrists, managers, college professors, and other professionals conduct *counseling interviews* to help find solutions to personal or professional problems of one of their clients, students, or subordinates. You may seek a counseling interview with any one of a number of professionals for help in finding out why you are always late for important appointments (except, of course, for this class).

Disciplinary interviews examine potential corrective action toward an employee or student. Although the disciplinary interview is generally called and controlled by the interviewer, the communication process should remain two-way in order for both parties to understand the causes and consequences of the problem at hand. (One of your authors was once the interviewee in a disciplinary interview after having been observed with a water pistol in a junior high algebra class. Not an experience to be repeated if one can help it.)

The final type of problem-solving interview—the *grievance interview*— serves the purpose of opening discussion on a coL plaint by an individual or group. Irate customers dissatisfied with the efficiency of their vacuum cleaners, students disgruntled over their grades, and employees fed up with substandard working conditions request such interviews with "people in authority." The success of the grievance interview (as with all types of problem-solving interviews) depends largely on the effectiveness of the interpersonal listening and speaking skills of both parties involved. It is exceedingly important that both parties listen to and understand the problem to be dealt with, examine possible solutions, and resolve the problem in a manner satisfactory for both parties. Indeed, effective interpersonal communication skills are vitally important to the success of the problem-solving interview.

Persuading interviews

In few situations is the regulatory function of speech communication so in evidence as in a persuading interview. Its purpose is acceptance of an idea, product, or service by the interviewee, and some subsequent action based on that acceptance. The success of the persuading interview can be measured by whether or not the interviewee engages in the desired behavior.

The most common type of persuading interview is the *sales interview*. That knock on the door or ring of the telephone just as you are seating yourself at the dinner table probably means that a sales interview is about to take place. The objective of the sales interview, of course, is to persuade you to purchase a product or service. (Although you don't have children *yet*, this set of fifteen encyclopedia volumes—plus twenty years of yearbooks—will someday be of invaluable assistance to them when writing term papers or preparing speeches for their speech communication classes. And all for a mere $39.17 a month for the next eight years.) It takes superior listening skills and straightforward questioning skills for you to become an effective interviewee in a sales interview. "Let the buyer beware. All sales are final!"

"Do you plan to vote in the upcoming election?" "Do you know who is running for city dog catcher?" "Are you aware that our candidate is campaigning in favor of incarceration for all roaming canines and felines?" Such questions are generally the content of *campaign interviews*. Whereas the objective of the sales interview is to sell a product or service, the objective of the campaign interview is to "sell" a candidate. The action requested is your vote.

As we have just seen, there are many types of interviews. All have certain elements in common—oral communication, two parties, a preconceived and serious purpose, and sharing of speaking and listening roles. Interpersonal communication skills are *transferable* from one interviewing situation to another. By examining them, you will become more *aware*, will better *understand*, and will be more able to *explain* effective interviewing skills. Whether you find yourself in the role of interviewer or interviewee, this knowledge can increase your ability to make effective and productive *choices* in interpersonal communication behaviors in the interviewing situation. The next two sections of this chapter will examine the responsibilities of and necessary skills for successful interviewers and interviewees.

WHAT ARE THE RESPONSIBILITIES OF THE INTERVIEWER?

The person in the role of the interviewer is the one who generally arranges for an interview. As the initiator, the interviewer develops the objectives and maintains control over the situation. Regardless of the type of interview, the interviewer has certain responsibilities which must be met for the interview to be productive and successful. We have identified five such responsibilities: (1) training, (2) preparing, (3) questioning, (4) listening, and (5) recording information. Various interpersonal communication skills are related to each of the interviewer's responsibilities.

Training

Although a single chapter of a book seldom makes an expert interviewer out of a neophyte, some amount of training in interviewing skills is preferable to none. The basic skills presented here can give you the theoretical and practical knowledge that will allow you to become a more effective interviewer. Specific training in verbal, nonverbal, and listening skills is also crucial for the competent interviewer.

General skills   First and foremost, the interviewer must become increasingly *aware of his or her own biases and prejudices.* As we discussed in Chapter 4, each of us has our own set of past experiences, beliefs, attitudes, and values through which we receive, interpret, and evaluate incoming stimuli. If accurate and useful information is to be shared in an interview, the interviewer must be more aware of his or her own perceptual processes. Important decisions are made during an interview, and accurate and objective interpretation of the interview data is needed. No one would want to be eliminated as a candidate for a job because of an interviewer's bias against red-headed applicants.

A second general skill to be developed by the prospective interviewer is a *thorough understanding of the interpersonal communication process.* The interview is a very specific form of interpersonal communication. The interviewer's interpersonal skills will determine the extent to which he or she can gather, share, and utilize information related to the interview objectives. The interviewer must develop the skills of putting the interviewee at ease, asking and responding to questions effectively, and evaluating and using information in a way that is as free as possible from personal bias. Barriers to communication flow should be removed by the interviewer to maximize information from the second party. Only through the successful practice of good interpersonal communication skills will the interviewer's purposes and objectives be realized.

Empathy is an important part of the interviewer's interpersonal communication skills. We have discussed the empathic process in Chapter 5. The interviewer must learn to "put himself or herself into the shoes of the interviewee." Without trying to understand the other party, the interviewer may misread verbal and nonverbal communication behavior and receive less than completely accurate information. Without the practice of empathy by an employer in a grievance interview, a disgruntled employee may not be able to fully explain the inadequacy of working conditions in an organizational setting.

A final skill which an interviewer must develop is that of *observing, evaluating, and adapting to the communication behavior of the interviewee.* No two interviews—no two interviewees—are exactly alike. The interviewer must recognize this fact and adapt communication behavior accordingly. This includes accepting any unusual or surprise questions or responses from the interviewee. Predetermined structure of questioning is useful, but an interviewee's question "How much money do *you* make for this job?" deserves a response. A flexible and adaptable communication style is a necessity for an effective interviewer.

Verbal communication skills   The necessary verbal skills include the use of *appropriate language and vocabulary.* The lawyer who liberally sprinkles legal terminology and Latin phrases throughout his or her speech might find that the client's next question is "What in the world are you talking about?" Language and vocabulary used by an interviewer should be at the level of understanding of the interviewee. Little is gained by the use of jargon, technical terminology, and ambiguous or vague terms. Words should be straightforward, simple, and specific. Care should be taken, however, not to use language that is too simple and might give the impression that the interviewer is "talking down to" the other person. Empathy is important here. Try to consider the interviewee's perspective in determining the most appropriate language and vocabulary for an interview.

Interviewers must also be careful when dealing with *sensitive content.* This aspect of verbal communication includes the wording and content of questions. Questions such as "Why were you fired from your last job?" make the interviewee feel anxious or defensive. Questions concerning an applicant's age, religious preference, marital status, and plans to start a family are illegal in selection interviews. To be an effective interviewer, one must be aware of these issues and attempt to put the interviewee at ease. "Prompt discussion of sensitive issues *if and only if* they are related to the purpose of the interview" might be a good guideline to follow when gathering or sharing information. Since the wording of a question is as important as the content, an interviewer might rephrase the "Why were you fired?" question in a less loaded manner: "How would you describe your relationship with your previous employer?"

A third aspect of verbal communication skills deals with *establishing rapport and diplomacy.* Although this element is important in any interviewing situation, it is crucial in problem-solving and persuading interviews. An interviewer must maintain an attitude of fairness, open-mindedness, and equality. The interviewer who begins a grievance interview by saying, "This probably won't do you any good, but let's hear your gripe" is not going to establish good relations with the complainant. A good interviewer will be genuinely friendly, tactful, and cooperative. Good interpersonal relationships between interviewer and interviewee do not assure a successful interview, but lack of rapport and diplomacy between the parties virtually condemns the interview to failure.

Depending on the type and objectives of the interview, an interviewer should make sure that his or her verbal communication includes the appropriate amount of *depth and relevancy.* Since the interviewer assumes the bulk of responsibility for directing the flow of communication, it is his or her duty to assure that the information shared is of sufficient amount and applicability. The police officer who asks only if the burglar was male or female, light- or dark-headed, and tall or short is going to gather insufficient information to make a positive identification of the criminal. The interviewer must, in addition, develop *persistence* in questioning to secure sufficient data. This may include restating or rephrasing questions, asking more specific questions, or telling the interviewee what information is being requested. Only through collecting/sharing information of adequate depth and relevancy will the interviewer's objectives be accomplished.

Nonverbal communication skills Many of the elements of *nonverbal communication* we discussed in Chapter 6 are applicable to the interviewing situation. The *setting* that the interviewer chooses should be comfortable and private. A person's previous employment record, career objectives, voting preferences, and medical or legal problems are personal information. The physical environment for the interview is also important. Would you rather sit on the opposite side of a huge desk from the interviewer, or would you prefer to sit in a padded chair facing the interviewer with a minimum of barriers to impede your discussion? Probably the latter. Seldom does an interviewer sitting behind a desk or other piece of furniture give the impression that a good interpersonal relationship is desired with the interviewee. Other nonverbal elements of the setting include a comfortable room temperature, adequate lighting, a minimum of auditory and visual noise which might be distracting, and as few interruptions as possible. Remember, it is the responsibility of the interviewer to make the interviewee as comfortable and at ease as possible.

Eye contact, if used appropriately by the interviewer, can project an attitude of interest and attention. However, constant eye contact can produce anxiety and lack of eye contact is interpreted as a sign of inattention or indifference. In like fashion, *body movements* certainly play a role in the development of a successful interview. Continuous finger tapping, note taking, leg bouncing, and clock watching are perceived as signs of inattention or impatience.

Besides being concerned with nonverbal aspects under his or her control, the interviewer also must *learn to read and react to the nonverbal behavior of the interviewee.* The interviewee who begins removing his or her jacket and mopping a perspiring brow is trying to tell you something. Weight shifting, finger tapping, fingernail cleaning, and voice cracking are usually signs that the interviewee is feeling anxious. Reacting appropriately to these and other nonverbal cues is a valuable skill, since a comfortable interviewee makes for a productive interview.

Listening training is vital to the successful interviewer. As with nonverbal communication behavior, the interviewer must learn to accurately receive, interpret, and evaluate verbal communication behavior. Not only does a half-awake "Huh?" in response to an interviewee's description of career goals exhibit ineffective listening skills, but the interviewer has probably missed some very valuable information as well. Listening is a major interviewer responsibility. Training in this communication skill is crucial to interviewing skills development.

Preparing

We advise the interviewer to "engage brain (mentation function) before opening mouth (linking and regulation functions)." Adequate preparation is needed *before* every interview. Being primarily responsible for setting goals and objectives, the interviewer should establish what information must be shared, how to structure the sharing process, and what must be done with the information.

The first preparation step involves the *establishment of objectives.* The "preconceived and serious purpose" element of an interview determines what these objectives will be. Do you need to collect accurate facts for a story? Do you want information on someone's attitudes toward gun control? Do you need to know why a group of workers called a "stop-work" action? Each of these purposes requires that the interviewer develop a well-defined set of objectives. Only by outlining the "what" of the interview ("What should be gained?") can the interviewer answer the "how" question ("How shall these objectives best be met?").

Once the objectives have been determined, the interviewer must *select an interviewing strategy*. This should include three elements: (1) opening and concluding statements, (2) key questions, (3) effective time management.

The opening statement should inform the interviewee of the purpose of the interview, put the interviewee at ease, and establish some interpersonal rapport. An opening statement for a grievance interview might go something like this:

> Hello, Elmer. I'm glad we could get together today. I understand that we have a problem with some interesting side effects as a result of our workers' breathing noxious fumes in the glue factory. I'm as anxious as you must be to resolve it as soon as possible.

Assuming both parties are in a state to deal with this problem effectively, a concluding statement to the interview might proceed along the following lines:

> Well, Elmer, I certainly appreciate your coming to me with this complaint. I assure you that I will investigate the problem further. I plan to do a little research on these unusual side effects and take the problem to the Health and Safety Department before the end of the week. I should be able to advise you of any action to be taken early next week. I look forward to talking to you again then. Until then, try not to breathe too deeply. Elmer? ELMER, ARE YOU OK?

At a minimum, the concluding statement should maintain a friendly relationship and inform the interviewee of the next action to be taken (if any). It is also useful and courteous to apprise the interviewee of an estimated time of the next contact.

The body of most interviews consists of a series of questions and answers. On the basis of the objectives of the interview, the interviewer should develop a set of key questions which form the body of the interview. The body of an exit interview might focus on the following set of questions:

1. Can you briefly explain your reasons for leaving Don's Trash Removal and Television Repair Service?
2. How do you rate the employee benefits program?
3. Were you satisfied with the promotion and salary structure of our company?
4. How would you describe your working relationship with your co-worker, Tony?
5. Have you any recommendations for improvements in working conditions at Don's?

Keep in mind that these are key questions, not all the questions that would make up the body of the interview. Other questions should supplement the major areas of concern.

The interviewer must effectively structure time to assure that adequate information be shared in the time allotted. Questions must be relevant. Subsequent questions should be anticipated. Discussion must be guided toward the interviewer's objectives. Adequate time must be given to all important points. Planning of time is a necessary part of preparing for the interview.

Valuable time may be saved by *gathering and evaluating pre-interview information* before the event. Then the interviewer can structure the interviewing strategy around particular areas or noticeable deficiencies in the information given.

A final step in the preparation process is *arranging the physical setting*. We have discussed the importance of the interview environment in previous pages. Part of the planning stage should include providing as pleasant, comfortable, and productive an environment as possible. Many of the previous preparation steps may go awry if adequate consideration is not given to the physical and psychological well-being of the interviewee.

Questioning

An interview is generally conducted as a set of questions and responses. Even though both parties question and respond, the interviewer has the primary responsibility for questioning. Depending on the type and objectives of the interview, the interviewer has various types and sequences of questions.

Bradley and Baird have furnished a useful categorization of the *types of interviewing questions*. They present three general types of questions: open, closed, and probing.

> Open questions are broad in nature and basically unstructured. Often they indicate only the topic to be considered and allow the interviewee considerable freedom in determining the amount and kind of information he or she will provide.[2]

Open questions are useful in determining opinions, values, and perspectives. The freedom of response which open questions encourage allows the interviewee to share information almost without restriction. Such questions as "What are your career goals?" "Why do you need my help?" and "How do you feel about the Equal Rights Amendment?" prompt personal and wide-ranging responses.

Closed questions serve to limit the range of information requested. They may require a simple "Yes" or "No" response ("Did you see the mugger's face?"), or they may allow the interviewee to select a response from a number of specific alternatives ("How often do you go to the movies? Less than once a month; once a month; twice a month; once a week?") Closed questions allow the interviewer to gather specific information, but allow the interviewee little freedom in expressing personal views or elaborating on responses. Closed questions are most often used when the maximum amount of information is desired in a relatively short period of time.

Probing questions encourage the interviewee to clarify or elaborate on partial or superficial responses. Through the use of these questions, the interviewer attempts to direct responses in a specific direction. Such questions as "Could you elaborate on your coursework in the area of speech communication?" "Do you mean to say that you already own *three* vacuum cleaners?" and "Will you discuss further your relationship with your foreman?" call for further information in a particular area. Probing questions are often spontaneous and used as follow-up questions to the key questions that the interviewer has prepared.

While preparing for an interview, an interviewer may develop a *questioning sequence*. Four such sequences have been suggested by Stewart and Cash: funnel, inverted funnel, quintamensional, and tunnel.[3] The *funnel sequence* begins with broad, open questions and proceeds toward more closed questions. The advantage is that it allows the interviewee to express views and feelings freely without restriction from the interviewer. It would be more useful to begin a grievance interview with the question "How would you describe your relationship with your supervisor?" than with the question "What makes you think your supervisor treats you like an idiot?" The former question allows the respondent to express feelings freely without bias or defensive posture on the part of the interviewer, as evidenced in the latter question. An example of the funnel sequence follows:

1. How would you describe your relationship with your supervisor?
2. How do you think your supervisor sees you as an employee?
3. Are you satisfied with how your supervisor treats you?
4. What do you believe to be the source of the conflict between you and your supervisor?
5. How satisfied are you with your job at this time?

The second questioning sequence—the *inverted funnel*—might go something like this:

1. Are you relatively satisfied with your job?
2. What conflicts, if any, do you have with your supervisor?
3. How satisfied are you with the manner in which your supervisor treats you?
4. How do you think your supervisor views you as an employee?
5. How would you describe your relationship with your supervisor?

The relatively closed questions that open the inverted funnel sequence can motivate the interviewee to begin talking about his or her job, and the progressively more open questions allow the interviewee to discuss the working relationship in increasingly general terms. The interviewer can encourage disclosure of more information as the interview progresses. The inverted funnel questioning sequence provides for this motivation by widening the range of information to be shared.

The *quintamensional sequence*[4] is used most appropriately in measuring the content and intensity of an individual's attitudes and opinions. It is a five-step sequence that assesses *what* an individual's attitudes and opinions are concerning a particular topic, as well as *how strongly* the individual feels about the relevant issues. The five steps and sample questions might proceed as indicated below:

1. *Awareness:* Tell me what you know about the race for Public Sanitation Engineer in the November elections.

2. *Uninfluenced attitudes:* What are the issues in this race as you see them?
3. *Specific attitude:* Which candidate do you plan to vote for in this race?
4. *Reason why:* What led you to favor this candidate?
5. *Intensity of attitude:* How strongly do you feel about your choice—strongly, very strongly, definitely not willing to change your mind?

Finally, the *tunnel sequence* consists of a series of parallel open or closed questions. This sequence has few probing questions, resulting in less depth of information than the previous three sequences. An interviewer may use the tunnel sequence to gather information concerning attitudes and opinions without regard for "reasons why" or intensity of attitudes. The following illustrates a tunnel sequence:

1. Are you aware of the race for Public Sanitation Engineer in the November Election?
2. What are the major issues in this race?
3. Which of these issues is most important to you in determining a favorite candidate?
4. Which candidate do you plan on voting for in this race?
5. Are you personally involved with the campaign of this candidate?

As you can see, the tunnel sequence provides limited background information but does allow the interviewer to gain important attitude information.

Listening

Earlier in this chapter we briefly discussed the importance of listening training to the interviewer. In Chapter 7 we looked at the role of listening in interpersonal and other levels of speech communication. Why is the skill of listening so critical to the interviewer? Well, no matter how thoroughly an interviewer has prepared for an interview, the preparation is useless if the interviewer is incapable of effectively listening to, interpreting, and synthesizing the information gathered during the interview. Each interviewee will answer each question in a slightly different manner. It is only through careful listening that the interviewer can be assured that information of adequate types and depth has been shared. If afterwards the interviewer finds that partial or tangential responses prevented the full sharing of information, the interview has not met its objective. Effective listening skills may help reduce this problem significantly.

Another reason for listening carefully is to aid the interviewer in *accurately perceiving and interpreting information.* This information includes the interviewee's responses to questions, as well as the interviewee's reaction to new information. The interviewer needs to be aware of when responses must be further probed and also when questions are being misperceived by the interviewee. The accuracy of shared information can be assured only to the extent that the interviewer practices effective listening skills.

Reading of an interviewee's beliefs/attitudes/values illustrates a third need for effective listening skills. An interviewer's proficiency in "reading between the

lines" may greatly influence the success of an interview. The interviewer who is able to perceive an employee's underlying attitudes toward the organization accurately in a grievance interview is more likely to deal productively with the problem than an interviewer who is not able to do so. It should be pointed out, however, that the interviewer should not *presume* these beliefs/attitudes/values. The effective listener will attempt to clarify interpretations through additional probing questions.

A final need met by effective listening skills is that of increasing the interviewer's *flexibility and adaptability*. By adapting to the needs of the interview on an individual basis, the interviewer is able to redirect discussion, clarify insufficient responses, and respond to the interview conditions as they develop. When the interviewer listens well, the objectives of the interview will be accomplished.

Recording information

A final responsibility of the interviewer is that of recording information from the interview. The information is useless if it is not recorded completely and accurately. Any decisions to be made or actions to be taken on the basis of interview data will be less than productive if they are based on partial or inaccurately recorded information.

The interviewer has two options for recording interview data: note taking or audio recording. In either case, the interviewee should be advised of the recording process that is taking place. In the case of taking notes, apologies might

168

be necessary and assurances given that the interviewee is being closely listened to in order to dispel any anxiety which might result from the interviewer's pencil-pushing behavior. If taking notes, the interviewer should practice listening skills even more intensely, so as not to miss anything being said. The notes should be as brief but complete as possible to ensure accuracy and thoroughness. Responses not recorded during the interview are seldom retrievable.

In the case of audio recording, the interviewee *must* be told for the sake of courtesy. Remember that Murphy's Law ("Anything that can go wrong, will; and usually at the worst possible moment") governs any attempt at using electronic recording devices. So take care to provide for effective microphone placement and adequate tape length when preparing for audio recordings. Be aware also that listening skills must be practiced effectively, even though you might have everything on tape. Questions not asked or responses not clarified during the interview might result in important information not being shared.

The bulk of responsibility for a successful interview falls on the interviewer, regardless of the type and purpose of the interviewing situation. The responsibilities of effectively communicating verbally and nonverbally, preparing, questioning, listening, and recording information all contribute to the successful interview. Consideration of and training in each of these areas are necessary prerequisites to the conduct of any type of interview. Similar responsibilities typify the role of interviewee.

WHAT ARE THE RESPONSIBILITIES OF THE INTERVIEWEE?

Although the bulk of responsibility lies with the interviewer, the interviewee also must take seriously the responsibilities of preparing, listening, and responding.

Preparing

In most cases, the interviewee has some knowledge of the *purpose and objectives* of an interview before the event. Preparation by the interviewee greatly influences the success of the interview in such situations as the grievance interview, the selection interview, and the exit interview. The interviewee can predict what some of the issues will be, and can prepare responses. For the selection interview, pre-interview consideration of career goals, salary requirements, and acceptable working conditions is useful. Statement of the problem, its causes, and possible solutions might be productively explored prior to grievance or counseling interviews. Examination of the facts should occur before a disciplinary, medical, legal, or exit interview. Pre-interview reflection on the interview objectives and the related informational requirements of these objectives allows the interviewee to contribute more to the success of the interview.

In addition to preparing for the interview objectives, an interviewee can gather other *pre-interview information.* You can learn about the company with which you are having the interview, its products or services, background, reputation, policies, and procedures on hiring, salary, and promotions. Knowledge of the types of questions asked or information shared, prerequisite skills or knowledge of terminology, and some background information concerning specific individuals or issues is useful preparation for a counseling, orientation, briefing, or instructional interview. We have found that it is generally advisable for students to have some knowledge of degree requirements and class schedules prior to academic counseling interviews. Without pre-interview information, the interviewee usually performs with varying degrees of effectiveness—usually below expectations—in the interviewing situation.

A third component of the preparing responsibility is the *nonverbal aspect*. This includes everything from being on time for the interview to maintaining an attitude of interest and consideration. Being on time, of course, is a matter of courtesy for the interviewer. Physical appearance should be appropriate for the situation, although slippers and a bathrobe may be the only option when the door-to-door opinion pollster gets you out of the shower. Belching, slovenly body posture, nose picking, and talking with your mouth full are nonverbal behaviors to be avoided at almost any cost. Appropriate eye contact, attentive body position, interested facial expression, and a firm handshake all contribute nonverbally to the positive image of an interviewee.

Listening

As crucial as listening skills are to the interviewer, they are even more important for the successful interviewee. The interviewing situation requires that the interviewee listen for the amount and depth of *information desired*. For a response to be appropriate and useful, the interviewee must know what is being requested. If a question is not understood, the interviewee should ask for clarification or restatement of the query. By doing so, the interviewee can respond more adequately to the interviewer's questions.

The successful interviewee will also practice *empathy*. It reinforces the importance of the interviewer as a person and of the interviewing situation as an interpersonal encounter. The interviewee should try to take into account the problems of the interviewer within the organizational setting. By considering these potential problems, the interviewee may assist the interviewer in accomplishing the interview objectives, not by saying what the interviewer wants to hear, but by responding directly, honestly, and completely.

The effectiveness of the interviewee's listening skills has its *nonverbal aspects*, also. The interviewee's eye contact is a significant measure of attention and interest. The interviewee should practice an appropriate amount of eye contact—not staring, but not avoiding. Body posture and hand and leg movements should be relaxed while exhibiting interest and involvement in the conversation. Though nervousness is natural, your nonverbal communication should project naturalness, involvement, and interest in the situation. By practicing sincerity in these nonverbal behaviors, the interviewee can listen more efficiently, showing interest in the interpersonal encounter, and can become a party to productive and fulfilling interviews.

Responding

Just as questioning is the primary responsibility of the interviewer, responding is the primary responsibility of the interviewee, even though any type of interview may require that both parties question and respond. Your responses to an interviewer's questions should be direct, honest, and appropriate in *depth and relevance*. In response to the question, "How would you describe your working relationship with your foreman?" an interviewer would not want to hear a 15-minute treatise on your problems with your husband's ex-wife, keeping the children in clothes, and finding a babysitter who doesn't let your children watch TV until midnight. When a question is posed, listen carefully, and take a few moments to think before you answer. A response that is well thought-out, straightforward, and relevant is more productive and appreciated than one that is "shot-from-the-hip," evasive, and unrelated to the question.

"I wanna cart the bread off in wheelbarrows" is inappropriate *language and vocabulary* in response to the question "What salary range did you have in mind?" *How* you say something may be as important as *what* you say. Language and vocabulary should not be stilted, jargony, slang-ridden, or overly formal. And it should be appropriate for you. It should be natural, understandable, and conversational. Don't get yourself into a situation where you're trying to explain what you mean by "appropriate nonverbal communication" when you don't know what it means yourself. (You do, of course, but use it sparingly.)

Finally, an interviewee should be *flexible and adaptable* to the needs of the interviewing situation. Interviewers may ask questions to "throw you off guard." When this happens, take a moment to think before you respond. Try to discover the motivation for the question and respond to the best of your ability. If you don't understand a question or its relevance, ask for clarification. A good answer to the wrong question might be worse than a mediocre answer to the right question. Listen carefully for content *and* intent of questions, so that you provide the information desired, especially when the interviewer changes topics. Development of flexibility and adaptability requires good listening, empathy, and accurate reading and interpretation of nonverbal communication. Once you develop these skills, flexibility and adaptability just take time and practice. Just remember, "Engage brain before opening mouth."

INTERVIEWING

PUTTING THEORY INTO PRACTICE

The interview is a more formal and structured interpersonal encounter than almost any other. For this reason, both parties must take their responsibilities seriously. Whether the interview is of the information-gathering, information-sharing, problem-solving, or persuading type, its success is dependent upon the knowledge and practice of effective interpersonal skills. Following are some guidelines for effective practice of interpersonal communication skills for interviewers and interviewees.

For the interviewer

1. Be aware of your personal values and biases as you interact with the interviewee.
2. Practice empathy; try to understand and accept the viewpoint of the interviewee.
3. Use language and vocabulary appropriate to the interview.
4. Be careful when dealing with sensitive content.
5. Attempt to establish rapport and diplomacy with the interviewee.
6. Make sure that the depth and relevancy of your verbal communication are appropriate to the situation. Be persistent when necessary.
7. Assure that the interview setting, your eye contact and body movements, and your reaction to the interviewee's nonverbal communication add to the efficiency of the interview.
8. Develop and practice effective listening skills; they are crucial to the success of the interview.
9. Select a questioning sequence and individual questions such that you gather/share the greatest amount of information in the time allotted.
10. Prepare for the interview: Establish objectives, select a strategy, and arrange for a comfortable interview.
11. Be flexible and adaptable to the process of each interview as it develops.
12. Record sufficient and accurate details of information gathered during the interview.

For the interviewee

1. Prepare for the interview: Establish objectives, gather pre-interview information, and prepare yourself physically and mentally.
2. Listen effectively to both the interviewer's questions and responses to your messages.
3. Respond to questions with appropriate depth and relevance. Make sure your responses are well thought-out, straightforward, and relevant.
4. Use language and vocabulary appropriate to the interview.
5. Be flexible and adaptable to the process of the interview as it develops.
6. Be aware of and utilize your nonverbal communication and that of the interviewer.

SUGGESTED ACTIVITIES

1. Choose a partner and plan a selection/employment or work-appraisal interview of 8–10 minutes. Develop a hypothetical or real-life employment situation and a question/response sequence for the interview. Perform this simulated interview for your class.

2. Select a hypothetical interviewing situation of one of the types discussed in this chapter. Develop funnel, inverted-funnel, quintamensional, and tunnel sequences of questions that might be used in the interview. Which of these sets of questions would be most effective in gaining the best information? Why?

3. Observe a sales interview in a naturally occurring setting. Notice and take notes on the nonverbal communication exhibited in the interview: physical environment, eye contact, proximity of participants, and bodily movements. List the observed nonverbal cues and briefly describe how they may have influenced the success (or lack of success) of that interview.

NOTES

[1]Robert S. Goyer, W. Charles Redding, and John T. Richey, *Interviewing Principles and Techniques: A Project Text* (Dubuque, IA: William C. Brown Company, 1968), p. 6.

[2]Patricia H. Bradley and John E. Baird, Jr., *Communication for Business and the Professions* (Dubuque, IA: William C. Brown Company, 1980), p. 128.

[3]Charles J. Stewart and William B. Cash, Jr., *Interviewing Principles and Practices*, 2nd ed. (Dubuque, IA: William C. Brown Company, 1978).

[4]George Gallup, "The Quintamensional Plan of Question Design," *Public Opinion Quarterly*, 11 (Fall 1947), 385–393.

UNIT IV

THE GROUP LEVEL OF SPEECH COMMUNICATION

As we stated in Chapter 2, the group level of speech communication is distinguished from other levels by the nature of the receivers of a message and by the degree of intentionality exhibited by a communicator. Group members attempt to satisfy the needs of several individuals *and* the needs of the whole group when they speak. Group communication requires a communicator to plan more effectively and produce messages which satisfy these two sets of needs. Thus, group communication necessitates increased intentionality over that of the interpersonal level.

The group level of speech communication serves the three functions discussed in Chapter 2 in much the same way as do the other levels. Individual group members are linked with their environment by practicing speech communication in groups, basically through the process of sharing information and opinions. By sharing this information, ways of thinking and individual opinions may be influenced or modified—the mentation function. And, as we shall see in th⁻ following chapters, behavior is influenced (regulation of behavior) as a result of communicating in groups.

In Chapter 9, we will take a descriptive approach to group communication. We will define what a "group" is, describe some characteristics that all groups have, and discuss some types of groups, some advantages and disadvantages of working in groups, and some potential communication problems associated with group work. This chapter is intended to make you more aware of the influences on speech communication at the group level and help you to understand them better.

Chapter 10 takes a prescriptive or "how to" approach to group communication. In this chapter we will provide some guidelines for becoming a more effective communicator as a group attempts to (1) solve problems and make decisions, (2) increase the effectiveness of its own communication, and (3) deal with conflict and leadership difficulties more effectively. It is our intention in this chapter to encourage you to recognize the many alternative methods of communicating in groups, toward the objective of producing more effective choices among the alternatives available to you in group situations.

9 GROUP DYNAMICS: A DESCRIPTIVE APPROACH

After studying this chapter you should be able to:

Define a "group" and identify four components of what makes up a group

Identify and explain eighteen characteristics of groups

Define and distinguish among four types of groups

Identify and briefly explain four disadvantages of working in groups

Identify and briefly explain four advantages of working in groups

Discuss eight potential communication problems often experienced in groups

---

Leslie: I think we should do our group project on shopping cart thefts. They cost us all money at the grocery store through increased prices.

Doug: Are you crazy? Who cares about a couple of pennies in comparison to the millions of dollars it costs taxpayers for airplanes and bombs? I think we should research the federal military budget.

Sharon *(Yawns):* Can we get this over with? *General Hospital* starts in 10 minutes.

Bill: All you think about is soaps! We're never gonna get this project done. I can't meet again on Sunday. The Steelers are playing the Rams on TV.

Doug: Let's go for a Coke. We can decide on the topic for our project next week.

Ross: But we gotta turn in a progress report during class tomorrow. What's easiest?

Sharon *(Looking at her watch):* Don't forget to list Debbie as among the missing for today's meeting. She's a real space cadet! Let's just do the project on shopping carts. That ought to give us something to do. If it doesn't work out, we'll just change the topic.

Leslie: Done. Let's go! Somebody write up the report for class tomorrow.

Sound familiar? Probably so, unfortunately. Working in groups doesn't have to be that bad, though, *if* you know how to go about it. But that's a pretty big "if." The purpose of this chapter (and the next) is to reduce the size of that "if."

As you may have noticed, in this unit we have shifted our focus from the interpersonal level of speech communication to the group level. In this chapter we intend to discuss what a "group" is, some characteristics of groups, several types of groups, and the process of speech communication in groups. The focus of the next chapter will be on the application of these concepts to a number of small group communication settings and tasks. The emphasis in both chapters is on skills—on what makes you a more effective communicator in small group situations. But first, let's look at how small group *theory* relates to *practice* at the group level of speech communication.

HOW IS A GROUP DEFINED?

Seven strangers sitting at a bus stop, reading their morning papers. Is this a group? Twenty people standing in the street observing a man perched on a fifteenth-story ledge. Is this a group? Eight department heads engaging in a spirited discussion concerning the possible acceptance of a new salary and promotion schedule. Is this a group? By definition, only the last of these collections is truly a *group*.

Marvin E. Shaw, a pyschologist, has defined a group as "two or more persons who are interacting with one another in such a manner that each person influences and is influenced by each other person."[1] Obviously, this definition fails to distinguish between the interpersonal and group levels of speech communication. For our purposes, it might be useful to modify Shaw's generally accepted definition slightly to make this distinction more clearly.

Group: Three or more persons who are interacting with one another in such a manner that each person influences and is influenced by each other person.

The number of people in a group, as we will be talking about them, is relatively small—*from three to about fifteen or twenty persons*. This lower limit of three people makes the distinction between *interpersonal* communication and *group* communication. Many groups (community planning committees, departmental faculties at the college or university level, organizational staffs or committees) consist of more than twenty members, but the potential for mutual influence decreases dramatically beyond twenty people. You will probably find that most groups of which you will be a member are made up of between three and ten members. We will be talking of this number (three to ten) when we discuss the typical small group.

Implied in our definition of a "group" is the assumption that members of

a group are in *face-to-face proximity* to one another. This aspect of our definition serves to differentiate group communication from telephone conference calls, electronically mediated messages, and written communiques. Certainly a number of people can communicate, get to know one another, and mutually influence one another through a variety of means. But feedback is most immediate and complete, and the potential for mutual influence is at its height, in a face-to-face setting.

The potential for mutual influence (". . . each person influences and is influenced by each other person") is perhaps greatest in a group situation. At a minimum, each member of a group should recognize the presence of each other member at a group meeting. It is much more likely, however, that each group member will be influenced by other members' personality characteristics, interactions with other members, and contributions to the task at hand as a result of one or more group meetings. It is often difficult *not* to be influenced by either the overtalkative group member or the member who sits in the corner and says nothing.

Mutual influence serves to differentiate group communication from public communication, which is essentially one-way communication. This is not to say that members of an audience cannot influence a speaker in some way, but the structure of the public communication setting provides the speaker with the bulk of responsibility for communicating a message. Such is not the case in group communication. The expectation in a group is that all members will participate, resulting in two-way communication and mutual influence.

In order for a number of people to be considered a group, some type of behavior must tie the people together. This behavior is *interaction* or *speech communication*. Through speech communication, group members come to know each other, influence each other, and generally develop feelings of group membership. It is through communication that seven people sitting at a bus stop decide to meet socially for a beer on Friday night. It is through communication that twenty people watching the man on the ledge become involved in collectively talking the man down. It is through communication that people influence one another and work toward the attainment of some goal or goals. It is through speech communication that individuals link themselves with one another in a group setting.

WHAT ARE THE CHARACTERISTICS OF A GROUP?

Company executives deciding where to locate the new plant. Students working on a group assignment. City planners wrestling with how to raise funds for the new sewage treatment facility. Twelve jury members deliberating on the guilt of an accused murderer. What do all of these groups have in common? The answer to that question is the subject of this section.

All groups are different, yet nearly all groups exhibit certain similarities. Central to these similarities is the fact that all groups communicate. The amount, types, and content of messages are influenced by and influence the other major characteristics of groups to be discussed in this section: group structure, group task, group climate, situation, group phases, and individual group member variable. Each of these major characteristics of groups has subcategories. We will discuss each of these in turn.

Group structure: Patterned regularities in feelings, perceptions, and actions that characterize aspects of the interaction among members of a group.

Group structure

Members of a group generally develop a set of feelings and perceptions about how others should contribute to the group, who should or may talk to whom, who the most prestigious members of the group are, and who should lead the group. Although these feelings and perceptions are not always discussed formally (or even at all) by group members, they may become evident to the astute observer through the actions and interactions of the members. Such actions and interactions take on regular patterns over time as the group develops. When we observe these patterned regularities of feelings, perceptions, and actions, we may say that a group has developed a structure. Four characteristics make up group structure: roles, status, leadership, and interaction patterns.

Role: The expectations shared by group members about the behavior associated with some position in a group, no matter what individual fills the position.[2]

Secretaries keep minutes and take care of correspondence. Treasurers handle and account for money. Leaders lead. Each position within a group carries with it a set of behavioral expectations that most group members agree upon, at least in principle. These roles are often formally identified and defined, depending upon the amount of formality associated with the group process. Many roles, however, are informal, in that the expectations of certain group members are not clearly defined and assigned to specific positions. These informal roles are often considered *functional roles.*

"Functional roles" is a term coined by Benne and Sheats to refer to those group member behaviors which are instrumental to accomplishing group purposes. They arrange these functional roles into three categories: (1) group task roles, (2) group building and maintenance roles, and (3) "individual" roles.[3] *Group task roles* are those behaviors that assist the group in achieving its purposes and goals. These roles are clearly related to the group's attempts at coordinating the efforts of all group members toward the successful accomplishment of the group task. *Group building and maintenance roles* serve to establish and maintain good interpersonal relationships among the members of a group. They are clearly behaviors that influence the way the group goes about dealing with personality conflict, the amount and types of communication evident in the group, and the motivational factors associated with the conduct of the group's interactions. Finally, *"individual" roles* are enacted in a group for the purpose of satisfying individual needs—needs associated with neither the group task nor the building and maintenance of good interpersonal relationships among group members. Many of you have probably encountered the individual roles of "recognition-seeker" or "playboy" in groups of which you have been a member.

Each of Benne and Sheats's group task roles, group building and maintenance roles, and "individual" roles is identified and briefly defined below. Remember that functional roles are not formally defined and, as such, are not identified with any position or single group member. Any of these informal behaviors may be enacted by one or more group members at any time during the life of a group. One or more individuals may perform a certain functional role at one time, and others may perform the same role or a variety of roles at another time.

Each of the behaviors listed may be *shared* by several group members, and their presence or absence depends on the needs of the group at any one time and on the group members' sensitivity to these needs.

FUNCTIONAL ROLES

GROUP TASK ROLES

The following analysis assumes that the task of the discussion group is to select, define, and solve common problems. The roles are identified in relation to functions of facilitation and coordination of group problem-solving activities. Each member may of course enact more than one role in any given unit of participation and a wide range of roles in successive participations. Any or all of these roles may be played at times by the group "leader" as well as by various members:

1. The *initiator-contributor* suggests or proposes to the group new ideas or a changed way of regarding the group problem or goal. The novelty proposed may take the form of suggestions or a new group goal or a new definition of the problem. It may take the form of a suggested solution or some way of handling a difficulty that the group has encountered. Or it may take the form of a proposed new procedure for the group, a new way of organizing the group for the task ahead.

2. The *information seeker* asks for clarification of suggestions made in terms of their factual adequacy, for authoritative information and facts pertinent to the problem being discussed.

3. The *opinion seeker* asks not primarily for the facts of the case but for a clarification of the values pertinent to what the group is undertaking or of values involved in a suggestion made or in alternative suggestions.

4. The *information giver* offers facts or generalizations which are "authoritative" or relates his own experience pertinently to the group problem.

5. The *opinion giver* states his belief or opinion pertinently to a suggestion made or to alternate suggestions. The emphasis is on his proposal of what should become the group's view of pertinent values, not primarily upon relevant facts or information.

6. The *elaborator* spells out suggestions in terms of examples or developed meanings, offers a rationale for suggestions previously made, and tries to deduce how an idea or suggestion would work out if adopted by the group.

7. The *coordinator* shows or clarifies the relationships among various ideas and suggestions, tries to pull ideas and suggestions together, or tries to coordinate the activities of various members or sub-groups.

8. The *orienter* defines the position of the group with respect to its goals by summarizing what has occurred, points to departures from agreed upon directions or goals, or raises questions about the direction which the group discussion is taking.

9. The *evaluator-critic* subjects the accomplishment of the group to some standard or set of standards of group-functioning in the context of the group task. Thus, he may evaluate or question the "practicality," the "logic," the "facts," or the "procedure" of a suggestion or of some unit of group discussion.

10. The *energizer* prods the group to action or decision, attempts to stimulate or arouse the group to "greater" or "higher quality" activity.

11. The *procedural technician* expedites group movement by doing things for the group—performing routine tasks, e.g., distributing materials, or manipulating

objects for the group, e.g., rearranging the seating or running the recording machine, etc.

12. The *recorder* writes down suggestions, makes a record of group decisions, or writes down the product of discussion. The recorder role is the "group memory."

GROUP BUILDING AND MAINTENANCE ROLES

Here the analysis of member-functions is oriented to those participations which have for their purpose the building of group-centered attitudes and orientation among the members of a group or the maintenance and perpetuation of such group-centered behavior. A given contribution may involve several roles and a member or the "leader" may perform various roles in successive contributions.

1. The *encourager* praises, agrees with, and accepts the contribution of others. He indicates warmth and solidarity in his attitude toward other group members, offers commendation and praise, and in various ways indicates understanding and acceptance of other points of view, ideas, and suggestions.

2. The *harmonizer* mediates the differences between other members, attempts to reconcile disagreements, relieves tension in conflict situations through jesting or pouring oil on the troubled waters, etc.

3. The *compromiser* operates from within a conflict in which his idea or position is involved. He may offer compromise by yielding status, admitting his error, by disciplining himself to maintain group harmony, or by "coming half-way" in moving with the group.

4. The *gate-keeper and expediter* attempts to keep communication channels open by encouraging or facilitating the participation of others ("We haven't got the ideas of Mr. X yet," etc.) or by proposing regulation of the flow of communication ("Why don't we limit the length of our contributions so that everyone will have a chance to contribute?" etc.).

5. The *standard-setter* or *ego ideal* expresses standards for the group to attempt to achieve in its functioning or applies standards in evaluating the quality of group processes.

6. The *group-observer and commentator* keeps records of various aspects of group process and feeds such data with proposed interpretations into the group's evaluation of its own procedures.

7. The *follower* goes along with the movement of the group, more or less passively accepting the ideas of others, serving as an audience in group discussion and decision.

"INDIVIDUAL" ROLES

Attempts by "members" of a group to satisfy individual needs which are irrelevant to the group task and which are non-oriented or negatively oriented to group building and maintenance set problems of group and member training. A high incidence of "individual-centered" as opposed to "group-centered" participation in a group always calls for self-diagnosis of the group. The diagnosis may reveal one or several of a number of conditions— low level of skill-training among members, including the group leader; the prevalence of "authoritarian" and "laissez faire" points of view toward group functioning in the group; a low level of group maturity, discipline, and morale; an inappropriately chosen and inadequately defined group task, etc. Whatever the diagnosis, it is in this setting that the training needs of the group are to be discovered and group training efforts to meet these needs are to be defined. The outright "suppression" of "individual roles" will deprive the group of data needed for really adequate self-diagnosis and therapy.

1. The *aggressor* may work in many ways—deflating the status of others, expressing disapproval of the values, acts, or feelings of others, attacking the group or the problem it is working on, joking aggressively, showing envy toward another's contribution by trying to take credit for it, etc.

2. The *blocker* tends to be negativistic and stubbornly resistant, disagreeing and opposing without or beyond "reason" and attempting to maintain or bring back an issue after the group had rejected or by-passed it.

3. The *recognition-seeker* works in various ways to call attention to himself, whether through boasting, reporting on personal achievements, acting in unusual ways, struggling to prevent his being placed in an "inferior" position, etc.

4. The *self-confessor* uses the audience opportunity which the group setting provides to express personal, non-group oriented "feeling," "insight," "ideology," etc.

5. The *playboy* makes a display of his lack of involvement in the group's processes. This may take the form of cynicism, nonchalance, horseplay, and other more or less studied forms of "out of field" behavior.

6. The *dominator* tries to assert authority or superiority in manipulating the group or certain members of the group. This domination may take the form of flattery, of asserting a superior status or right to attention, giving directions authoritatively, interrupting the contributions of others, etc.

7. The *help-seeker* attempts to call forth "sympathy" response from other group members or from the whole group, whether through expressions of insecurity, personal confusion, or depreciation of himself beyond "reason."

8. The *special interest pleader* speaks for the "small businessman," the "grass roots" community, the "housewife," "labor," etc., usually cloaking his own prejudices or biases in the stereotype which best fits his individual need.[4]

Status: The worth of a person as estimated by a group or a class of persons. The estimate of worth is determined by the extent to which his attributes or characteristics are perceived to contribute to the shared values and needs of the group or class of persons.[5]

A group member's *status* in a particular group is determined by the group. If an individual has a personal attribute or characteristic (for example, knowledge of a wide range of computer systems) that is related to the group task or goal (the selection of a new computing system to manage the need of a large manufacturing firm), then that individual might be afforded high prestige or status in a group of executives in that organization who are charged with making the decision concerning which system to purchase. The same person may be assigned high status in one group and a relatively low status in another, dependent upon the needs and values of the group. An advertising executive might be assigned high status in a church group planning to raise money by raffling off a car, where the objective is to sell as many tickets as possible. The same advertising person could be perceived as having little value (status) in a group of college graduates whose charge is to recommend curriculum changes in the School of Music.

Leadership: Interpersonal influence, exercised in a situation and directed, through the communication process, toward the attainment of a specified goal or goals.[6]

All groups exhibit leadership behavior. Note that we did not say that "All groups have a leader." Leadership behavior is shared by several or all group members. "Interpersonal influence" may be performed by any group member. The functional roles discussed in a previous section may be enacted by any number of individuals at any time. These roles, especially the group task roles, are all directed toward the attainment of a particular goal or set of goals, either directly or indirectly. Although most groups have a designated leader, this person is seldom the *only* group member to exert interpersonal influence. Many or all group members exhibit goal-directed influence at one time or another.

As our "leadership" definition indicates, this interpersonal influence occurs through the process of communication. Four styles of leadership communication have been identified. These styles differ according to the amount of control or influence attempted by a group member. The *authoritarian* leadership style attempts to limit member participation, in favor of maintaining a majority of control over the process of the group. This style of leadership dictates all procedures and tasks and preserves sole responsibility for presenting material, deciding on the method of discussion, and evaluating the group.

A second style of leadership—the *democratic* style—helps and guides the group toward accomplishing its goal. The democratic leader selects materials for and methods of group discussion with the assistance and approval of the group. The communication behavior related to this style provides the group with guidance through questions, clarification, and encouragement. The democratic leader directs discussion, but remains essentially uninvolved with the issues. The responsibility for evaluation of the group rests with the group, but within a framework suggested by the leader.

The *group-centered* leadership style is characterized by an almost total lack of directing the procedures of the group. Instead, the group-centered leader attempts to understand the thinking and feeling of group members so that this understanding may be reflected back to the group through supporting, clarifying, accepting, and reflecting on the contributions of other members. The content and methods of discussion are left completely to the discretion of the group, and the assessment of the group experience is the responsibility of the individual group member.

"Leadership in name only" may be the most suitable definition for the *laissez-faire* leadership style. A person exhibiting this style rejects any and all responsibility for directing the group. Participation by this leader is infrequent, and then only when asked. All decisions and assessments are made without the laissez-faire leader's involvement and encouragement. Perhaps the most productive communication behavior contributed to the group by this leader is to ask for a motion for adjournment.

Which leadership style is appropriate for a particular group depends largely on the needs of that group. When a group needs to complete a task quickly or when group members find it difficult to define the task clearly, an authoritarian leadership style might be most appropriate. Authoritarian leaders furnish much-needed structural and procedural guidance in this situation. The democratic leadership style is most useful in groups where the task is relatively well defined and where the group members know each other and get along well together. The help and guidance provided by the democratic leader assist the group when needed, but mainly in a supportive and counseling manner. This leadership style generally results in an extended period of time for the group to reach its goal, but with greater overall member satisfaction than with the authoritarian leadership style. The group-centered style of leadership is most appropriate in counseling and therapy types of groups. The aim of such groups is usually sharing of information, feelings, and thoughts, with no clearly defined objectives set for the group as a whole. What group members need in such groups is the supporting, clarifying, and reflecting communication behaviors that the group-centered leader provides. Our "leadership in name only" or laissez-faire leadership style warrants limited discussion. Since communication behaviors by a "leader" of this kind are nearly nonexistent, this leadership style is appropriate only when the person has no power or authority in the group and when other group members exhibit useful and productive leadership behaviors.

Interaction patterns: The processes by which group members communicate or interact with one another as they conduct their activities according to some recurrent patterns.

A useful way at looking at how groups conduct their business is to see who talks to whom. *Interaction patterns* aid us in defining the roles, status, and leadership behaviors in any group. The frequency and content of messages exchanged among certain group members often provide valuable information concerning how each member contributes (or fails to contribute) to the effective functioning of the group. Remember that these interaction patterns are just that—regular patterns. They do not imply that certain members may talk to certain other members and not to certain others, or that communication *never* takes place between selected members. They only indicate the *relative* frequency with which members communicate with one another. For instance, it has been found that more communication is directed toward a deviant in a group (that person who refuses to agree with a majority of group members on a certain point or points). This communication pattern would be reflected in the total group's interaction pattern. Some common interaction patterns in five-person groups are graphically represented in Figure 7.

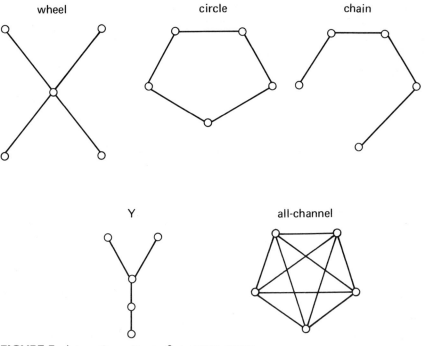

FIGURE 7 Interaction patterns: five-person groups.

Group task

All groups are formed for some reason. Regardless of the type of group, all groups have some job to perform.

Group task: Generally the reason why the group was formed, the job the group must perform. Includes purpose and goal(s).

A *group's task* may be assigned or suggested by a source external to the group itself, or the group may define its own task. The nature of the task may be clearly defined prior to the establishment of the group, or part of the group's process may involve more specifically defining the task. The publicly stated problem or job that the group is dealing with is generally the group task. However, efforts to identify and perform group roles, methods of discussion and decision, and criteria for task completion are also important facets of the task.

Purpose: The reason the group was formed, as opposed to working as individuals.

Many tasks or problems can be dealt with more effectively in groups than on an individual basis. Sharing of expertise, sharing of individual thoughts, feelings, and attitudes, and more effective creation of new ideas or approaches to the solution of a problem are all *purposes* of groups. The vice-president of an insurance company may wish to change the employee benefits package offered to its workers. If perceptive and concerned with others' contributions to this decision, that VP may compose a decision-making group of managers and workers to deal with this problem. The *purpose* of this group, then, would be to share perceptions, feelings, attitudes, and needs of a number of people from a variety of organizational levels in an attempt to decide upon (or at least make recommendations for) an employee benefits program suitable for the greatest number of employees. The vice-president alone might not be able to compile and consider the bulk of information necessary to make a decision that would be most beneficial to *all* employees.

Goal(s): The objective(s) of the group against which the effectiveness of the group may be evaluated.

A group seldom attempts a task without some *group goal(s)*. The assumption here is that someone, either internal or external to the group, sets a number of objectives for the group to accomplish. The group is then evaluated according to its relative success in completing its task. The goal or goals that the group is working toward may include both short- and long-range goals, both individual and collective goals.

A homecoming planning committee might have several short-term goals, such as selection of a specific date, specific activities, and specific times for the various activities. The long-range goal of the group might be to have a homecoming week during which as many students as possible participate and are satisfied. The collective goal of the group might be identical to the long-range goal, but individual goals may influence the nature of the group's interaction and focus. Some members might be interested in having a delightful homecoming dance, others might concentrate on picking a football game their team can win, while still others might be most interested in planning competitive activities that will make their fraternity or sorority look good. Thus, a group's goals consist of a variety of subgoals, both long- and short-term, both individual and collective.

Group climate

All groups develop a certain climate or atmosphere. Each member has feelings about each other member and about participation in the group as a whole. Most groups also develop some expectations for behavior in the group—what is permitted and what is not permitted. Should disagreements arise within the group, some members attempt to exert their influence by trying to work out the problems so that the group may proceed toward the accomplishment of its goal(s).

These perceptions and relationships among group members constitute what we call "group climate."

Group climate: The feeling that group members develop toward the group and the other members of the group. Includes cohesiveness, norms, and conformity pressure.

Frank: I think we should split into two separate groups. Terry is a real pain, and Jeff never shows for our meetings.

Lisa: Yeah, and Craig always seems to start arguments with Amy and me.

Mary: But Dr. Biggers said we have to work as a *group* on this project. How is he going to take this?

Harry: He didn't say we couldn't work as subgroups on two different aspects of the project.

Lisa: That could be a problem. First, let's call a mandatory meeting of the whole group, and whoever doesn't show up, they're out of the group and we'll tell Biggers why.

Evidently the *group climate* in the eight-member group being discussed by four of its members is not very good. Personality and procedural conflicts exist, the group (at least four members of the group) wants to split, and some standards of behavior are under consideration in order to influence certain members to attend meetings. Frank, Lisa, Mary, and Harry don't have very positive feelings toward the group or toward particular members in the group, but they are trying to improve their group's climate in a positive manner.

This group, like most other groups, will not effectively proceed toward its goal without a positive working climate. How members feel about other members and about the total group experience, as evidenced by their communication about these feelings, determines how efficiently and quickly the group will achieve its goals. Not that group members always agree—they don't. Mutual positive regard and respect, acceptance of (not necessarily agreement with) others' feelings, ideas, and contributions, compliance with agreed-upon standards of behavior, and a willingness to adopt group values and decisions—these factors all contribute to a positive group climate. Only under conditions approaching these ideals will a group function effectively.

Cohesiveness: The "stick-togetherness," degree of solidarity, or identification of the individuals with the group as a whole; "the forces acting on group members to remain in the group."[7]

Most of us are encouraged to remain in groups as long as we feel that we are a part of the group, we are attracted to other group members or the group as a whole, or we are aware of the pressure of external forces supporting our continuing within the group. We can speculate concerning the conditions influencing the *cohesiveness* of the student working group we referred to earlier. Certainly the group is encouraged to work together by an external force (Dr. Biggers). But this encouragement may not be sufficient for the group to maintain a high level of cohesiveness. Personality conflicts and behavioral conditions (not attending meetings and arguing habitually) are working as divisive forces within this group. These negative forces seem to be overpowering the authoritarian support of the instructor, at least for Frank, Lisa, Mary, and Harry. The conditions encouraging us to remain a member of any group must be stronger than the opposing forces, or we may leave the group. We must be attracted to some or all group members or the activities of the group, or the external pressure for continued group membership must be sufficient for us to remain. Some or all of these conditions must exist among group members for a relatively high level of cohesiveness to exist and for the group to work as a collective whole.

Norms: The standards group members have about how they should behave in the group. May be either implicit or explicit.

Robert's Rules of Order sets forth a very formal and explicit procedure for conducting group meetings that is commonly called "parliamentary procedure."[8] Many formal and long-term groups use parliamentary procedure as a set of *norms* or behavioral standards for the conduct of their meetings. But not all groups follow such a formal and clear-cut set of norms. Just as our four students in the discussion above attempted to set norms for their group, many groups, both formal and informal, develop behavioral expectations for their members. Members of an informal group of friends may decide that if all individuals who wanted to go to a movie together don't arrive by 8:15, "we'll leave without them." "Group members who interrupt others while talking will become the recipients of a long, cold stare" might be an example of an implicit norm developed in a group where one or more members typically interrupt others. Thus, some norms may never be actually stated in a group, but the verbal or nonverbal communication behavior of the group members when a norm is broken often indicates that norms do indeed exist. Some norms do exist in all groups, and these behavioral expectations and compliance with them serve to increase the efficiency of the group process.

Conformity pressure: Interpersonal influence intended to increase the degree to which a group member's behavior corresponds to the norms of the group.

Just as all groups have norms, all groups attempt to gain group members' compliance with these norms through interpersonal influence. *Conformity pressure* may take many forms: the cold stare, verbal reprimands, the assignment of boring or difficult tasks, or even ejection from the group. The amount and type of conformity pressure may vary according to the norm violated, the status of the deviant, and the point in the group's interaction at which the norm is violated. Norms often change as the mood or interaction of the group changes. A severe verbal reprimand may be leveled at a person who deviates from the norm during a heated argument, where the same person deviating from the same norm during a time of casual conversation might receive little notice or conformity pressure.

Situation

Situation: The physical arrangements in which a group finds itself. Includes setting and proximity.

Although many people would define a group's *situation* in terms of all the conditions existing in a group at any one time, we have chosen to discuss "situation" more generally in terms of the *physical environment* in which a group conducts its meetings. As we discussed in Chapter 6, the characteristics of a physical environment may greatly influence communication behaviors performed in that environment. Arrangement of furniture, lighting, temperature, colors, and the placement of group members within the physical setting all have potential influence on the interaction among group members.

Setting: The physical surroundings in which the group is meeting at a particular time.

Some people prefer to meet in the home of a group member. Others prefer a more formal atmosphere in which to conduct business. Some group tasks lend themselves to sitting on a thickly carpeted floor, whereas a large conference table and straight-backed chairs with hard seats are more appropriate for some jobs. One of your authors selected a setting for his oral defense of his dissertation which encouraged a *brief* meeting. A small conference room with a bare wooden table and wooden chairs and no air conditioning, in mid-July at 3:00 P.M.—this may have had something to do with the fact that the meeting lasted just short of one hour. (Of course, the quality of the dissertation may also have had an influence.) Indeed, the physical surroundings in which a group meets may have a great effect on group climate and effectiveness.

Proximity: The arrangement in which the group members place themselves, or in which they are placed, in group meetings.

Are you aware that the Vietnam peace talks in Paris in 1968 were held up for weeks because of a discussion concerning the shape of the conference table to be used and where representatives of various nations would be seated around the table? "What difference does that make?" you may ask. "Plenty" would be the response of many people. The person at one end of a rectangular table may be perceived as the leader or the person with highest status. The group member to the right of that person may be perceived as second in importance. If certain subgroups sit together in a group meeting, they may be seen as a force to be dealt with as a group. Although they might not *intend* to influence other group members strategically, they may be believed to be doing just that.

Some group members feel more comfortable if they can see the faces of all other members clearly. This gives them the advantage of being able to read the facial expressions of all group members. Some prefer to place themselves so that direct eye contact with particular or all group members is accessible. Certain members might be placed or place themselves at a specific location within a group so that they may be perceived as leaders, have access to nonverbal cues, or strategically influence the interaction within the group. Look at Figure 8. What kinds of assumptions would you make about the placement of individual group members in the seating arrangements?

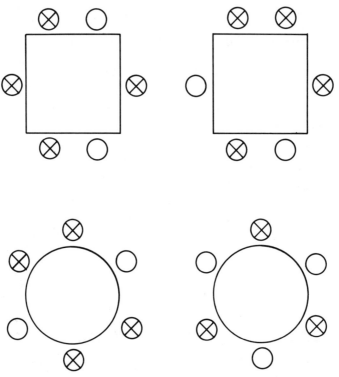

FIGURE 8 Four seating arrangements.

Group phases

Groups grow and develop over a moderately long period of time, just as people do. And just as there are phases in the growth of human beings (infancy, childhood, adolescence, adulthood), there are relatively well-defined "phases" in the development and growth of groups. Researchers interested in the development of groups, especially task-oriented groups, have identified from three to five such phases. For example, Schutz [9] identified three phases (inclusion, control, affection) based on how group interactions are influenced by individual and group needs. Fisher[10] and Tuckman[11] each recognized four phases (orientation/forming, conflict/storming, emergence/norming, reinforcement/performing), and Caple[12] observed five phases (orientation, conflict, integration, achievement, order). We have chosen to discuss Fisher's categorization of group phases, because of its emphasis on the speech communication behaviors characterizing each phase.

Fisher's first phase is that of *orientation.* During this early stage, group members attempt to become familiar with the group and with other members. The group begins to develop a group climate, and to settle questions concerning leadership, norms, status, and group task. The communication in this first phase is characterized by ambiguity and uncertainty related to both interpersonal relationships and attitudes on how to go about defining and accomplishing the group task. The *conflict* phase follows orientation. The major characteristic of the communication in this phase is heated and emotional discussion, frequently over interpersonal issues. Attempts to persuade dissenting members concerning task issues is also prevalent. Leadership, norms, and roles begin to take shape, and task-related attitudes and ideas are expressed more tenaciously. In comparison with the interaction in the first phase, that in the conflict stage is characterized by much less ambiguity and uncertainty.

Ambiguity again is expressed as a major characteristic of communication in the third phase—*emergence.* Conflict is less evident in this phase, although not completely lacking. Resolution of the issues argued in the second phase begins as dissenters ambiguously express their ideas and attitudes in a way that shows other group members that they are "coming around." Attitude change is a gradual process, so publicly stated and tenaciously held attitudes change slowly from disagreement through ambiguity to agreement. It is during this phase that the group members begin to see "the light at the end of the tunnel." *Reinforcement* is the final stage of group development. Positive reinforcement of prevailing attitudes and accomplishments is evident in this phase. If major decisions were made during the emergence phase, these decisions are supported and reinforced during the reinforcement stage. A spirit of unity, amicable cooperation, and "pats on the back for a job well done" are the communication behaviors most often associated with this final phase of group development.

Not all groups proceed through these phases in the order discussed, or even necessarily through all four phases. Long-standing groups often make decisions with a minimum of orientation and/or conflict. Some groups cycle through several conflict and emergence phases as they make various decisions on their way to accomplishing a single task. Moreover, these phases are generally not clearly distinguishable, as groups make gradual transitions between phases. It is interesting to note, however, that most students in our small-group communication classes are able to identify and analyze communication behaviors in these four phases. If this analytic procedure is possible as a result of a limited amount of time spent learning about group development, then the information gained from this analysis should be efficiently utilized to help us understand and explain the small-group communication process. After all, we need to make informed and effective choices as to how to improve our own speech communication behavior, especially in the small group setting.

Individual group member variable

A long-time researcher and author in the area of small groups has stated that " . . . evidence from research indicates that people do, in fact, behave differently in groups than when alone."[13] Although this group characteristic is still ill-defined by small-group researchers, we believe that its presence in the small group has important implications for and influences on understanding and explaining communication in groups.

Individual group member variable: The influence that an individual group member's personal characteristics and abilities have on other members of a particular group and on the group as a unique entity. Includes (but is not limited to) (1) individual personality characteristics, (2) group role(s), (3) group status, (4) interpersonal communication repertoire, and (5) individual group communication personality.

The final characteristic—individual group communication personality—has not been adequately defined by small group researchers to this time, so little emphasis has been placed on its existence or study. How an individual's communication behavior differs among various communication settings is not known, and methods to use in an attempt to study these differences are nonexistent.

We do know, however, that groups are made up of individuals, and that the characteristics and abilities of each individual serve to influence other group members and to make each group a unique entity. As any individual in a group changes, as a group's membership changes in any way, the group itself changes. Even as only one group member is deleted or added, all other characteristics of the group—even its process of communication—change with that difference in group composition.

Considerable research has shown that the personal characteristics and abilities of any group member influence in some undefinable way the group as a whole. Such characteristics as expertness in a particular subject area, age, sex, physical characteristics, intelligence, personality characteristics, and popularity all affect the climate, structure, task, development, and communication of a group so as to make that group different from any other group. If a city planning committee should discover that a certain group member is an architect, they might look to this member to lead a discussion concerning plans for the construction of a new city hall building, and direct more interaction toward that member. The single male member in a student group may find that he is perceived as an outsider and unworthy of making contributions to the group's problem-solving efforts. Older group members are often looked to for support or leadership. The most dependable group member, as perceived by the group, will probably be assigned the tasks most crucial to the effective and productive accomplishment of the group's goals. The list could go on and on.

It is generally accepted that the combination of all individual group members' characteristics makes a group unique in that the group itself is more than the sum of its parts. Although the individual group member variable is still ill-defined, its presence and influence is undeniable. The characteristics that have been discussed to this point in the chapter are all indications of the belief that a group is more than just a number of people thrown together at the same location.

Communication

The final characteristic of a group (and the most important) is the message or communication. Through communication, group members link themselves with one another (linking function), share and utilize knowledge (mentation function), and influence one another (regulation function), in an attempt to achieve goals that they believe to be important. Through communication, groups develop a group structure and a group climate, grow and mature through various phases, and solve problems or conduct business. There is *mutual* influence between communication in a group and all other group characteristics. The communication that takes place in a group influences all other characteristics; the group's structure, task, climate, situation, phases, and composition determine the types, content, and frequency of messages produced in a group. Further discussion of these relationships will be deferred until the next chapter.

WHAT ARE SOME TYPES OF GROUPS?

Think of all the groups to which you have belonged and belong now. How many are there—fifteen? fifty? one hundred? Regardless of how many groups you can think of, most of them probably would fit rather neatly into five basic categories or types: primary, social, educational, problem-solving or decision-making, and therapeutic.

Primary groups serve the purpose of developing close interpersonal relationships. Our family and our closest friends may constitute *all* of our primary groups. Although our family and close friends may also act as any other type of group for us, their main purpose is the establishment and maintenance of close interpersonal relationships.

We expand our circle of interpersonal relationships by becoming members of *social groups.* Joining a fraternity or sorority, having friends over for dinner or

a beer, going out to the movies with people we meet in classes or at work, and joining a number of coworkers for lunch all expand our range and number of interpersonal relationships through membership in social groups.

In both these types of groups—primary and social—the main purpose is to develop and maintain interpersonal relationships. Although we may perceive this purpose as involving task-oriented behavior at times, the other three types of groups are generally associated with identifiable tasks and goals. The task to be accomplished in an *educational group* is to disseminate or acquire some amount of knowledge in a given subject area. Classes and seminars, training sessions, group orientation sessions, and public forums are examples of learning or educational groups. Through interaction with other group members, we dispense or gain information on a topic of interest to all group members.

Probably the type of group that comes most readily to mind when "group communication" is the topic of discussion is the *problem-solving/decision-making group.* That's not so surprising—it is the most common type of group. Imagine that you are 35 years old. Imagine also that you have a family of two children and a spouse, and a job as assistant manager of a clothing store. A typical day in the life of *you* may go something like this:

    7:00 Up with the alarm
    7:30 Breakfast with the spouse and kids; topic of discussion: what plans to make
        for the upcoming weekend.

9:00   Meeting with store manager, head buyer, advertising manager, and franchise owner; topic of discussion: what to do about slumping sales.

12:00   Luncheon meeting with Lions Club; topic of discussion: how to raise money for the Lions' sponsored football team.

1:30   Meeting with store department managers; topic of discussion: how to reduce employee turnover.

5:30   Home for dinner

6:30   Dinner with spouse and kids; topic of discussion: how to buy new bicycles, pay the gigantic phone bill, and save money for the weekend planned this morning, all out of two small paychecks.

8:00   Meeting with the Church Renovations Committee; topic of discussion: which part of the church building or grounds needs renovation the most.

11:00   Home and bedtime; topic of discussion: who takes the dog out.

Had enough? Problem solving and decision making are everywhere! We will defer further discussion of this topic until the next chapter. (After all, the authors made this decision as a group.) Suffice it to say that problem solving and decision making are the most common types of group activities.

The final type of group—the *therapeutic group*—has as its objective personal change in the individual group member. The alcoholic or the drug addict joins a group to "get off the stuff." Marriage partners attend group counseling sessions to share with other couples their feelings and dealings in hopes of bettering their relationship. The ex-convict joins a support group with the objective of becoming a more productive member of society. The common characteristic in all these situations is the desire and attempt to effect some personal change in the group member through interaction with others who have problems in common.

WHAT ARE SOME DISADVANTAGES AND ADVANTAGES OF WORKING IN GROUPS?

Given your knowledge of and past experiences in working in groups, you may be tempted to ask: "Why assign a task to a group, when a well-informed, intelligent individual might perform this task just as effectively?" The "might" in this question is a vitally important word, and it provides the motivation for this discussion of some positive and negative aspects of group work.

Suppose you were asked to nominate a person for candidacy for the office of President of the United States. What criteria would you use for the selection of this person? Personality characteristics, knowledge of foreign and domestic affairs, public image, political background and experience, financial status—all these items might appear on your list of selection criteria. How would you develop each of these items? *Which* personality characteristics? *How much* knowledge of foreign and domestic affairs? *What kind* of public image? *What type* and *amount* of political experience? *Which* financial status? Once you have adequately defined your criteria, how might you go about finding the ideal person who meets those criteria as closely as possible? To aid you in this enormous task, you might enlist the assistance of your parents, friends, instructors, maybe some political figures, business associates, the person on the street. (What, *you* aren't that "well-informed, intelligent individual who might perform this task just as effectively"?) You could even have a meeting with some of these people so that you might all share your perceptions and ideas about this selection process. Yet another *group!* Well, groups must have some advantages. But let's look at the disadvantages first.

Disadvantages of groups

It wouldn't be hard to convince most people that working in groups takes *more time* than working alone. Because group members share information and discuss alternatives and issues, groups are less efficient than most people working by themselves, in terms of using time and ease of achieving task goals. You might be able to decide fairly easily and quickly what movie to see on a Friday night, but when two or more friends are involved in making the same decision, disagreements must be worked out and alternatives must be considered. These processes add to the time and lessen the efficiency of the decision-making process in comparison with making the same decision alone.

Certain socio-emotional variables within a group may lead to a decrease in task efficiency commonly known as the *"groupthink"* phenomenon.[14] In highly cohesive groups, members often suspend critical judgment and the maintenance and presentation of personal opinions in an attempt to preserve a false sense of unanimity within the group. Once a tentative decision has been reached, negative information is ignored and discussion of other alternatives is suppressed. The group develops a shared illusion of invulnerability, and the moral and ethical consequences of its decision are not considered. Thus, victims of the groupthink phenomenon resist the free and open discussion of many alternative solutions and issues (which we will discuss as an advantage of groups).

Another disadvantage of group work is an interesting aspect known as the *"risky shift"* phenomenon. Groups tend to select problem solutions or decision alternatives that are less conservative and have a lower probability of success than would an individual working on the same task. Why and how this happens is not fully explainable at this time. It may be that individuals in a group feel that the responsibility for making the decision is not personal, since several group members must bear the consequences. It may also be true that the risky shift phenomenon occurs in groups where a leader or a leading subgroup is inclined to take risks, and other group members follow along. The less conservative and less probable alternative may also be an ideal solution, but not really feasible or comprehensive in its scope. The group stands to be less effective in its decision-making or problem-solving attempts if the most workable and intelligent selection from alternatives is not made by the group.

Without a doubt, group work provides *more opportunity for conflict* than does working alone. Whenever three or more meet, discussion, disagreements, and some amount of conflict generally result. You may be in conflict with yourself over what to do about a deteriorating love relationship, but when you get a group of friends together for the purpose of discussing this matter, various attitudes and opinions will be expressed, some of which will conflict. Disagreements will arise, and possibly some heated arguments will ensue as your friends attempt to assist you with this problem. Don't get the idea that conflict is *always* a disadvantage in groups—it isn't. Most groups need some healthy conflict to reduce the chances that either groupthink or risky shift will occur, and so that a variety of attitudes, opinions, and alternatives will be openly discussed. When a number of individuals, all with different personality characteristics, get together to discuss various topics through collective sharing of opinions, ideas, and alternatives, some kind and amount of conflict will surely result. It is not the *presence* of conflict that is the disadvantage to working in groups—it is the *method of dealing with that conflict* that often provides a major stumbling block to effective group functioning. In the next chapter we will discuss some suggestions for effectively dealing with group conflict.

Advantages of groups

We believe that the advantages of working in groups far outweigh the disadvantages. Generally there is a *greater availability of materials* in groups than there is in individual work. This is accomplished through an effective division of labor. Individual group members can work on various aspects of a problem or decision and share that information with the group. This saves time and increases group efficiency.

When there is group participation in problem solving or decision making, the result is *higher interest in the task* and *greater commitment to the outcome.* Individuals who make decisions or solve problems unilaterally and then hand down those decisions to others find themselves without whole-hearted support. Wouldn't you rather have a voice in deciding how your student fees should be spent?

Other important advantages to group work are consideration of *a wider range of issues and alternatives, increased chances for in-depth analysis,* and *higher-quality decisions.* All group members are provided the opportunity to suggest issues and alternative solutions in a group meeting, and several heads are better than one when critically analyzing various problem solutions or decision alternatives. Research has shown that, for the reasons discussed above, groups also make *higher-quality decisions.* Groups can amass, synthesize, and analyze a greater amount of information than can an individual. When individuals take active participation in group problem-solving and decision-making tasks, they are more interested and committed to the task and its outcome. The result is a decision of higher quality and with more enthusiastic support than would be the case with an individual decision passed down from above.

Now who do you think could make the more effective selection of a candidate for the President of the United States—you or a group including you? Right! That's probably why it's done that way now.

WHAT ARE SOME GROUP COMMUNICATION PROBLEMS?

Before leaving this chapter, it might be useful to identify some potential communication problems that you face in groups. Some are problems with individual behavior; others concern the group as a whole.

One individual problem is that of the *dominating talker.* This person has something to say about everything, and attempts to control the discussion. Whether or not the dominating talker's contributions are useful, this person diminishes group effectiveness by denying equal participation by all group members. On the other end of the "talking" continuum is the *nonparticipator.* Imbalance in group participation is the result of this communication problem, also. You never know what's going on inside the head of a nonparticipator, and potentially productive contributions stay there, unexpressed.

The *insensitive group member* says whatever comes to mind, regardless of how it affects others. Personality and group conflicts arise when this group communication problem persists. "That's a stupid idea," "You don't know what you're talking about," and "We already talked about that, don't you listen?" flow from the mouth of the insensitive group member. You might want to send this one across town for coffee.

Some group members conceal personal goals, objectives, or needs in hopes of achieving or satisfying them through the group's interaction. These concealed needs or goals are called *hidden agendas.* Suppose you have just opened a quick copy printing service and you need new contacts to develop your clientele. You might join a civic or social group to meet businesspeople and office personnel for the express purpose of selling your service. Your hidden agenda is the motivating factor for membership in these groups, not the goals or activities of the group itself. Group members with hidden agendas detract from group effectiveness by usurping group time and energy for personal gain.

Related to the group member with a hidden agenda is the *personal interest pleader.* A member might encourage a youth activities planning committee to schedule a roller skating party if that group member is the owner of a roller skating rink. Or a member of the city planning committee might support the placement of the new utilities office building in an economically depressed area if that individual is the owner of four acres of land in that locality. The personal interest pleader impedes group productivity by limiting the alternatives that the group might consider.

Groups also experience problems not directly related to the communication behavior of an individual. Restrictions in time, energy, or information may influence a group to yield unnecessarily to *conformity pressure.* A group might accept a good solution at the expense of a better one if group members are short on time or energy. Or the desire to finish and go home may make a mediocre alternative look good if presented and supported at the right time by the right individual. A group's productivity will be reduced if members *submit to a high-status member.* You may be delighted to know that a famous heart surgeon socializes with the group of heart surgeons who are considering whether or not you need open-heart surgery. But would you want those surgeons to make their decision by submitting to this high-status member of the weekend golf group? Probably not. Group effectiveness suffers when high-status members get the conformity nod.

Lack of cohesiveness disrupts efficient group functioning. Groups that don't develop an atmosphere of openness, supportiveness, and friendliness spend valuable time and energy coping with *interpersonal and decisional conflict.* Personality conflicts, close-mindedness, pettiness, and inflexibility lead to tense interpersonal relationships and indecision. Some conflict is to be expected and is constructive in all groups. But when divisiveness and hostility are prevalent and persist within a group, a decline in motivation and productivity is the result.

GROUP DYNAMICS: A DESCRIPTIVE APPROACH

PUTTING THEORY INTO PRACTICE

Working in groups can be a fulfilling yet frustrating experience. In this chapter we have defined what a small group is and identified a number of characteristics which are distinctive to all groups. We have performed the mentation function of speech communication by discussing four types of groups, some advantages and disadvantages of working in groups, and several communication problems experienced in small groups. You may have noticed that we have said little pertaining directly to skills development. We have basically *described* what to look for when observing or participating in groups.

But all is not lost for the cause of small group communication skills development. As you may remember from Chapter 1, learning is a four-step process: (1) awareness, (2) understanding, (3) recognition of alternatives, (4) choice. Our discussion of group communication in this chapter has focused on the first two of these steps: awareness and understanding. In describing the various characteristics, advantages and disadvantages, and potential communication problems associated with working in groups, we hope we have helped you achieve *more awareness* and *better understanding* of some of the concepts that influence the effectiveness of communication in small groups.

We have already seen, for example, that overtalkers and nonparticipators often serve to lower the effectivenss of group communication. We have described how groups usually make higher-quality decisions when taking more time to make those decisions. These and other observations should have resulted in your becoming more aware of and more enlightened about the complexity of the speech communication process in groups. You are on the road now to being able to apply these observations to a better understanding of what it takes to become a more effective small group communicator.

The intent of this chapter extends beyond these first two steps in the learning process, however. You should, at this point, be able to recognize some of the alternatives available to you when you communicate in small groups. You know that there should be a balance between nonparticipation and domination of the communication process. You know that you must be patient when making decisions in groups and must avoid the "groupthink" and "risky shift" phenomena. You also know that there are definite advantages to working in groups, as opposed to working as an individual, to solve a problem or make a decision. Knowing these things should enable you to recognize certain communication alternatives and, to some extent, encourage you to make informed and productive choices when participating in groups.

As we indicated in Chapter 1, speech communication *practice* improves through *theory*-informed and -enlightened choices. The next chapter will shed further light on the learning steps of recognition of alternatives and making productive choices in small groups.

SUGGESTED ACTIVITIES

1. Observe a group in its natural setting: a city council meeting, a college/university committee, or a fraternity/sorority meeting. Make notes and/or diagrams of the situation (setting and proximity) in which the group is working. How do you think setting and proximity are influenced by status, roles, and leadership characteristics of that group? How do you think these group characteristics influenced the communication that you observed in the group?

2. Designate five classmates to work on a problem-solving exercise in class. (Your instructor might have some fun exercises to use.) Observe the members of that group closely

for 10 to 15 minutes as they work on the exercise. Note which functional roles each group member performs. How did you know which group member performed which role? What degree of success did each group member have at performing the role(s) attempted? How might certain roles have been performed more successfully?

3. In your everyday dealings with people (friends, parents, instructors, coworkers), observe leadership behaviors and identify which style of leadership communication is exhibited by those people: authoritarian, democratic, group-centered, or laissez-faire. On the basis of the descriptions of these four styles of leadership communication given in this chapter, list the communication behaviors which enabled you to categorize these leaders. Remember, these leadership styles are seldom distinct categories. See if you can assign a *predominant* leadership style.

[1]Marvin E. Shaw, *Group Dynamics: The Psychology of Small Group Behavior,* 3rd ed. (New York: McGraw-Hill Book Company, 1981), p. 8.

[2]Paul A. Hare, *Handbook of Small Group Research,* 2nd ed. (New York: The Free Press, 1976), p. 4.

[3]Kenneth D. Benne and Paul Sheats, "Functional Roles of Group Members," *Journal of Social Issues,* 4 (Spring 1948): 41–49.

[4]Benne and Sheats, pp. 42–46. Reprinted by permission of The Society for the Psychological Study of Social Issues.

[5]Paul F. Secord and Carl W. Backman, *Social Psychology* (New York: McGraw-Hill Book Company, 1964), pp. 294–295.

[6]Robert Tannenbaum, Irving R. Weschler, and Fred Massarik, *Leadership and Organizations: A Behavioral Science Approach* (New York: McGraw-Hill Book Company, 1961), p. 24.

[7]Secord and Backman, *Social Psychology,* p. 269.

[8]*Robert's Rules of Order* (New York: Bell Publishing Company, 1978).

[9]William C. Schutz, *The Interpersonal Underworld* (Palo Alto: Science and Behavior Books, 1966).

[10]B. Aubrey Fisher, "Decision Emergence: Phases in Group Decision-Making," *Speech Monographs,* 37 (1970): 53–66.

[11]Bruce W. Tuckman, "Developmental Sequence in Small Groups," *Psychological Bulletin,* 63 (1965): 384–399.

[12]Richard B. Caple, "The Sequential Stages of Group Development," *Small Group Behavior,* 9 (1978): 470–476.

[13]Shaw, *Group Dynamics,* p. 46.

[14]Irving L. Janis, *Victims of Groupthink* (Boston: Houghton Mifflin Company, 1972).

10 GROUP DISCUSSION: A PRESCRIPTIVE APPROACH

After studying this chapter you should be able to:

Distinguish between problem solving and decision making

Explain the eight steps in decision making/problem solving

Direct a group through a problem-solving discussion, using any one of four problem-solving formats

Influence a group to increase its communication effectiveness

Influence a group to manage conflict more effectively by exerting influence over the communication in the group

Influence a group's leadership by exerting influence over the communication in the group

Only a working understanding of communication and the group process, coupled with the experience of group membership, enables the member to be effective.[1]

Developing effective communication within a group is not easy. Anything short of a combination of knowing about (theory) and knowing how (practice) leaves the individual less than completely effective in groups. There are no tried-and-true methods for improving effectiveness in group situations. There are only alternatives to be experimented with by the concerned group member in aiding group productivity. The guidelines in this chapter are not to be followed blindly as authority. They are merely *suggested alternatives* which you might apply as your experience in groups widens and your sensitivity to group needs matures.

Each group is unique in its composition, structure, goals, and climate. To attempt to dictate what you should do in a specific group situation would be doing you a great disservice. We would be wrong—you would not become more effective. We can only provide the theoretical stimulation for your practical application of group communication principles. *You* must practice and grow.

"Practice makes perfect" should be the guiding principle applied to your group communication skills.

The guidelines presented in this chapter are certainly applicable to any group situation. They may be appropriately instituted whether you find yourself on a church fund-raising committee, a civic planning board, or a group of business executives. In the following pages we will help you increase your awareness, understanding, and realization of alternatives. The choice from among these alternatives is up to *you*. Only you can select from and apply these alternatives as you develop a keener sense for what needs to be done in a group and when.

Our focus in this chapter is on task-oriented groups—problem-solving and decision-making groups specifically. We have chosen this focus because they are the most common and difficult types of groups in which to communicate effectively. Participation must be shared and active, leadership must be of high quality, conflicts must be resolved, and group needs must be recognized and satisfied—all in the name of effective problem solving and decision making. No, developing effective communication within a group is *not* easy.

HOW DO GROUPS SOLVE PROBLEMS AND MAKE DECISIONS?

Many writers use the terms "problem solving" and "decision making" interchangeably. Brilhart, however, makes an important and useful distinction between these two terms, as shown here.

Problem solving: A procedure by which an individual or group moves through time from a state of dissatisfaction with something to a plan for arriving at a satisfactory condition. A series of stages or steps is always involved in problem solving, and entails many decisions.[2]

Decision making: Choosing among two or more possible alternatives.[3]

Brilhart's distinction is important because you, as a member of a group, might approach a task differently if your group were selecting a single alternative from a number presented to you, rather than starting from a state of dissatisfaction, developing a number of possible solutions, and selecting from them. Problem solving involves making a number of decisions while attempting to solve a problem.

For example, you may be faced with the problem of taking a foreign language to fulfill a graduation requirement. True, you do need to choose from a number of foreign languages. This seems to be a *decision.* But your *problem* goes deeper than simply selecting from among the available alternatives. You may feel that you are not good at learning foreign languages, so your problem might be stated: How can I most effectively fulfill the one-year foreign language graduation requirement? *Which* foreign language should I attempt? To *whom* should I turn for guidance? *When* should I enroll in a foreign language course? *What* other courses should I take that will give me enough time to study my foreign language? These are all *decisions* which must be made in attempting to resolve this *problem.*

STEPS IN PROBLEM SOLVING/DECISION MAKING

Order and organization are two important prerequisites to effective group problem solving and decision making. We have identified eight general steps that any group might use to ensure this order and organization in their group processes:

---

1. Clearly identify and define the task.
2. Prepare for discussion.
3. Analyze the problem/decision within the group.

4. Identify and clarify alternatives.
5. Thoroughly evaluate the alternatives.
6. Select from the alternatives.
7. Implement the solution/decision.
8. Evaluate the success of the solution/decision.

Each group member should *identify and define the task* of the group before the first group meeting, if possible. This definitional process encourages the group member to develop a personal perspective on the problem, and to formulate possible solutions, issues, and informational needs. Personal perspectives and formulations of this sort enable the group member to develop a personal point of view from which to draw during group discussion. Individuals should not attempt to solve the problem or make the decision alone during this step, as these predispositions and their presentation in the group might hamper free and open discussion. What groups don't need is a personal interest pleader in each group member.

Once this personal perspective is developed, each member should *prepare for the discussion*. Researching the problem or decision area is necessary for the intelligent and productive group member. All facets of the problem should be researched, not just those aspects which support the individual's personal per-

spective. Background of the problem, successful and unsuccessful alternatives attempted in the past, the current status of the problem, and criteria for an effective alternative are all areas that the group member should be concerned with and be prepared to discuss. A group member who is not well informed and well prepared will not be a productive group member.

Perhaps the most important step in any problem-solving/decision-making endeavor is to *analyze the problem/decision task within the group.* Many groups falter as a result of failing to analyze the group's task completely. Each group member brings to the group slightly different perspectives and definitions of the task. These perspectives must be discussed and differences resolved prior to any discussion of solutions/alternatives. By completing this step in its proper sequence—early in the group's interaction—considerable frustration and conflict can be avoided.

The importance of this analysis process cannot be overstated. No group can hope to accomplish a task without a full understanding of what that task is. Discussion of alternatives is useless if the group has not thoroughly defined and collectively agreed on what the problem is or what decision must be made. Could a group of architects and engineers design a building before they know how the building will be used? Should members of a "Greek Awareness Week" committee consider inclusion of various activities before they find that their charge is simply to advertise the event on campus? The answer to both of these questions is an emphatic "no!" Don't put the proverbial cart before the horse. The selection of the right solution or alternative for the wrong problem is worse than useless. Increased efficiency in the use of time and energy will result when groups clearly define and analyze their task prior to any other step.

Next, group members must *identify and clarify the alternatives* available to them. Attitudes of openness, supportiveness, and creativity are a necessity in this step. Group members should be encouraged to share ideas and opinions freely, without fear of being laughed at or ridiculed. All alternatives and possible solutions should be considered. No matter how preposterous an idea or solution might sound, it should be given equal and fair consideration. Many a farcical idea has provided the impetus for more feasible and workable solutions. Although all options should be explored, care should be taken during the discussion to insure relevance and feasibility so that group efficiency is not impaired.

One method of identifying sufficient and creative solutions or ideas is the *brainstorming* approach. The brainstorming technique was first developed by Alex Osborn, an advertising executive who felt a need to develop a creative problem-solving technique that would rule out evaluation and criticism of ideas and focus on developing solutions that were imaginative and innovative.[4] The emphasis of this approach is on creativity and quantity of ideas without evaluation and criticism during the generation process. Some rules for employing the brainstorming approach should be presented to the group before the process begins:

1. All judgments and criticisms must be put aside during brainstorming.

2. Think of as many solutions as possible. The wilder, the better. Encourage creativity.
3. Record and display all ideas.
4. Modify previous ideas to develop new ones.
5. Make sure each group member abides by the rules. If not, remind the group of the rules, ask the uncooperative group member to be silent or leave the group.
6. Try to draw suggestions from all group members.
7. Evaluate ideas once all ideas are shared, possibly at a later session.

Brainstorming may not work for all groups. It takes time, and some groups do not have enough for the purpose. The problem must be clearly defined prior to the generation of ideas. If a group allows sufficient time and desires quantity and creativity of possible solutions, brainstorming is a productive alternative.

A part of this step is the development of a set of criteria against which alternatives may be assessed. If the group has adequately defined and analyzed its task, these criteria should be easy to produce. The group should have its goals and objectives firmly in mind by this time, and the process by which the group will be evaluated must be related to these goals. The criteria for the best solution or decisional alternative must enable the group to achieve these objectives. For example, a group of top executives in a manufacturing firm may be assigned the task of deciding upon a marketing strategy to advertise a new product: newspapers and magazines, radio and television commercials, supermarket demonstrations, or free samples mailed to selected neighborhoods. Their objective would be to reach the greatest number of people, in the most affordable way, in the least amount of time, with the maximum possibility for sales. Their selection of the best marketing strategy should meet the following criteria:

1. Which strategy will reach the greatest number of people?
2. Which strategy will be most cost efficient?
3. Which strategy can be implemented within the next two months?
4. Which strategy will allow us to reach the greatest number of people in a one-month period?
5. In the past, which strategy has proven to be the most effective in producing sales of products similar to ours?

The fifth step in problem solving/decision making is the *complete evaluation of alternatives*. This is the point at which unworkable and unfeasible alternatives should be discarded, conflict and/or groupthink is most likely to occur, and open, honest (but responsible), and active discussion by all group members must take place. Discussion during this step must be critical but empathic, active but not dominating, cohesive but not overly conforming. All disagreements should be idea-centered, not person-centered.

Now the group should be ready to *select from the available alternatives*. Finally the group is going to solve its problem or make its decision. As with the previous step, caution is the guideline. Resist making hasty decisions and avoid groupthink. Discussion should be free and open, and continue to be idea-centered rather than person-centered. Contributions from each group member should be encouraged and taken seriously. In-depth analysis of each remaining alternative and application of the solution criteria are a must. Members should resist conformity on the grounds of status or power. A decision that all members can accept and agree to is superior to one in which some members "win" and some "lose."

Once decisions are made and solutions are selected, part of your group's task may be to *develop a plan to implement the solution/decision*. If the group in the manufacturing firm example above selected the radio and television commercial marketing strategy, they might also be required to devise a plan of action. This plan of action could include fiscal planning (sources and amounts), production of the commercials (who, when, how many), test market selection (how many, where, when), and timetable development for implementation. All these areas require more problem solving and decision making. Many groups are not required to develop a plan of action. It is useful for you as a group member to know whether this implementation process is an objective of your group as you proceed through step 3 above—analyzing the task. If it is, your group must plan for this step. If it isn't, you should know that, too.

A final step in the problem-solving/decision-making process is to *evaluate the success of the solution/decision*. What is involved in this step (if it is part of your task) is to conduct follow-up research concerning how your group's solution/selection met the criteria and improved the unsatisfactory conditions it was meant to improve. Organizational superiors, sales figures, recipients of the improved conditions, opinion polls, and a variety of other individuals, groups, and devices often serve as evaluation agents. If your decision or solution was a productive one, congratulations! If not, back to the drawing board.

These are the eight sequential steps that serve to guide groups through problem-solving/decision-making discussions. They are prescriptive in that they provide a step-by-step procedure to follow in the quest for effective problem-solving and decision-making discussions. They are provided in hopes that you, as a member of any group, may guide your fellow group members toward more productive group discussion. In the next section, we will present several problem-solving formats that further detail steps 3 through 6 discussed above. They provide specific patterns for guiding a group's thoughts and interactions during problem-solving discussions.

WHAT ARE SOME PROBLEM-SOLVING FORMATS?

Groups often need added organization and order in their problem-solving discussions. Problem-solving formats furnish guidelines or steps by which a group may structure its efforts. *Which* format to use, if any, depends on the type of problem being considered, group composition, the clarity of the group's task and objectives, and the amount of group structure desired. Some groups function productively with a free-flowing, informal discussion process; others need more specific direction. Select the problem-solving format that seems most appropriate for your task and group, or modify one if necessary.[5]

The reflective-thinking format

1. What is the nature of the problem facing us?
2. What are the causes and consequences of the problem?
3. What things must an acceptable solution to the problem accomplish?
4. What solutions are available to us?
5. What is the best solution?

Research concerning the effectiveness of this format has cast some doubt on its usefulness. Although it was intended to parallel an individual's problem-solving thought processes, it may not be as adaptable to group problem solving as once thought.

The ideal-solution format

1. Are we all agreed on the nature of the problem?
2. What would be the ideal solution in terms of all parties involved?
3. What conditions within the problem might be changed in order to accomplish this ideal solution?
4. Of the solutions available to us, which one most closely approaches the ideal solution?

This format focuses on the "best" solution in terms of all parties involved. It encourages the group to look at how conditions within the problem might be changed and to recognize the obstacles related to those changes. The group's task would be to overcome those obstacles and to effect changes which would most closely approximate an ideal solution for all parties involved in the problem.

The single-question format

1. What is the question that the group must answer in order to accomplish its purpose?
2. What subquestions must the group answer before it can answer this single question?
3. Does the group have sufficient information to answer these subquestions?

   If the answer to question 3 is yes, answer them.
   If the answer to question 3 is no, proceed to 4.

4. What are the most appropriate answers to these subquestions?
5. Assuming that the group's answers to the subquestions are correct, how might the single question be answered to solve the problem?

The focus of the single-question format is identification of issues (subquestions). A discussion of subquestions assists the group in considering the major question relevant to adequate solution of the problem. The emphasis in this format is on a step-by-step resolution of issues toward the goal of answering the single question that will most effectively solve the group's problem.

Nominal group technique

1. Individual generation of solutions in writing.
2. Round-robin sharing and recording of ideas.
3. Group discussion of ideas one at a time for purposes of clarification and evaluation.
4. Rank ordering of alternative solutions and public tabulation of results.
5. Group discussion concerning results. If the results of the first vote are inconclusive, another vote may be taken. Some alternatives may be eliminated at this point.
6. Second vote (if necessary) and selection of best alternative.[6]

The nominal group technique provides the advantage of individual creativity and withholding of evaluation and criticism of ideas until all are made public. The technique is "nominal" in that alternative solutions are generated by individuals, but the decision-making process is accomplished by the group. Once these ideas are presented to the group, the clarification and evaluation process begins. Finally, all group members order their preferences from best to worst and these results are opened for discussion. If a "best" solution is not agreed upon, a subsequent vote may be taken. Thus, the nominal group technique combines the advantages of individual creativity and group discussion and decision making. This technique might also be used in conjunction with any other problem-solving format during any of its stages. For instance, the nominal group technique might be used to generate ideal solutions in the second step of the ideal-solution format.

Our list of problem-solving formats is not exhaustive, but each may be useful in some group situations. We do not suggest that any one of them be used indiscriminately. They do, however, provide suggestions for groups that desire or require added organization, order, and direction in their problem-solving efforts. Analyze your group and your task before deciding *if* you need a problem-solving format. Not all groups do.

HOW ARE DECISIONS REACHED IN GROUPS?

Groups arrive at decisions through a variety of methods: (1) majority vote, (2) decision by expert or high-status member, (3) decision by leader, and (4) consensus. Each of these methods is common in groups, but the preferred method is the last—consensus. You will see why as we discuss these methods.

Groups often use the *"majority rules"* method of making decisions. At first glance, this democratic procedure seems to make the most sense. After all, we do elect our own President in this manner. If given a second consideration, this method might not seem the most appropriate for *group* decision making. If the objective of a group is for all members to be satisfied with and committed to the decision (as we believe they should be), the majority rule method does not meet this important aspect of a group process. Some members win, others lose. More likely than not, those who lose will not be completely satisfied with the group's decision and they may not be fully committed to its implementation and support.

When majority voting decides issues, subgroups form and bargain with other members or subgroups to muster support for their points of view or subgroup goals. When this happens, group discussion deteriorates to a political or personal struggle. Minority members are especially resistant to supporting the "group" decision. In such cases, high-quality decisions are seldom the result, and group effectiveness plummets.

The next two decision making methods—*decision by expert/high-status member* and *decision by leader*—are decisions in name only. Groups often conform to the wishes of an expert, a high-status member, or a leader in attempting to make a decision. In some isolated cases, a group might even *assign* decision-making authority to such a group member. In essence, the "group" denies any authority or desire to make a decision, and allows itself to be nothing but a sounding board for ideas. These methods of decision making have their disadvantages. Lack of support for the decision, failure to utilize the ideas, opinions, and expertise of other group members, loss of group cohesiveness and credibility, and members' failure to understand the reasons behind the decision are only a few of the negative consequences possible with these methods of decision making.

Decision by consensus is the most appropriate method for problem solving/ decision making in groups. A decision by consensus is one that *all* members of the group agree is the best that they can all accept. This does not necessarily mean that *all* members agree that the decision is the absolute best, but all members agree to accept some alternative, regardless of individual points of view. In a consensus, no one loses. If all members agree to accept a decision, all members should be at least moderately satisfied with the outcome of the group discussion. Thus, *shared* judgments, ideas, opinions, and decisional responsibility result in *shared* decisional satisfaction and productivity. Unanimity is not always possible in group decision making; consensus is the best alternative to it.

HOW CAN YOU INCREASE GROUP COMMUNICATION EFFECTIVENESS?

One thing that you *cannot* do is control the communication behavior of others. You can't force another group member to take an active role in group discussion, any more than you can control another's thoughts and opinions. You can *influence* others in various ways, but you *cannot control*. You can exert influence on yourself, other group members, and the group as a whole—influence that will result in more proficient group communication. As the quotation at the beginning of this chapter indicated, your effectiveness and the effectiveness of your influence blossom from the marriage of your understanding of and your experience in communication and group processes—the marriage of theory and practice.

We all maintain integrated and interdependent sets of beliefs, attitudes, and values. These B-A-V systems influence our perceptual, thinking, and speaking processes. As we experience our world, we attempt to make sense out of that world on the basis of these B-A-V systems and to assign meaning to it. The result of these experiencing, sense-making, and meaning-assigning processes is the development of a point of view or perspective concerning our world. In like fashion, we experience, make sense of, and assign meaning to that segment of our world we have labeled "group communication." And, in like fashion, we develop a perspective concerning the process of group communication. This perspective determines our own group communication behavior and, in turn, affects the degree to which we are effective in influencing the communication behavior of other members in a group. Our objective in the remainder of this chapter is to add to your working knowledge of group communication in a way that will assist you in developing healthier intrapersonal, interpersonal, and group perspectives toward that part of our world we call "group communication." (The following discussion is adapted from Fisher's categories of intrapersonal, interpersonal, and group factors for improving group communication effectiveness.[7])

Developing an intrapersonal perspective toward group communication

Dance and Larson have stated that "intrapersonal speech communication plays an essential formative role in the development of an individual's interpersonal speech communication."[8] They went on to say that the levels are cumulative and reciprocally influence one another. In other words, any disruptions at the intrapersonal level of speech communication are visible at other levels. It makes sense, then, that any discussion of developing healthier perspectives toward group communication should begin at the intrapersonal level of speech communication. A group member must develop a healthy intrapersonal perspective toward group communication prior to contributing to healthier interpersonal and group perspectives. Five intrapersonal guidelines may assist you in developing a more effective intrapersonal perspective:

1. Develop an attitude of openmindedness.
2. Develop habits of honesty and responsibility.
3. Develop a willingness to criticize and to be criticized.
4. Develop a readiness to share your ideas and opinions.
5. Develop an attitude of commitment to the group.

Openmindedness is essential when approaching a group communication situation. Don't prejudge ideas, people, or groups. Remember that no one knows everything there is to know about a topic, not even you. Become more aware that you can be wrong as well as right, you can learn as well as teach, and you can follow as well as lead. Try not to think that you've got everything figured out and that everyone should agree with you. They won't. Be open to and consider the ideas and opinions of others. Others can make useful suggestions. Group communication effectiveness depends on openmindedness on the parts of all group members. Contributions to the group process are wasted if they fall on deaf ears.

Group members should develop and maintain *honest and responsible* approaches to interacting in groups. They should feel free to express their ideas freely, openly, and candidly. Silence and conformity to group pressure *simply* for the sake of minimizing conflict has no place in effective groups. Individuals should also practice responsibility in their interactions, not only in terms of taking responsibility for their own actions and contributions, but also in terms of taking responsibility for the effects of their actions on the feelings and attitudes of other group members. *Practice empathy* in group situations, just as you would in interpersonal communication situations. A comment such as "Gee, that's a stupid idea!" can hardly be stated more honestly, but can certainly be stated more responsibly.

Closely allied with the honest and responsible approaches to group interaction is the development of a *willingness to criticize and to be criticized.* Groups can hope to be most effective when members feel free to objectively evaluate and criticize ideas, opinions, and solutions. Remember that once an idea or alternative is presented to the group, it becomes the possession of the group and not of the individual who presented it. Focus evaluations/criticisms on the idea, not on the individual. Critical analysis should be issue-oriented, not person-oriented. Try to keep this in mind when your idea is being critiqued and when you critique another's idea.

Fourth, you should develop a posture of *readiness to share your ideas and opinions.* You may feel that others know more or are more adept at communicating than you are. They often aren't, *so speak up.* Your contributions are just as valuable as anyone else's. Don't monopolize group interaction, but don't be content to sit idly by while others shoulder group responsibility. Your contribution may be the one that solves the problem.

To be effective, group members must be enthusiastic, positive, and *committed to the group and its process.* Don't prejudge the group and its task. Assume that the group task is important and necessary, and that your participation in the group is desired and needed, and will be appreciated. Provide the group with the time and energy that it needs to be a productive group. Do the research that needs to be done. Contribute when you think it's appropriate and beneficial. A group is only as effective as the members that make up that group. Members who think the group's task and processes are important will think the group is important. Members who think the group is important will find the internal motivation to influence and contribute to the group's productivity. The seed from which this internal motivation grows is the commitment of each member to the group.

Developing an interpersonal perspective toward group communication

Just as your intrapersonal perspective toward group communication influences the group process, so does your perspective concerning interacting with other group members. How you interact with others, of course, is up to *you.* The following five guidelines may help you in communicating with other group members:

1. Expand and use your knowledge of communication processes.
2. Develop a habit of active verbal participation.
3. Integrate your speaking and listening behavior with interpersonal sensitivity.
4. Practice supportiveness in your interactions with others.
5. Listen and provide feedback effectively.

This book is intended to increase your awareness and understanding of the speech communication process. It is designed to widen the range of alternatives available to you in choosing which speech communication behaviors are appropriate and effective in a specific situation. *Use them in groups.* Be aware of how your beliefs, attitudes, and values may distort what someone is saying. Consider the feelings of others when you respond to them—use empathy. Realize how your choice of language and nonverbal communication may be misinterpreted and misunderstood by others. Utilize self-disclosure and confirming responses to increase group cohesiveness. Use your *knowledge of the speech communication process* to increase the effectiveness of your interactions with other group members.

Develop a habit of active verbal participation in groups. It's one thing to *think* about saying something; it's quite another to *say it.* When one of the authors was in a graduate-level speech communication course, during one class session the class wrestled with the question "When do you know when to say something?" The only answer that we all could agree on was "When you feel a need to say something, say it." This is good advice. The relevancy of the contribution and its possible effects on other group members should be considered before speaking, of course. If the message is relevant and is produced honestly and responsibly, go ahead! The shy, silent group member stands little chance of contributing to group effectiveness. Keep in mind, however, that the "dominating talker" also contributes to group effectiveness—in a negative manner.

When interacting with other group members, your listening and speaking should show evidence of *interpersonal sensitivity.* When listening, practice empathy. Try to take the other person's point of view for a moment, and respond accordingly. Although we have indicated previously that evaluation and criticism should be issue-oriented and not person-oriented, sensitivity to the motivations and feelings of another group member allows you to "read between the lines" and practice more effective listening and responding skills. When responding, show evidence of your concern for and understanding of the other's point of view. Through the practice and exhibition of interpersonal sensitivity, interpersonal relationships with the group are strengthened, cohesiveness is established and maintained, and the effectiveness of group communication grows.

Supportive communication has been discussed in Chapter 5. Communication that exhibits supportiveness indicates that you are openminded, empathic, concerned, and considerate of the ideas and opinions of other group members. Conditional and issue-oriented statements provide evidence that you are adaptable and flexible to the needs and conditions of the group process. Being supportive shows that you have the best interests of others at heart, and that you want the group process to be as egalitarian and open as possible.

The final guideline for developing a healthier interpersonal perspective is to *listen and provide feedback effectively.* We have discussed effective listening and feedback skills in Chapter 7. These skills are especially important in the group situation. Important decisions are made and problems are solved in groups. For these decisions to be made effectively, group members must ensure that they understand and utilize information efficiently and completely. Discussing and accepting contributions some group members do not understand serves to limit group effectiveness. If you don't understand or think you don't understand something someone has said, say so and ask for clarification. Listen carefully. If you don't, something might slip past you and you may agree with something you only partially heard or understand.

Developing a group perspective toward group communication

It may seem strange to talk about developing a *group* perspective toward *group* communication. "After all, groups develop their own perspective, don't they?" you might be thinking. "That's true," we respond, "but they don't always develop a healthy perspective." With all the potential problems associated with working in groups, as discussed in the last chapter, we know that groups may settle for a barely acceptable perspective simply to get the job done. But if "simply getting the job done" is not what you consider to be an effective group strategy, read and utilize the following five guidelines for developing a healthy group communication perspective:

1. Encourage active participation.
2. Develop group sensitivity to group processes.
3. Engage in metadiscussion.
4. Develop patience toward group slowness.
5. Avoid formula answers.

We have discussed at length the importance of *active and full participation* by all group members. Groups are formed for a purpose, and this purpose evolves from some need to *share* ideas, opinions, and thoughts through the group communication process. Without active and balanced participation by all group members, this purpose will not be well served. You can aid in this sharing process by encouraging the development of free and open discussion. Ask for ideas and opinions from those members who talk little or not at all. Suggest to dominating talkers that other members should be given the chance to speak. Contribute yourself. It just might be that shy or silent member who is most able to provide the all-important idea for goal-accomplishment, *if given the chance.* Support the group's purpose of active participation.

You may assist the group in becoming *more sensitive to group processes.* The group must function as a group before it can *productively* work toward its goals. Disagreements and conflicts are natural and expected occurrences in groups. Inform the group of this fact and help the group deal with them constructively. Help the group remain issue-oriented and not person-oriented. Encourage active participation and supportive communication. Direct criticism toward a more honest, responsible, and empathic channel. Discourage name calling and personal interest pleading. Disclose hidden agendas tactfully and allow the group to deal with them *as a group.* With your knowledge of group processes, you can make the group more aware of and sensitive to group communication problems and their productive solutions.

Engage in metadiscussion. In other words, talk about the communication in the group. Groups should continually be made aware of how they are doing. This self-evaluation process occurs all too infrequently. Comments such as "So far we seem to have defined the problem clearly" or "I think we're getting a little off the track" illustrate characteristics of the group's communication process that are useful or constructive. The group's awareness and understanding of these positive characteristics of their own communication behavior may serve to motivate the group to loftier heights. In the case of negative or impeding forces, the group needs to become aware of these forces so that they can be avoided or effectively dealt with by the group. They can't be corrected if they aren't recognized. Talk about your talking!

As we have mentioned before, groups take longer to solve a problem or make a decision than do most individuals. Groups should be aware of this fact and must *develop patience toward the slowness* of the group's process. Not all group tasks can be accomplished in one meeting. Any group takes time to become *a group.* Many groups attempt to skip the orientation phase of group development and get down to the job at hand. Unfortunately, such groups find that they must return to an orientation phase of some kind because they are not functioning effectively as a group. Our experience in working in or with groups indicates that what happens prior to achieving "groupness" is a waste of valuable time. Groups get impatient. They may feel that orientation or conflict phases serve no useful purpose in task-oriented groups. Because of factors either internal or external to the group, members want to get the job done as quickly as possible and be done with it. Our experience with classroom work groups provides evidence that the quality of projects produced by such groups is inferior to those produced by groups that have taken the time and effort to attain "groupness" *prior to* work on the group's task.

Help develop an attitude of patience in groups. Problem-solving formats add structure to group discussion and assist the group in using its time more efficiently. But they don't always work for a particular group. Establish and maintain flexibility and adaptability as a group goal. If something doesn't work, try something else. Encourage active participation. This all takes time, and the group must be patient enough to expend this time and effort in order to function and accomplish its task with maximum effectiveness.

Closely related to this attitude of patience is our final guideline—*avoid formula answers.* Formula answers are obvious and easy to arrive at, but often unrealistic. For example, one of your authors assigned a group project which necessitated each group's working toward and presentation of the "best" solution to a problem of the group's choice. One of these classroom groups selected the problem of how to deal with the influx of Cuban refugees into the south Florida area in 1980. Their best solution was to educate the residents of south Florida about these people and about how to incorporate them more effectively into our society. No recommendations for *who* might conduct this process, *how* it was to be conducted, or *who* should be educated. This was a formula answer. Obvious? Yes. Easy to arrive at? Well, maybe. Realistic? Not in the terms in which it was presented. Groups must avoid formula answers. They generally lack detail, are unrealistic, and prevent the group from effectively solving a problem or making a decision.

HOW CAN GROUPS MANAGE CONFLICT MORE EFFECTIVELY?

Conflict: Perceived disagreement between two or more interdependent parties concerning the acceptance of some idea, action, or goal.

Groups inevitably experience disagreement and conflict. Not all group members get along well together, nor do they always see eye-to-eye on certain issues. Conflicts may be either perceived or real. They may be only *perceived* when individuals misunderstand, inaccurately perceive, or personally dislike one another. Conflicts may be *real* when individuals fully understand, accurately perceive, and even like one another, but they find that they still disagree. Conflicts may also be either destructive or constructive. They are *destructive* when members refuse to accept others' contributions as valid, argue for the sake of argument, focus on personality characteristics of other group members, or in any other way, unnecessarily interrupt the effectiveness of the group process. They can be *constructive* in that they may stimulate creativity and active participation in the group, encourage the group to engage in criticism and evaluation of ideas and goals, or focus discussion on issues rather than on personalities.

Finally, conflicts may be either person-oriented or task-oriented. *Person-oriented* conflicts arise when individual personalities clash, group members criticize others' reasons for holding a particular belief or attitude rather than the relevancy or efficacy of the idea, or verbal "sparring" for the sake of argument occurs. *Task-oriented* conflicts ensue when the disagreement—perceived or real—deals directly with some aspect of the group's actions, goals, or task-related objectives. Regardless of the nature of the conflict, there are several communication behaviors that encourage groups to deal with conflict effectively:

1. Don't always argue for your own position.
2. Don't assume that someone must "win" and someone must "lose."
3. Don't change your mind too quickly simply to avoid conflict.
4. Avoid easy conflict-reducing techniques.
5. Seek differences of opinion.
6. Encourage active participation by all members.
7. Use group pronouns rather than self-oriented pronouns.
8. Avoid opinionated statements that indicate closed-mindedness.

9. Make an effort to clarify misunderstandings in meaning.
10. Keep the discussion goal-oriented.
11. Use metadiscussion frequently.[9]

We have discussed many of these guidelines or related suggestions in previous sections of this book. They are particularly important to the effective management of conflict. Continually arguing for your own position results in making others defensive and limits the range of alternatives to be considered by the group. The ideal decision-making strategy—consensus—dictates that group members not assume that some must win and others must lose. Consensus encourages a sense of acceptance and satisfaction by *all* group members. Don't give in too quickly and try to avoid easy conflict-reducing strategies such as groupthink or formula answers. Thorough discussion and evaluation of issues and alternatives takes time and effort. Be willing to use this time and effort rather than opting for the "easy way out." A balance between habitual personal interest pleading and groupthink must be found if a group is to engage in effective decision making/problem solving.

Seek out differences of opinion and encourage active participation by all. Conflicts often arise when some group members dominate discussion and others refrain from speaking. These over-talkers plead for their own point of view and often form coalitions to muster support. This strategy promotes divisiveness and conflict. Shared participation by all group members directs the group toward more open, satisfying, and productive discussion. When everyone contributes, the number and quality of alternatives increase, chances for open and sincere criticisms of issues increase, and the final group product reflects the acceptance and satisfaction of all group members. Under these circumstances, conflict is more likely to be constructive than destructive.

The chances that conflict will be constructive are influenced nearly as much by *how* something is said as by *what* is said. The use of group pronouns ("we," "our," "us") rather than self-oriented pronouns ("I," "mine," "me") builds cohesiveness and a sense of concern for *group* involvement. The same holds true for avoiding opinionated statements, which are evidence of closed-mindedness and speaking from a basis of personal opinion rather than from fact. Although personal ideas and opinions are important to a group's process, offer your ideas with the intent of contributing to group effectiveness, not of controlling the group or directing it in the way that you think it should go. Use of group-oriented pronouns and unopinionated statements helps reduce the destructive nature of conflict by promoting an atmosphere of objective involvement in the group's process, a feeling of acceptance, supportiveness, and satisfaction among group members, and an attitude of openness, cohesiveness, and equality in regard to group interaction.

Make efforts to clear up misunderstandings in meanings. As we have discussed, not all conflicts are real—some arise from differences in perception and misunderstandings in meaning. Try to clarify these inaccuracies. If ambiguous terminology or usage of language is exhibited, try to clear it up as soon as possible. If the group doesn't understand what you're saying, it's impossible for group members to agree or disagree, to know whether or not the information is useful. All conflict will not disappear once perceptions and meanings are clarified, but a group need not waste valuable time and effort arguing over ideas that members already agree on, simply because of these types of misunderstandings.

Finally, conflict can be managed more effectively through frequent use of metadiscussion and maintenance of goal-oriented interaction. Comments about how ugly Mary's new hairdo is and what an idiot Bob is have no place in most task-oriented groups. Should these comments occur in your group, use metadiscussion to talk about their inappropriateness and to redirect communication in the group to a more goal-oriented and constructive channel. Talking about your talking can keep the group on track, increase the awareness, acceptance, and satisfaction of the group process, and allow the group to utilize its time and energy more efficiently.

As we have seen, conflict is a natural, expected part of communication in groups. It should be accepted as such, but it must be managed effectively if a group hopes to attain its objective. Conflict in a group should be real, task-oriented, and constructive. Conflict serves several useful purposes in groups, but to be constructive it must be handled openly, objectively, and positively by all group members. Use these guidelines toward the goal of fostering increased group productivity through managing conflict effectively.

HOW CAN LEADERSHIP EFFECTIVENESS BE INCREASED?

By now you should be able to answer this question for yourself. In Chapter 9, we defined "leadership" as "interpersonal influence, exercised in a situation and directed, through the communication process, toward the attainment of a specified goal or goals." We also stated that this interpersonal influence is very often shared by several or all members of a group, and that what a leader should do in any particular situation depends upon *the needs of the group at that time*. Fisher summarized this point of view concerning leadership effectiveness in the following manner:

> In conclusion, then, a functions approach to group leadership is not necessarily an attempt to discover what specific behaviors or functions a leader performs and non-leaders do not perform. Rather, the functions of a group leader may be the discrimination of which functions should be performed with whom and at what times.[10]

In other words, any group member should be able to perform leadership behaviors or functions (exert goal-directed interpersonal influence) in any group situation. The effectiveness of that attempted leadership will depend on that group member's sensitivity to the needs of the group and of the individual group members and on the enactment of communication behaviors and functional roles (see

Chapter 9) which satisfy these individual and group needs. Those individuals who most accurately perceive and appropriately respond to those needs will be practicing leadership communication most effectively.

How can this be done? In Chapter 9, we presented a descriptive approach to group communication. In it we defined and discussed a number of characteristics of groups and their interrelationships with each other and with the focus of group communication—communication. We also described some types of groups, some advantages and disadvantages of working in groups, and some communication problems associated with groups. Our intent in that chapter was to increase your *awareness* and *understanding* of the group communication process—to increase your knowledge of communication and group processes. In this chapter we have taken a *prescriptive* approach to speech communication at the group level. We have provided some ideas for increasing your effectiveness in problem-solving/decision-making groups by presenting the steps in the problem-solving/decision-making process, some formats for problem-solving discussions, and some procedures for making decisions. In addition, we have presented some guidelines for developing healthier intrapersonal, interpersonal, and group perspectives toward group communication, and for dealing more effectively with conflict in groups. In other words, we have attempted to increase your *realization of alternatives* for working in groups, so that you might make more effective *choices* when engaging in group communication.

Return to the quotation from Fisher at the beginning of this chapter and apply it to these two chapters and to leadership effectiveness. What remains for you to do is to widen your experience in group communication and to use the knowledge that you have gained, both in these two chapters and in your own experiences, to become more effective in exerting interpersonal influence in groups through speech communication. The knowledge—both descriptive and prescriptive—is here. The experience will come. The *choice* is up to *you*.

GROUP DISCUSSION: A PRESCRIPTIVE APPROACH

PUTTING THEORY INTO PRACTICE

In this chapter we have taken a prescriptive approach to group communication. We have described the intent of this chapter as to suggest alternatives from which you might select—not haphazardly or indiscriminately—to increase the effectiveness of speech communication at the group level. In attempting to realize this intent, we have suggested some steps you should follow in solving a problem or making a decision. We have provided some problem-solving formats and decision-making procedures that groups might use to add structure and organization to these processes. Then we presented some guidelines that should help any group member communicate more effectively in and about groups at the intrapersonal, interpersonal, and group levels. We suggested some guidelines for managing conflict more efficiently, and proposed how you might incorporate all these guidelines in your attempts at exerting your influence more productively through the practice of leadership communication.

Put this theory into practice. Some learning comes by trial and error. Such is often the case when working in groups. But an informed trial is superior to a naive trial. We have attempted to reduce your naiveté concerning group communication, in the hope that your trials will be informed and frequent and that your errors will be few.

The choice is yours.

SUGGESTED ACTIVITIES

1. Divide your class into groups of five or six members. As a group, identify a problem that needs solving. It might be a personal problem, a college/university problem, or a social problem. Using as a framework the eight steps of decision making/problem solving discussed in this chapter, list at least some of the decisions that must be made at each step in order to effectively solve the problem. You don't necessarily need to solve the problem; just outline the problem-solving strategy in terms of the decisions that need to be made along the way.

2. Divide your class into four groups of nearly equal size. Identify a problem that all groups agree would be interesting to all. (This is a problem in itself.) With each group using a different problem-solving format, have all groups attempt to solve the problem. Then compare notes. Which format was the easiest to use on this problem? Which group arrived at the best solution? Which group took the most time to solve the problem? The least time? Did the amount of time used by various groups have anything to do with the problem-solving formats used?

3. Solicit volunteers to form a discussion group on the topic "What can be done to decrease the use of illicit drugs in high schools?" Once the group has been formed, direct each group member to think of his or her own solution to the problem—the wilder the better. When each participant has answered the question individually, have the group discuss the problem and possible solutions for 10 to 15 minutes. Each group member should be directed to argue for his or her own solution during this time, directing all comments toward the goal of group acceptance of that solution. At the end of this time, have the group attempt to arrive at a consensus concerning the best solution, using all the guidelines for effective group communication outlined in this chapter. In other words, have the group develop a *group perspective* toward group communication for 10 to 15 minutes. At the end of this second period, discuss as a class the relative effectiveness of the two perspectives toward group communication—individual versus group. Which perspective was more effective? More pleasurable for the participants? Which yielded less conflict in the group?

NOTES

[1] B. Aubrey Fisher, *Small Group Decision Making*, 2nd ed. (New York: McGraw-Hill Book Company, 1980), p. 284.

[2]John K. Brilhart, *Effective Group Discussion*, 3rd ed. (Dubuque, IA: William C. Brown Company, 1978), pp. 120–121.

[3]Brilhart, *Effective Group Discussion*, p. 121.

[4]Alex F. Osborn, *Applied Imagination* (New York: Charles Scribner's Sons, 1962).

[5]The presentation of the first three of these formats is adapted from Alvin A. Goldberg and Carl E. Larson, *Group Communication* (Englewood Cliffs, NJ: Prentice-Hall, 1975), pp. 149–150.

[6]Andrew H. Van de Ven and André L. Delbecq, "Nominal Versus Interacting Group Processes for Committee Decision-Making Effectiveness," *Academy of Management Journal*, 14 (1971:203–207).

[7]Fisher, *Small Group Decision Making*.

[8]Frank E. X. Dance and Carl E. Larson, *Speech Communication: Concepts and Behavior* (New York: Holt, Rinehart and Winston, 1972), p. 56.

[9]Adapted from Steven A. Beebe and John T. Masterson, Jr., *Communicating in Small Groups: Principles and Practices* (New York: Scott, Foresman and Company, 1982).

[10]Fisher, *Small Group Decision Making*, p. 218.

UNIT V

THE PUBLIC LEVEL OF SPEECH COMMUNICATION

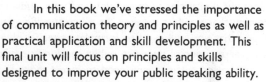

In this book we've stressed the importance of communication theory and principles as well as practical application and skill development. This final unit will focus on principles and skills designed to improve your public speaking ability.

At this point you may wonder what the differences are between the public communication level and the other levels of speech communication. Do public speaking skills require a different body of theory than do interpersonal or group communication skills?

The most obvious feature of the public communication level is its context—one person speaking while a substantial number of people are listening. But consider also the following specific distinctions:

1. Because the public communication level is more formal than other levels, the listener has *more specific expectations* of the speaker. We will discuss the importance of audience analysis before a speech.
2. The speaker directs the message to many people simultaneously and attempts to *identify common attitudes, beliefs, values, and needs* shared by the audience members and the speaker.

227

3. The speaker has a *greater intent* to communicate a specific message; public communication is less spontaneous than speech at other levels.

4. The speaker has *more control* over the communication process. A public speaker is more responsible for selecting the approach to the subject, organizing the ideas, and delivering the ideas than a speaker on the intra- or interpersonal communication level.

5. Because the public communication level is more formal and the audience has more specific expectations of the speaker, it is appropriate to be *more prescriptive*—to provide a more specific list of do's and don't's for effective communication.*

Will knowing these characteristics really help you become a better public speaker? We think it can, because it helps you better understand what happens when you talk to a large audience. And, more importantly, it can give you a basis on which to develop your public speaking skills.

Because the listeners have certain expectations of you as a public speaker, you will need to identify those expectations and decide what you must do to live up to them. Knowing that you are speaking to a group of many individuals, you should try to identify similarities between you and your audience (interests, attitudes, etc.). Knowing that a public speaker has more specific goals for his communication should tell you that you will need to formulate specific objectives for your talks. Since you have greater control over the public speaking situation than over other communication settings, you need to invest more time in preparing for a public speech than in preparing to talk casually with a small group. Finally, because a formal speaking occasion permits us to provide specific suggestions for preparing for the speaking event, you should learn all you can to help improve your skills. And that is the purpose of this unit.

Specifically, in Chapter 11 we will identify six steps for preparing a public speech. These should help you organize your approach to most public speaking situations. We will also suggest some ways of managing the anxiety you may have about speaking in public.

In Chapter 12 we will focus on persuasion. We will suggest methods of enhancing your credibility and identify strategies for developing logical arguments, using emotional appeal, organizing persuasive messages, and adapting your message to your audience.

---

*Adapted from Frank E. X. Dance and Carl Larson, *Speech Communication: Concepts and Behavior* (New York: Holt, Rinehart and Winston, 1972).

11 **THE ESSENTIALS OF PUBLIC SPEAKING**

After studying this chapter you should be able to:

Analyze your audience to help you achieve your speech objective

Identify appropriate criteria for selecting a topic for a speech

Differentiate between speeches to inform, persuade, and entertain

Write a specific purpose for a speech

Select and use appropriate supporting material for a speech

Clearly and logically organize your major ideas in a speech

Identify the purposes of speech introductions and conclusions

List suggestions for managing speech anxiety

You're proud of being a philatelist. Ever since your father got you started with your hobby in the second grade, you have enjoyed learning as much as you can about stamps, and you have acquired quite a sizable collection. It's because of your interest in stamps that you accepted the invitation to give a 15-minute speech about your collection to a local stamp club next week.

You've known about the commitment for four weeks, yet you still haven't started preparing the speech. Aside from your anxiety about standing up and speaking to a group of people, you're just not sure how to go about preparing a speech. What should you do first? How do you limit the topic to fit the time limit? What's the best way to organize the speech?

What are your options? Just try to "wing it"? Write some of your thoughts out word for word and read them? Cancel? Perhaps if you knew a little bit about how to prepare a speech, the task would not seem so forbidding.

To help you prepare for any speaking engagement, we will identify techniques and principles for planning, preparing, and presenting a public speech. We will list a sequence of six essential steps involved in public speaking. In the next chapter we will elaborate on speaking to persuade.

First, we will talk about audience analysis, why it is important, and how to do it. Second, we will give you guidance in selecting a topic. Third, we will present some suggestions for narrowing your topic so that you can zero in on a specific purpose. Fourth, we will give you advice on gathering information to support the major ideas you want to communicate. Fifth, we will suggest ways in which you can organize the information and ideas you have assembled. And, finally, we will give you some pointers on delivering your message. These six steps for preparing and presenting a speech should serve as an efficient approach to most speaking assignments. While these steps suggest that each stage should be completed before the next, remember that communication is a *process*. Many of the steps may thus overlap.

I. ANALYZE YOUR AUDIENCE

You may wonder why analyzing your audience is listed as the *first* step in public speaking. You might think that picking a topic should be first or that researching a topic should be listed ahead of audience analysis. The simple truth is: your audience has a clear influence on the types of topics you select and on just about every other aspect of public speaking.

Earlier we talked about the process of decentering—trying to view the world as others view it. Audience analysis is really an exercise in decentering. Your objective is to understand how the audience is going to react to you and your message. How will they respond to your topic? Will they be impressed with you and what you say? Knowing as much as you can about your listeners and their expectations will help you make some of the other important decisions as

you prepare your speech. But don't get the idea that audience analysis is something you do *only* before you begin the other speech preparation tasks. Audience analysis is an ongoing activity. Try continually to learn as much as you can about your listeners, even as you research, organize, and rehearse your speech.

We will talk about audience analysis from two perspectives, *demographic* and *psychographic* audience analysis. Demographic analysis involves finding out such things about your audience as their age, sex, race, religion, education, and political affiliation. Psychographic audience analysis consists of attempting to identify the beliefs, attitudes, and values your audience holds toward various issues and concepts. You may recall from Chapter 4 that a belief is the way in which we structure reality—what we think is true and what we think is false. If you believe in something, you have structured your reality to believe that it exists. Do you believe the sky will fall tomorrow? Is the world round? Do you believe in God? Your answers to these questions reflect your beliefs.

An attitude has to do with your likes and dislikes. "What's your attitude," someone may say, "toward President Reagan?" Do you like him, dislike him, or simply tolerate him?

We defined values as judgments we make about the relative importance of things. Our values play a major role in influencing our attitudes and our beliefs. Knowing what values an audience holds can help you better anticipate how they will react to your message.

In comparing the concepts of attitudes, beliefs, and values, some scholars feel that values are the most stable, least resistant to change. Beliefs are less stable, more changeable than values. And attitudes change more frequently than either beliefs or values. "But why," you may ask, "is it important for me to know these things?" The answer is that if you decide to persuade your audience to change their attitudes, beliefs, values, or behavior, it is essential to know which of these constructs you are attempting to change. Changing an attitude will probably be easier than changing an audience's ideas about something they value highly—such as honesty, justice, or freedom. We will talk more about selecting persuasive strategies relating to beliefs, attitudes, and values in the next chapter.

Besides trying to identify an audience's demographic and psychographic attributes, you should discover other important information. It is important to identify your audience's expectations of you as a speaker and of the speaking situation itself. What does your audience expect from you? To be entertained, informed, bored? Are you the sole reason for the audience's congregating, or are you going to be sandwiched between a business meeting and punch and cookies? The answers to these questions can help you to select a topic (if you have that choice) and to know what types of supporting information to use in clarifying and illustrating your talk.

You should also be interested in the physical setting for the speech. Is it a large room with a public address system, or will it be a small room with chairs arranged in a circle? Will there be a lectern available for your use? Several studies suggest that the physical environment has an important effect upon how people behave. A well-decorated room will have a more positive effect upon your audience than will a barren room with uncomfortable chairs and poor ventilation and lighting. There are, of course, limits to what you as a speaker can change in the physical environment. But you can be prepared to compensate for various factors that may make it more difficult for your audience to attend to your message. Again, the topic, the kinds of examples and illustrations, and your delivery style can help you reach an audience in an environment that is working against you.

Let's summarize the types of questions you may want to ask. While the following list is not comprehensive, it should help you begin to analyze both your audience and your speaking situation.

Demographic audience analysis

1. What is the age level of the audience?
2. What is the breakdown between males and females in the audience?
3. What is the education level of the audience?
4. What is the racial makeup of the audience?
5. What are the religious and political affiliations of audience members?

Psychographic audience analysis

1. What are the audience's attitudes (likes and dislikes) toward my topic?
2. What strong beliefs does the audience hold about my subject?
3. What underlying values does the audience hold?
4. What expectations does the audience hold for me and the speaking situation?

Environmental analysis

1. What are the physical arrangements for the speaking situation?
2. How many people are expected to attend the speech?
3. Will I be expected to speak with a microphone from a lectern?

We have so far stressed prespeech audience analysis questions. But audience analysis, like the communication process itself, is continuous. Keeping your audience in mind as you select a topic and a purpose, and as you research, organize, and rehearse your speech is important. It is also crucial to analyze your audience while delivering your speech. Audience analysis is a thread that is woven through the entire fabric of speech preparation and delivery.

2. SELECT A TOPIC

In some speaking situations you won't have to worry about selecting a topic. It is not uncommon for you to be asked to speak on a specific subject. But rest assured there will also be many times you will be asked to speak and not be given a topic—it will be up to you. For many people, selecting a topic is frustrating. In trying to find that one best idea for a speech, they come up empty-handed. They might think of several plausible ideas, but that "best" speech idea eludes them.

What often happens is that these persons' desire to find the ideal topic is so strong that they become overly critical of their creative processes. Here's where audience analysis and taking an inventory of your own interests can help you. Usually, the best topics and ideas for a speech are ones that come from your own experiences. What are issues you feel strongly about? Have you had any interesting or unusual jobs? Don't forget to look in newspapers, magazines, and news programs for suggestions of important, recent, relevant topics. Another place to find ideas for a speech is the calendar—what anniversary of a famous person's life or death occurs close to the time you are to speak? There will also be many times when the speaking occasion itself will dictate what an appropriate topic should be.

Consider the technique of brainstorming if you really get stumped for a topic. Begin with a blank sheet of paper, or talk to a tape recorder. List as many possible speech topics as you can. Don't evaluate them. Just keep the ideas coming. Once you have twenty or fifty or eighty ideas, then evaluate them. In doing so, apply these criteria: (1) Is this a topic I'm interested in? (2) Can I find resources and information to develop my ideas? (3) Do I have some personal experiences that would add greater interest to my topic? (4) Would my audience be interested in the topic? If you can answer "yes" to each of those questions, you are on the road to developing an interesting speech.

While generating enough ideas for a speech topic is a problem for some people, others have just the opposite problem. They have too many ideas and are uncertain which one would be best. If this is your situation, your audience analysis can help determine which topic would be most suitable.

3. DEVELOP A PURPOSE

Before launching into researching your topic and organizing your speech, you need to decide upon your purpose. You first should decide what your *general purpose* will be. There are three general purposes of public speeches: to inform, to persuade, and to entertain. Let's take a closer look at them.

First, speaking to inform is an important objective of many of the speeches you hear. Class lectures, seminars, and workshops are examples. When your task is to inform others, your purpose is one of teaching, defining, illustrating, clarifying, or elaborating on a topic. In this chapter we are focusing on the essentials of public speaking primarily for informative presentations.

A second major purpose of public speaking is to persuade. Political speeches, advertisements on radio and TV, and sermons are examples of presentations in which the speaker's objective is to induce the audience to change or reinforce their attitudes, beliefs, values, or behavior. For this kind of speech, you generally follow the same basic process of planning and preparing your message as we are presenting in this chapter. But when your objective is to persuade, you are also extremely concerned about your audience's attitudes toward you and your topic. These will have an important impact upon the choices you make in designing a persuasive message. In the next chapter we will discuss this further.

A third general purpose is to entertain, as in after-dinner speeches and comedy monologues. Often the key to presenting an effective entertaining speech lies in the selection of stories, examples, and illustrations and in your speech delivery. A speaker's ability to use humor is also important. Of course, humor can be used when your objective is to inform and to persuade. We do not discuss entertaining speeches at length, but speakers who effectively entertain apply many of the principles we do discuss in this chapter and in Chapter 12. Though distinctions can be made among informing, persuading, and entertaining speeches, in many cases a speech may include two or all three general objectives.

You next need to decide what your *specific* objective should be. Perhaps, listening to a speaker, you have nudged someone next to you and whispered, "What's this person talking about, anyway? I don't understand the point of the speech." You may have some idea of the general topic and a hint of the general purpose, but the specific purpose of the speech escapes you. When this happens, it's usually because the speaker has failed to narrow the topic sufficiently.

Suppose, for example, after analyzing your interests and your audience's interests, you decide to speak about the economic problems facing consumers today. Your general topic area is obviously current economic problems. But you now need to narrow that topic and formulate a more specific objective. Assume you have been given a 10- to 15-minute time limit for a talk to a local chapter of a consumer organization. How can you fit the topic into that time limit? First, think of the variety of topics you could talk about under the heading of "current economic problems"—inflation, unemployment, or the housing shortage. There would be enough information on each one of those subtopic areas to fill several scholarly volumes. So it is clear you need to narrow your topic further. You could talk about the effects of the local economy on the housing industry in your community—that is a bit more specific. But exactly what do you want your audience to know about this topic? That it is a serious problem? After much deliberation, you finally arrive at the following specific purpose for your talk: "At the end of my speech, the audience should be able to identify two major causes of the current housing shortage and two of its effects on our community." As you continue your reading and research on the topic, your specific purpose may be even further refined, but for now your topic is much more workable than a general one like "current economic problems."

You may notice that the above statement of purpose is phrased in terms of what it is the speaker would like the audience to be able to know, do, or feel at the end of the speech—specifically, to identify the major causes of the current housing shortage and its effects on the community. Another specific purpose could be, "At the end of my speech the audience should be able to list and define three contributing causes of inflation in the United States." This again clearly identifies the type of information you want to communicate to your audience.

Yet another specific purpose might be, "At the end of my speech the audience should write to Congress to express their opposition to the current government approach to rising crime in our community." This statement indicates that you will be trying to influence the behavior of the audience members. Still other purpose statements might indicate that you want to evoke a certain emotion. You might want your audience to feel happy, sad, sympathetic, or angry about a given topic or issue.

Once you have formulated your specific speech objective, write it down on a piece of paper or a note card and keep it in front of you as you read and gather ideas and information on your topic. Your specific purpose should guide your research efforts, helping you to eliminate irrelevant materials. But as you continue to read and learn more about your topic, you may decide to modify your specific purpose. In other words, formulating a specific objective should serve as a tentative destination as you develop your speech, but as you continue to work on your speech, your destination may change. You may decide to modify your original purpose statement. The important point to remember is that you should have *some* destination in mind at all times during your speech preparation.

4. GATHER SUPPORTING MATERIAL

With a specific purpose decided upon, you are ready to continue the process of speech construction by gathering material to support your major ideas. Of course, you have probably been thinking about possible sources and ideas since you first considered your topic. But now you can begin gathering information with a clear goal in mind.

Supporting material for a speech consists of the facts, examples, statistics, and testimony from others that illustrate, amplify, clarify, and provide evidence for your major ideas. A speaker does not just string a series of major ideas together, but fills in the outline with definitions, explanations, facts, personal and hypothetical examples, analogies, statistics, and testimony from a variety of sources. A speaker's selection of supporting material has an important effect upon maintaining audience interest. Chances are good that, if you find a speech boring, the speaker has not selected appropriate supporting material. Almost any subject can be made interesting with supporting material that commands the attention of the audience. To help you find such material, we will present a list of several types of supporting material and will provide some tips for their use.

Types of supporting material

1. Definition A *definition* is simply a way of explaining unfamiliar terms or concepts to others. There are several ways to do this in a speech. You can define something with examples. You can explain how the thing or concept is similar to other things or is different from other things in its class. Of course, you can just quote the definition from a dictionary. Some dictionaries, notably the *Oxford English Dictionary,* trace the origins of words (etymology). Such information can sometimes give an audience new insight into the term you're using.

Definitions can be overused in a speech, however. Define words and new concepts when you need to, but don't select a topic that is so technical that you need to spend a great deal of time defining terms. Just defining a word with other words may not be very interesting to your audience.

2. Examples   When you use an *example,* you are providing a specific instance to clarify or dramatize a point. If you are talking about problems of violent crime, you can clarify what you mean by simply listing specific examples (murder, rape, armed robbery). Examples can also be more lengthy. If your topic is violations of human rights, you may describe the policies of a certain country or provide detailed accounts of cases involving rights violations.

To maintain interest and hold attention, one of the most effective types of supporting material is *personal examples.* Most audiences enjoy hearing about personal experiences that are relevant to the point you are trying to develop. When your speech includes such material, you may also be perceived as more competent to talk about your topic.

But what if you haven't had any outstanding personal experiences with the subject? You can still enhance audience interest by using hypothetical examples. A *hypothetical example* is one that is devised to illustrate a given point, even though the example may not have occurred. It is never presented to an audience under a guise of truth; instead, a hypothetical example usually begins with such a phrase as "Imagine yourself in the following situation. . . ." or "What would you do if . . . happened to you?" Phrases like these indicate to your audience that while your example may be quite plausible, it never actually happened.

A key to using examples, whether true or hypothetical, is to describe them so that the experience comes alive to your listeners. Appeal to your listeners' senses. Describe the sights, sounds, smells, and textures of the image you want your audience to imagine. The more concrete and vivid your example, the more likely it is to gain and hold audience attention.

3. Illustration   An *illustration* is a story, fable, or anecdote with a theme, moral, or purpose that supports a point you wish to communicate. Illustrations can range in tone from humorous situations to poignant or tragic stories. A lengthy illustration can even serve as the basis for an entire speech.

Don't assume that the moral or purpose of the illustration will be so clear to your audience that you need not state it. Provide a preview to your story, giving your audience something to look for in the illustration. Or, if you tell the story without identifying the theme beforehand, state your point afterwards.

4. Analogy   Another word for *analogy* is *comparison.* You can sometimes support a point by comparing one object, concept, or principle with another. There are two types of analogies—literal and figurative. A *literal analogy* involves comparing or contrasting things of the same class. Comparing one senator with another senator, in terms of their ability to get bills passed, is an example of a literal analogy.

A *figurative analogy* requires comparing or contrasting things of different classes. A figurative analogy is a good tool to help clarify relationships and add interest to your speech. One student wanted to convince her class that whole wheat bread is more nutritious than white bread, because it contains more wheat germ. To illustrate the point, she had her listeners imagine that the room in which she was speaking was a loaf of white bread and that her listeners represented portions of wheat germ within the bread. "Imagine," she said, "that there are twice as many people in this room right now. That gives you some idea of the increased amount of wheat germ in a loaf of whole wheat bread." Though this may not have proved that whole wheat bread is better than white bread, it did clearly illustrate her point. Exert caution in trying to *prove* any point with only a figurative analogy for support. But employ figurative analogies liberally to add clarity and interest to your speeches.

5. Statistics   *Statistics* are numbers that summarize several facts or examples. They are often used as evidence to show how significant a problem is or is not. One often-used statistic is a *percentage,* which indicates proportion. A speaker employing a percentage can indicate the significance of some figure by showing what part of a whole it represents. An *average* is another popular kind of statistic. Averages can easily mislead an audience, however, if not used or interpreted properly. When you give someone an average number, unless you also provide some indication of the variation of the numbers used to reach the average, the figure can be misleading. The average of 2, 3, 4, 2, 2, and 22 is 5.8. The number 22 makes that "average" score higher than all but one of the numbers. The average does not accurately represent all six scores.

While statistics are an important type of supporting material, too many statistics, because of their abstractness, can detract from the interest of your speech. Fortunately, there are ways of using statistics to make them more meaningful to your listener. For example, you can make any statistic less abstract by comparing the statistic to something that your audience can visualize. Do you think your audience really understands how many a billion, a million, or even several thousands of anything is? Relating a number to something tangible can add clarity to your ideas. Rather than just saying that 55,000 people were killed in auto accidents last year, note that this is the equivalent of a large sports arena full of people, gone because of careless driving. Another suggestion for using statistics is to round off the figures, unless you have to be very precise. Saying "nearly a million" instead of "998,376" aids in audience comprehension and recall.

6. Testimony   A *testimony* is a statement made by someone else that supports an idea or position that you are trying to develop. The best testimony, of course, does not come from just anyone. It comes from someone whom your audience will recognize as qualified and reliable. When using expert testimony to support your own position, make sure that the person you quote (1) is an expert in the field involved, (2) is not biased, (3) will be respected by your audience as competent and trustworthy, and (4) is quoted by a reputable source.

Using visual aids   Tammy was planning to give a speech about types of creative financing available to potential home buyers. She had spent many hours in researching her speech and had ample facts, statistics, examples, and testimony to support her major ideas. She realized, however, that she needed to communicate in a clear and concise way. She wisely decided to use such visual aids as a bar graph, a poster, and the chalkboard to help present her material.

Visual aids can effectively and dramatically help you clarify a point. Let's briefly consider several types of visual aids and some ways to use them effectively.

Visual aids consist of any type of visual material, such as a picture, chart, or diagram, that can help you make your point more clearly. The following list should give you some ideas for selecting visual aids for your talks.

Types of visual aids

1. Objects or models of objects (e.g., model cars, trains, etc.)
2. Chalkboard diagrams or drawings
3. A large picture
4. Diagrams
5. Slides
6. Movies
7. An overhead projector
8. Line, bar, or pie graphs
9. Organizational charts
10. Clothing or costumes
11. Handouts of printed information
12. Maps

Suggestions for using visual aids   Though the list above should give you some ideas for selections visual aids, you still may need some pointers on how best to use them in a speech. The following suggestions should guide you in both your selection and your use of visual aids:

1. Make sure your chart, poster, picture, etc., is large enough to be seen clearly by everyone in your audience. Don't use a small picture from a magazine or a photo that you took unless you are sure everyone can see it.
2. If you use the chalkboard, prepare your drawing ahead of time but keep it covered so the audience won't be distracted by it before you are ready to refer to it. The chalkboard is best used during your speech when you want to make a very quick diagram or write a word or phrase on the board.
3. If possible, try to conceal your visual aids until you are ready to refer

to them. If you display all of your charts, posters, and objects before you speak, some of the impact may be lost.

4. Use visual aids to control your audience's attention. When using an overhead projector, for instance, turn the projector on when you want your audience to refer to your statistics or diagram. When you move on to another point, turn the projector off, so the audience will focus their attention on you and the point you are making.
5. Rehearse your speech, using your visual aids.
6. Double check your visual aids just before you begin your speech. Are they in the proper order? Does the projector work? Do you need an extension cord? Do you have chalk?
7. Keep charts and diagrams simple. Use dark markers to make your charts and posters. And remember, it is better to use two or three simple posters than to try to cram everything you need onto one poster.
8. If you feel you need to use dittoed or Xeroxed handouts, make sure they do not distract from your oral presentation. You may want to wait until the end of your speech to give your audience a handout. Or, if you need to give your handout to the audience early during your presentation, tell them why you are doing so and try to keep their attention focused on your presentation rather than on your printed material (unless, of course, you want them to concentrate on the handout).
9. Try not to pass objects around to your audience while you are speaking. This creates a distraction. If there is no other speaker following you on the program, you may want to invite interested audience members to view your visual aids after your speech.
10. Talk about your visual aids, don't just show them. Help your audience understand the important facts or statistics on a chart or poster you display. Don't just hold it up and expect the audience to know why you are showing it.

Sources of supporting material We have talked about the types of supporting material, briefly noted some of their virtues, and pointed out how they can be misused. We have also provided a few pointers for using visual aids. But you may still need help in locating sources of supporting material.

As a student, you are no doubt familiar with the library and how to use it. Knowing how to use the card catalogue to find a book, *Readers' Guide to Periodical Literature* to find a magazine, or more specialized indexes like the *Social Science Index, Education Index,* or *Psychological Abstracts,* can add greatly to your ability to find appropriate examples, definitions, statistics, and testimony for your speeches. Besides the more traditional library resources, don't overlook other materials available to you. Books of collected quotations can add much interest to your talks. Song lyrics, poems, jokes, or fables can be used to support ideas and major points you want to develop.

Personal interviews can also be used as supporting material. And you might conduct a survey yourself to find out more about how the community or your audience may feel about a subject. You may decide to analyze your audience by taking a survey of their attitudes toward or beliefs about a given issue. The results can be summarized statistically or used to formulate approaches for presenting your information to your audience. The search for interesting, accurate, and relevant supporting material will pay dividends in the form of an attentive and appreciative audience.

5. ORGANIZE YOUR IDEAS

A well-organized speech can enhance the probability that your talk will be well received; audience members will also remember more of your presentation if you announce your organizational plan early in your presentation and then stick to it. In addition, you will feel more comfortable delivering your speech. The longer your presentation, the more you need to take care to organize the information in a logical, orderly manner.

There are three major parts to any speech: the introduction, the body, and the conclusion. Since the body of a speech contains the bulk of ideas and information, it provides the greatest challenge to the speaker in terms of organization.

It may seem that the best way to prepare a speech is to conduct some research and then just to sit down and write the speech out, starting from the beginning and working until the speech is finished. This approach, however, is not advisable, for several reasons. It is not a good idea to write your speech as you would a term paper or an essay for English composition, because there is a difference in style between a speech (oral communication) and a paper (written communication). Specifically, an oral style, as compared to a written style, should be (1) more personal (greater use of the personal pronouns "I" and "you"), (2) more informal, and (3) more repetitious—in a written document the reader can stop, reflect, or reread for additional clarity; the listener does not share these advantages. Nor is it a good idea to start from the beginning and work until you've written your conclusion. Instead, it is better not to develop your introduction until you have completed the body of your speech. One purpose of an introduction is to provide an overview of what follows. It is difficult to plan an overview if you haven't developed the major ideas of your presentation. Therefore, resist writing your speech from beginning to end. Consider another approach.

We recommend that you begin to organize the speech by working on an outline of the body. Then develop the conclusion. And, finally, work on your introduction.

Preparing a speech outline

A written outline is the most efficient tool to employ in organizing your speech. The first task in preparing an outline is to decide upon your main supporting points. Sometimes these may be reasons your thesis, or central idea of the speech, is true. The main points for a speech supporting the passage of a particular legislative bill would probably be reasons the bill should be passed. Sometimes the main points of a speech are simply steps to be taken to achieve some goal. For example, a speech on how to make a sand sculpture would offer a sequence of steps one must take to construct the finished product. Other speeches may simply fall into logical divisions. A speech setting forth the requirements for success in college would probably utilize the requirements under consideration as its main points. Keep the main points fairly few in number—an audience will remember three or four major ideas, but not nineteen! List your main points on a sheet of paper, leaving plenty of space in between. (Look at the sample outline below.) Note that Roman numerals are used for major ideas, letters are used for subpoints. Also note that all points at the same level should be parallel in form— if I is a sentence, II should be a sentence; if A is a prepositional phrase, B should be a prepositional phrase.

Now look at the points you've written down—don't worry about what order they are in; in the next section we will talk about strategies for organizing these major ideas. As we noted in the previous section, supporting materials (subpoints) may include examples, definitions, statistics, and so forth. In developing your outline, you may find just a word or phrase adequate for some of these ideas; others you may want to write out in more detail. There is really no limit to the number of supporting materials you use for each main point. Just be sure all the main points have adequate support, but not so much that you will violate your time limits if you include everything.

Sample outlines The following two sample outlines serve as models for appropriate outline formats.[1] The outlines that you prepare for your speeches may be either more or less detailed than those we have included here. The content and length of your speech will affect how detailed your outline will be.

Note that both outlines begin with the title of the speech followed by a specific purpose sentence. Note also that each outline includes well-developed ideas for an introduction, body, and conclusion. A bibliography is also included.

The first outline, "The Human Voice: Index to Personality," would be appropriate for a visual aid speech. Note that each major idea in the body of the speech will be illustrated by a chart, model, or poster.

The second outline, "The Great Debate," is organized using visual images (e.g., Preparation of Kennedy, Arrival of JFK at the Ambassador East Hotel, Preparation of Nixon, etc.). Organizing a speech based on images rather than facts, statistics, or abstract ideas can help you and your audience remember a speech more effectively. As we have already discussed, your selection of specific and concrete stories, illustrations, and examples adds interest to the audience plus giving you the benefit of helping you remember the speech more effectively. Remember, these sample outlines illustrate one approach to speech outlining. Use them as general models.

THE HUMAN VOICE: INDEX TO PERSONALITY

Purpose sentence: At the end of the speech the audience should be able to identify the three basic areas of speech production.

INTRODUCTION

I. Dorothy Sarnoff's story about New York executive who sounded angry without knowing it
   A. The man was totally unaware of his voice's impact on others
      1. Sound is conducted through cranium or bounced off walls
      2. Neither provides a reliable indicator of how we sound to others
   B. Most people have reactions similar to the executive's if they haven't heard their voice in some time
II. The voice is extremely important both as a primary indicator of personality and as an instrument in public speaking

BODY

I. The power triangle: (show chart)
   A. The diaphragm:
      1. Large double dome-shaped muscle below the rib cage
      2. Can be very important for producing power for singers and individuals who do a lot of public speaking
   B. The lungs:
      1. Serve to store air before it travels upward
      2. The difference between inhalation and exhalation
      3. Bronchial tubes
   C. Trachea
II. The larynx (voice box): (bring out model)
   A. Vocal cords or bands
      1. Air pressure builds up and blows the cords apart
      2. Size of vocal cords determines pitch
   B. Thyroid (Adam's apple)
   C. The epiglottis and esophagus
III. The resonators: (show poster)
   A. The phayrnx or throat
      1. Determines the quality of the sound after it leaves the larynx
      2. The naso-pharynx
   B. The nasal cavity
      1. Is the largest of the resonators and is important in producing a pleasant sound
      2. The problem with a cold or sore throat
   C. The mouth
      1. Important in speaking distinctly
      2. Three parts: lips, tongue, teeth

CONCLUSION

I. The advantages of practicing with a tape recorder or video unit
   A. In conversation
   B. On the telephone
   C. In public speaking
II. You can always do your homework

Sources:

Peter B. Denes and Elliot N. Pinson, *The Speech Chain* (Bell Telephone Laboratories, 1964).

Giles Wilkeson Gray and Claude Merton Wise, *The Bases of Speech,* 3rd ed. (New York: Harper & Row, 1959).

Raymond Rizzo, *The Voice as an Instrument,* 2nd ed. (New York: Bobbs-Merrill Company, 1978).

Dorothy Sarnoff, *Speech Can Change Your Life* (New York: Dell Publishing Co., 1972).

THE GREAT DEBATE

Purpose sentence: At the end of the speech the audience should be able to list the steps both candidates went through to prepare for the first Kennedy-Nixon debate.

INTRODUCTION

I. A very popular book a few years ago was *The Selling of the President* by Joe McGuiness, about the 1968 campaign.
   A. The author went to Humphrey's campaign manager and then to Herb Klein, Nixon's chief adviser.
   B. McGuiness shows how Nixon aides hired a public relations firm to improve their candidate's image through meticulous preparation.
   C. This tactic has been criticized, but it won for Nixon a close victory in the 1968 election.
II. The careful preparation of the 1968 campaign seems to have been a product of the lesson that Nixon learned during the first Kennedy-Nixon debate, on September 26, 1960, in Chicago.

BODY

I. Preparation of Kennedy:
   A. Sunday, September 25:
      1. JFK arrived at the Ambassador East Hotel with his three "brain trust" advisers, Sorensen, Goodwin, and Feldman.
         a. Ted Sorensen was a speech writer and chief tactician
         b. Richard Goodwin was a brilliant young lawyer
         c. Mike Feldman was a law instructor and later a successful businessman
      2. The four brought with them a portable library of information on any topic that might come up during the debate.
         a. They put in a long study session, preparing for the debate like college students getting ready for an exam
         b. Stress was placed on the latest information
   B. Monday, September 26:
      1. The four held another "skull session" in the morning.
      2. JFK then had lunch with Sorensen, Robert Kennedy, and the public opinion analyst Louis Harris.
      3. After lunch, Kennedy gave a brief speech to the United Brotherhood of Carpenters.

4. He took a nap until five, when he woke up refreshed.
5. He put in another study session.
6. He then ate what he terms a "splendid dinner" by himself in his room.
7. Preparation at the Chicago TV studio:
   a. JFK inspected the set
   b. He purposely had worn a dark suit, which would contrast with the gray studio background
   c. He sent back for a light blue shirt, since studio advisers said a white shirt would glare under the lights
   d. He had no make-up

II. Preparation of Nixon:
   A. Sunday:
      1. Although Nixon had been advised to arrive in Chicago a day early to rest, he disregarded the advice and arrived tired at the Pick-Congress Hotel late Sunday night.
      2. Aides had tried to reach Herb Klein, Nixon's chief adviser, but Klein could not be found.
   B. Monday:
      1. Nixon gave a speech to the United Brotherhood of Carpenters during the morning—a speech which Nixon felt was not favorably received.
      2. The rest of the day Nixon spent by himself, mostly in his hotel room.
         a. TV advisers could not get in to see him
         b. He received one visitor for 5 minutes
         c. Henry Cabot Lodge called long distance to advise Nixon to try to destroy the "assassin image"
      3. Preparation at the studio:
         a. Nixon struck his already injured knee when he got out of the car and his face turned white
         b. Nixon inspected the set
         c. One adviser applied a light pancake make-up called "Lazy-Shave" to hide Nixon's five o'clock shadow

CONCLUSION

I. The results of that first crucial debate are history: most experts agree that it was won by Kennedy because he appeared much better prepared.
   A. The Committee on the 1960 Presidential Campaign—an impartial group—stated by a vote of 20 to 6 that JFK won.
   B. All but one of the committee agreed that Kennedy had made the greatest political gain.
   C. The *New York Times* stated that the debates were "really the deciding factors" in Kennedy's vistory.

II. Although some may criticize the always interesting Nixon for employing a PR firm to build a new image, most political experts agree that Nixon had learned his lesson and prepared carefully for the 1968 presidential victory.

Sources:

Austin Freely, *Argumentation and Debate* (Belmont, CA: Wadsworth, 1966), pp. 398–418.

Joe McGuiness, *The Selling of the President, 1968* (New York: Trident Press, 1969).

The *New York Times*, November 6, 1960, Sec. 4, p. 1.

Theodore White, *The Making of the President, 1960* (New York: Atheneum, 1961), pp. 311–318.

Patterns of organizing a speech

Some speeches will seem to fall easily into natural divisions and orders of major ideas and supporting points. But other speeches will require more effort to organize the ideas into a meaningful and logical sequence. To help you arrange your ideas, we will discuss several patterns of organization.

1. Chronological A speech organized *chronologically* is organized according to a time sequence. If, for example, you are talking about how to build or make something, a chronological arrangement may be best. Historical events and speeches based upon personal experiences also lend themselves to a chronological speech pattern.

2. Spatial A spatial speech organization is arranged according to geography or space. If you are giving a speech about your home town, it would make sense to talk about the East Side, the downtown area, and then the West Side. If you are describing a hospital, you may want to talk about each floor in sequence. Spatial organization is flexible enough to allow you to exercise your prerogative about where to begin; it requires only that you proceed sequentially.

3. Topical A *topical* speech order is simply arrangement by the obvious or natural division of topics. A speech about the federal government can be arranged by talking about the executive, legislative, and judicial branches. Or, in the example of the hospital that we used in illustrating spatial arrangement, you may decide to organize your speech by talking about the functions of the hospital, rather than about the physical plant. Topical arrangement allows you fairly free rein in deciding which division to discuss first, which second, and so on. Many speeches with a general objective to inform follow a topical organizational pattern.

4. Complexity You can organize a speech following the *complexity* pattern if your first points are about the simple aspects of your topic and your later points develop more complex ideas. Usually biology, chemistry, physics, and other science classes discuss elementary principles first and more complex ideas and concepts later on. The syllabi for these classes illustrate organization by complexity.

5. Problem-solution The *problem-solution* organizational pattern is practically defined by its name. Because it is usually not a good idea to present solutions before your audience understands or appreciates the nature of the problem, you first talk about a problem; then you talk about the solution or solutions to the problem you've discussed. The problem-solution organizational pattern lends itself to both informative and persuasive speaking.

6. Cause and effect *Cause-and-effect* patterns discuss known causes and then discuss probable or actual effects of the causes. For example, you could first discuss what caused Mount St. Helens to erupt and then talk about the effects this volcano had upon the country. The cause-and-effect organizational pattern can help an audience understand complex issues and events. There is always the risk, however, of oversimplifying cause-and-effect relationships. Just because we know event *A* happened and we also know event *B* immediately followed event *A*, it doesn't necessarily mean that event *A* caused event *B*. Make sure you have adequate evidence to infer cause-and-effect relationships.

7. Pro and con A speech organized by a *pro-and-con* method first presents an advantage or advantages of a particular issue and then identifies its disadvantages. An entire speech or a single point in a more lengthy speech could be arranged according to a pro-and-con pattern.

8. Primacy Studies suggest that a point presented in either the first or last position in a speech will be remembered more easily than one placed in the middle.[2] A *primacy* speech arrangement places the strongest, most important point first. If you are speaking to an apathetic group and know you need to capture their attention early, a primacy pattern may be in order. Or if you feel you are facing a hostile audience, you may want to place your most important point first, so they do not become even more hostile. If you placed you best point last, they might not be listening to you by that time.

9. Recency *Recency* is just the opposite of primacy—you place your strongest or most significant idea last. If your audience is not unduly hostile or apathetic, place your best idea last—build to a climax. Most trial lawyers like to summarize their cases to the jury last. The final position has a psychological advantage of emphasizing your key idea.

Additional suggestions for organizing a speech There will usually be several ways to organize each speech you give. Here again, careful analysis of your audience and the speaking situation can guide you. You may decide to use one or a combination of the patterns we have suggested. Remember, it is impossible for you to have an "unorganized" speech—organization simply means an arrangement or sequence of information. All speeches have a sequence of ideas, but the sequence may be illogical or unclear. To insure that you have a clear sequence of thought, reflect upon your speech purpose, your time limits, and the expectations of your audience.

Transitions Once you have your major ideas and subordinate ideas well organized, you should consider how you can provide a smooth transition from one point to the next. Audience members should never have to wonder why you're talking about a particular idea at a given point in your speech.

One technique for clear transitions is a brief internal summary and preview. Note what you have said thus far and identify what the audience still needs to know.

Another technique is the use of a rhetorical question. You might say, "We've talked about some of the causes of cancer, but perhaps you're wondering, 'What are some of the methods of curing cancer today?' That brings me to my next point." You do not need a formal transition statement inserted between each minor or subordinate point in your speech. Transitions should be explicit, however, between major ideas or major shifts in the direction of your speech. Transitions between the introduction and the body of your speech, as well as between the body and the conclusion, are also appropriate.

Concluding the speech   After outlining the body of your speech, developing ideas with supporting materials, and providing clear transitions, your next task is to prepare a conclusion.

The primary purpose of most speech conclusions is to summarize (see the sample outlines). The conclusion does not need to be a "let's-hear-everything-one-more-time" approach, but rather a statement that lets the audience know what you feel your most important points are. You can restate your main points, or you can provide one final example or illustration to support the purpose of your speech. A visual aid can be used to summarize your ideas graphically.

In addition to summarizing, many speakers use their conclusion to challenge their listeners, move them to take some action, or stimulate them to learn more about the subject.

Finally, conclusions should provide a note of closure or finality. A good technique is to make a reference to an early example or question that you posed to the audience. If you began by using a hypothetical example, you can again refer to it, noting how the outcome of the example may be affected by the information you shared with the audience. Or you may answer a rhetorical question that you posed earlier.

Developing an introduction   After the body and conclusion of the speech have been outlined, you need to develop an introduction to your talk. As you recall, the reason the introduction is the last part of your speech rather than the first is that you need to formulate the bulk of your speech before you can prepare a proper overview of your major ideas. Giving your audience a preview of your major ideas is an important function of your introduction.

Besides providing an overview of your speech purpose, your introduction should catch the attention of your audience and help establish interest in your subject. There are several techniques for developing an opening statement that will catch attention. You could begin by asking a question: "If you and a friend were dining in a restaurant and your friend choked on a piece of food, would you know what to do?" The question you formulate should capture your audience's interest and make them want to hear more. You could also begin with a personal example that pertains to your topic. Still other suggestions include:

> ➤ Use a startling fact or statistic
> ➤ Use a quotation from a poem or famous person
> ➤ Use a hypothetical example
> ➤ Make a reference to the occasion
> ➤ Make a reference to a person in the audience
> ➤ Use an analogy

Given all these possibilities, your opening line should *not* be, "The purpose of my talk today . . ." True, somewhere in your introduction you should state your purpose or make it clear to the audience. But your opening sentence need not unimaginatively announce it.

Besides providing an overview of your subject and catching attention, your introduction should establish a motive for your audience to listen to you. In essence, you will need to convince your audience that what you have to say will be relevant to their needs. Even when presenting an informative talk, you need to consider, "Why should this audience listen to me on this particular subject?" The more you know about your audience, the easier this task will be. And the answer to this question should be considered as you plan the introduction.

In addition to the above objectives for introductions, if your audience is unfavorably prejudiced toward you or toward your topic, it would be useful to deal with that prejudice in your introduction. You might also try to make some effort to enhance the perception of yourself and your subject matter. In the next chapter we will talk more about techniques for improving your credibility as a speaker.

6. REHEARSE AND DELIVER THE SPEECH

With your speech outline, introduction, and conclusion in hand, you are now ready to work on your speech delivery. What do you think is more important: the content of your speech, or your delivery of the speech? During the early part of this century, elocutionists, forerunners of today's speech teachers, felt that delivery was more important than content. Speech training largely consisted of techniques and exercises for improving posture, movement, and vocal quality. While contemporary speech teachers certainly don't discount the importance of speech delivery, they prefer a more balanced approach to delivery and content.

In our discussion of nonverbal communication in Chapter 6 we identified applications of nonverbal communication research to public speaking situations. The following discussion should help you apply some of the suggestions for improving your speech delivery. We will also review such key delivery variables as gesture, eye contact, movement, and vocal cues.

Styles of speech delivery

We will discuss four styles of speech delivery. The first is called *manuscript speaking*. A speech delivered in manuscript style is completely written out and then read, word for word. Undoubtedly you have heard speeches delivered this way. Perhaps a professor, lecturer, or member of the clergy simply stands and reads from prepared remarks. You've probably wondered, "Why don't they just hand out copies of their speech and forget about reading it to us?" Manuscript delivery style is usually not preferred by audiences. Few speakers read well enough to make it interesting. But speakers persist in using manuscript delivery style, for a variety of reasons. If someone has written the speaker's speech, as is often the case with politicians, the speaker has to read it or memorize it. One advantage of manuscript speaking is that the speaker can choose words very carefully, a fact that often makes it a preferred manner of delivery for someone in power who is dealing with a sensitive and critical issue. Yet other speakers adopt a manuscript speaking style because of the anxiety they experience when they stand before a group to speak. "If," they think, "I can just refer to my manuscript, I won't get as nervous. I won't have to worry about forgetting what I want to say." While it is true they won't forget their lines, the audience suffers, because most manuscript speech presentations lack the vitality and spontaneity needed to hold the audience's attention.

A second delivery style requires *memorization*. The speaker delivers the speech from memory, without notes. While the speaker has an abundance of eye contact with an audience (a good thing), most memorized speeches *sound* memorized—stilted and over-rehearsed. As we noted earlier in the chapter, there are significant differences between oral and written communication style. The personal and informal qualities are usually missing from both the manuscript and the memorized style. Therefore, these styles are not recommended for gaining maximum audience interest and approval of the speech.

A third style is called *impromptu*. Impromptu speaking involves virtually no advance preparation or rehearsal. A speaker speaks as one idea leads to another. The advantage of impromptu speaking is that the speech is usually delivered informally, with the speaker using direct eye contact with the audience. But unless the speaker is extremely talented, an impromptu speech often lacks logical organization and thorough research. There are times, of course, when we are called upon to speak without advance knowledge of the invitation. But if you are forewarned of your speaking assignment, impromptu speaking is not the best style.

If not manuscript, memorized, or impromptu, what's left? An *extemporaneous* speaking style is usually recommended as best for most situations. When delivering a speech extemporaneously, the speaker speaks from an outline, but not from a word-for-word manuscript. The speaker has rehearsed the speech so that key ideas are fixed in mind, but not enough so that the speech sounds memorized. The extemporaneous style eliminates many of the disadvantages of manuscript, memorized, and impromptu speaking, while retaining the advantages of a well-organized presentation delivered in an interesting and vital manner. Let's turn our attention to specific suggestions for enhancing your skill in delivering an extemporaneous talk.

Gestures

The next time you are having an informal conversation with someone, notice how both you and the other person use your hands and bodies to communicate. You emphasize important points with your gestures. You may also gesture to point to objects, to direct attention, to enumerate, and to describe objects. Gestures serve these same functions for a public speaker. Many speakers aren't sure what to do with their hands. They try putting them behind their backs (standing at parade rest), burying their hands in their pockets (to hide them), clutching the lectern, or just letting their hands flop around without much purpose or control. Rather than prescribing specific things for your hands to do, we will identify some important criteria for your use of gestures.

First, your gestures should not appear tense or rigid, but relaxed. Second, they should be definite, rather than accidental brief jerks of your hands, arms, or body. Third, gestures should seem appropriate to the content of your speech—they should be timed to coincide with the corresponding verbal message. Fourth, strive for variety and versatility in your use of gesture. Don't use just one hand or one all-purpose gesture. And finally, your gestures should appear natural, not artificial or contrived. Your audience should not focus upon the beauty or appropriateness of your gestures, but upon your message.

Eye contact

Several studies suggest that one of the most important delivery variables in a public speaking situation is eye contact.[3] Looking at your audience communicates that you are interested in them and that you want them to be interested in you. It signals that the communication channel is open—you want to talk and you want them to listen.

Looking at your audience is also important because it helps you know what they are doing while you talk. Are they interested in your speech? Are they looking back at you? Do they seem restless? Bored? Are they leaving? You will only discover the answers to these questions if you are looking at your audience, seeking feedback. If your audience is not responding as you want them to, you may need to adjust your presentation to regain their interest. You could pick up the pace of your delivery, delete or include information as seems appropriate, or point out that the information you are presenting has important implications for the audience. You will only be able to adapt to your audience during your speech if you are looking at them and are aware of their behavior.

Movement

Should you feel free to walk around during the speech presentation, or should you stay in one place? If there is a lectern, should you stand behind it, or would it be acceptable to stand in front of it or to the side of it? Would it be all right to sit down while you speak? Or could you walk around in the audience, as Phil Donahue does on his TV talk show? You may well find yourself musing over one or more of these questions while preparing for a speech. The following discussion can help you answer them.

You may want to walk around during your presentation, but the walking should not detract from your message. If the audience is watching your movement, rather than focusing upon what you are saying, it would be better to remain standing in one place. If you want to, step from behind the lectern (assuming this does not interfere with the public address system) and move closer to your audience, creating a more intimate climate. As you move into a transition statement or change from a serious subject to a more humorous one, movement may be a good way to signal that your approach to the speaking situation is changing. In short, your movement during your speech should make sense. It should not be perceived as random pacing in front of your audience, nor should it appear overly dramatic.

Vocal cues

Vocal cues, including the pitch, rate, quality, and volume of your voice, play an important role in communicating feelings and attitudes. It is primarily through our voices, as well as our facial expressions, that we communicate whether we are happy, sad, bored, or excited. If your vocal cues suggest that you are not very interested in your presentation, your audience will probably not be very interested, either. Appropriate variation of vocal pitch, rate, quality, and volume can add interest and help maintain audience attention.

Vocal pitch is the consistent tonal range of your voice. Some speakers have high-pitched voices; others speak in deeper pitches. A monotone is a voice that evidences little pitch variation. The speaker who drones on in a monotone does little to enhance interest in the speech or enthusiasm for the presentation. On the other hand, random variation in pitch just for the sake of vocal variety should be avoided. The pitch of your voice should be appropriate for the meaning you wish to communicate.

Your voice can vary in volume to give added emphasis to words. Sometimes speaking softly can emphasize a point, just as can speaking loudly. Increased vocal intensity can signal an intensity that you feel about your subject. Variety in speech rate can also help maintain interest. Use a pause before or after key ideas, after you ask a rhetorical question (to give the audience time to think about an answer), or after you have presented technical material, to give the listeners a chance to let it sink in.

The best advice we can give you about both your physical and vocal delivery is to be yourself. Strive for a natural style. The elocutionists tried to make all speakers move and gesture the same way. Not good advice today! Let the motivation for delivering your message stem from your desire to communicate, not from your desire to be dramatic. Each speaker has a unique approach to delivering a message. Don't try to pattern your delivery upon someone else's behavior.

Managing your anxiety

Before concluding our discussion of the essentials of public speaking, let's talk about a very real concern—yes, even a fear—that you may have about speaking to others in public. One of the most anxiety-arousing sentences in the English language is, "And it gives me great pleasure to introduce our speaker for this afternoon, *(fill in your name)*."

The anxiety that you experience before and during public speaking situations is related to our discussion of intrapersonal communication earlier in the book. Your perception of the speaking assignment, your self-image, and your self-esteem interact to create anxiety. You want to do well, but you're not sure you can or will. Your body responds to this conflict by an increased breathing rate, more adrenalin, and more blood rushing through your veins—in short, you have more energy. This increased energy can explain your increased perspiration, more rapid beating of your heart, and sometimes shaking hands and knees. Your body is trying to help you deal with your uncertainty. The challenge is to put this extra energy to work rather than letting it demoralize you.

This anxiety and uncertainty that you may have felt before a speech is shared by many people. A few years ago a survey of common fears concluded that fear of speaking in public ranked first, while fear of dying ranked sixth![4] But just knowing why you experience anxiety or that your fear of public speaking is shared by many people does not make your fear any less important or significant. You may feel you need some help in dealing with your anxiety. Here are some suggestions for managing your fear of public speaking.

1. Talk about something you are familiar with. Try to avoid a subject you feel uncomfortable with or that you don't enjoy.
2. Prepare! Prepare! Prepare! Do your homework. Research your topic.
3. Try not to focus on your anxiety, but on the speech and the message that you want to communicate to your audience.
4. Try to anticipate your actual speaking performance situation as much as possible. Stand, walk to the lectern, wait to be introduced, and imagine your audience in front of you as you practice.
5. Make sure your speech is well organized, including appropriate transition phrases, so that you feel comfortable with the information and know how to get from one idea to the next.
6. If your anxiety is overwhelming, seek help from your instructor or counselor. Remember, it is not abnormal to experience anxiety.

THE ESSENTIALS OF PUBLIC SPEAKING

PUTTING THEORY INTO PRACTICE

This chapter has focused on public communication—speaking to several people at once. We have offered some specific suggestions to help you translate the theory of public speaking into practice. We have identified several overlapping steps.

We're sure you realize, however, that just being able to list six steps in preparing a public speech is not automatically going to make you a better public speaker. The trick is to apply the principles that we have discussed in this chapter to your own speaking efforts. The best way to learn is to take the plunge and begin working on your first speech. To help you get started, we would like to review some key concepts we have recommended.

I. Analyze Your Audience

- Try to find out as much as you can about the listeners' demographic characteristics, such as their ages, education level, and religious and political preferences.

- If possible, also try to determine the audience members' psychographic profile, by identifying the attitudes, beliefs, and values they hold toward you and your topic.

2. Select a Topic

- The best speech topic is one in which (1) you are interested, (2) you can find information to help you develop your ideas, (3) you have some personal experience, and (4) your audience will be interested.

3. Develop a Purpose

- Develop a specific purpose that is phrased in terms of what it is you want your audience to know, do, or feel at the end of the speech.
- Write your specific purpose down and keep it in front of you as you gather ideas and supporting material for your speech.

4. Gather Supporting Material

- The secret to an interesting talk is interesting supporting material.
- Select a variety of supporting material.
- A key to using examples is to describe them so that the experience comes alive to your listeners. Appeal to your listeners' senses.
- Make sure the point of your illustration is clear to your audience.
- Be sure to relate your statistics to something the audience can visualize.
- Use visual aids that are simple, clear, appropriately revealed, and well rehearsed with your speech.

5. Organize Your Ideas

- Develop an outline rather than writing your speech out word for word.
- Select a pattern or patterns of organization that will help give your speech a structure clear to your audience.

6. Rehearse and Deliver the Speech

- Don't read or memorize your speech.
- Strive for a natural, conversational, extemporaneous speaking style.
- Look at audience members. You cannot have too much eye contact with your audience. (However, you should not just stare at one or two people, because that would make them uncomfortable.)
- Your vocal delivery should include variety in pitch, rate, volume, intensity, and quality.

Suggestions for Managing Your Speech Anxiety

- Talk about something you are familiar with.
- Try to concentrate on communicating with your audience rather than on your anxiety.
- When you rehearse your speech, try to recreate the speaking situation.

SUGGESTED ACTIVITIES

1. Select a recent speech reprinted in *Vital Speeches in America*. Prepare an outline of the speech and identify the organizational pattern.
2. Select from the following list of speech topics one that particularly interests you, then prepare a *specific purpose sentence* for an informative speech.
   Nuclear power plants
   Inflation
   Term life insurance
   Higher education
   Cancer
   Republicans
   George Washington
   Terrorism
   Crime in your community
3. Watch a television broadcast of the evening news. Analyze the visual aids (photos, charts, symbols, etc.). Provide a critique of the broadcast based on the discussion of visual aids presented in this chapter.
4. Find a good example of each of the types of supporting materials mentioned in this chapter. Consult a variety of sources, such as newspaper articles, magazine articles, and advertisements.

NOTES

[1] The two outlines were written by Harry Hazel, Associate Professor of Communication Arts, Gonzaga University, Spokane, Washington. Professor Hazel has graciously granted permission for their use in this book.

[2] See, for example, C. I. Hovland, I. L. Janis, and H. H. Kelly, *Communication and Persuasion* (New Haven: Yale University Press, 1953); C. I. Insko, *Theories of Attitude Change* (New York: Appleton-Century-Crofts, 1967).

[3] See for example, Steven A. Beebe, "Eye Contact: A Nonverbal Determinant of Speaker Credibility," *Speech Teacher,* 23 (1974):21–25.

[4] Survey reported in *London Sunday Times*, October 7, 1973.

12 PERSUASIVE SPEAKING

After studying this chapter you should be able to:

Identify differences and similarities between informative and persuasive speaking

Discuss how persuasion occurs

Identify suggestions for enhancing speaker credibility

Effectively organize a persuasive speech

Identify suggestions for effectively using emotional appeals to motivate an audience

Apply appropriate tests of evidence and reasoning to the development of logical arguments

Effectively adapt a persuasive message to friendly, neutral, and hostile audiences

On the television screen we see the image of a tall, frosty glass of orange juice. We hear the announcer intone, "Florida orange juice. Brimming with flavor. Cool, delightful, and delicious. Refreshing. It's not just for breakfast any more." After seeing this commercial, we are quite aware of the fact that the advertiser is attempting to persuade us. Those who prepared the commercial certainly want to change our behavior—they want us to buy Florida orange juice. Yet when we examine the message presented in the commercial, on the surface it appears to be informative. At no time did the announcer say, "Buy it," or "Try it today." The announcer simply described a glass of orange juice and implied that many people were consuming it at times other than at breakfast.

What is persuasion? Or, to be more specific, what's the difference between communicating to inform and communicating to persuade? In the previous chapter we presented six basic steps of preparing a public speech, emphasizing informative presentations. In this chapter we will focus upon persuasive speaking. We will first provide an overview of the persuasive communication process. We'll note several principles that help explain why we are persuaded to change our attitudes and behavior. Then we will discuss how the speaker can enhance his or her effectiveness as a persuasive communicator, by noting how we can enhance our perceptions of credibility. Third, we will suggest how to best select and organize ideas for maximum persuasive impact. And finally, we will examine how the audience plays a vital role in affecting the types of persuasive strategies we should select in preparing a persuasive message.

256

PERSUASION DEFINED

As discussed in Chapter 11, the primary purpose of informative speaking is to teach, describe, illustrate, define, and clarify ideas. Informative speakers present new information and ideas in a way that they hope will help listeners comprehend and remember what they are trying to communicate. Persuasion, on the

other hand, is the process of trying to *change* or *reinforce* an attitude, belief, value, or behavior.

When first comparing the definitions of informative speaking and persuasive speaking, it would seem that there is a clear and obvious distinction between these two types of oral communication. Yet when we take a further look at the objectives of persuasive and informative speaking, the two purposes become less distinct.

Why inform an audience? Why do teachers teach? Is the information that we, your textbook authors, provide in this text going to have an effect upon your attitude toward speech communication? Yes, it probably will. Information, then, can and does affect your attitudes and may affect your behavior.

To some extent, all communication potentially affects attitudes, beliefs, values, or behavior. It may be more accurate to distinguish between speeches to inform and speeches to persuade as differing in degree. All attempts to persuade an audience rely upon information to some extent. But the selection and organization of the information are strategies of persuasion.

HOW DOES PERSUASION OCCUR?

Why do people change their attitudes and behavior in response to something someone else says? Social scientists have tried through numerous theories to identify those factors that help us explain why people are persuaded. One of the most widely written-about theories attempting to explain how persuasion occurs is called *cognitive dissonance*.[1]

Cognitive dissonance theory is based on the principle that humans strive for consistency in their thoughts and actions. Leon Festinger, the researcher credited with cognitive dissonance theory, suggests that each of us operates from an organized, logical set of thoughts about ourselves, about other people, and about everything with which we come into contact. We attempt to organize our thoughts about our world so that each attitude or belief that we hold is consistent with other thoughts we have about our world. Each time we are presented with new information that is inconsistent with the way we have organized our thoughts, we experience a state of disorganization called cognitive dissonance. Such disorganization is uncomfortable and prompts us to reestablish consistency or balance. This phenomenon is not restricted to mental processes. The human body, say physicians, also operates on the same principle. If you cut yourself or become bruised, your body begins to correct the problem. Whether it is through the production of more white blood cells, a rise in body temperature, or a change in respiration, your body attempts to respond so that physiological balance is restored.

This is the same type of process that, according to dissonance theory, occurs psychologically. A person who is attempting to persuade us (to change our attitudes, beliefs, values, or behavior) usually tries to point out a certain problem or need that we have. Then the persuader offers a solution or suggestion as the best way to solve the problem or meet the need. Thus, the persuader first "creates" dissonance and then attempts to relieve it by noting some change that should occur. The change, of course, is the specific solution that the persuader wants the listener to adopt.

A politician who aspires to the Presidency of the United States usually tries to remind listeners of the various problems confronting our country—inflation, unemployment, the energy shortage, and the like. Once the dissonance has been created, the presidential candidate suggests that the problem can be alleviated, or at least somewhat diminished, if he or she becomes President. A candidate, in effect, says, "If I become President, I can restore balance to the country once again." The candidate can also help you feel more peace of mind (cognitive *consistency*) if you agree to support his or her candidacy. Thus, persuasion is more likely to occur if you first experience cognitive dissonance. Then the persuader will suggest how you can reorganize your thoughts and achieve cognitive consistency by adopting some proposal. The suggested solution, however, is only one of several options the listener may adopt. The next section considers several others.

WHAT HAPPENS WHEN YOU EXPERIENCE DISSONANCE?

When you experience dissonance, you may respond in a variety of different ways to restore consonance.[2] First, you could *attack the credibility of the source* of the information that created the dissonance. If, for example, you hear a speaker tell an audience that the university you attend is not a high-quality school, you will probably experience some dissonance. You may conclude that the speaker does not know what he or she is talking about—you attack the speaker's credibility. Or imagine that your speech instructor has given you a grade which you feel significantly underestimates your speaking ability. You could conclude that your teacher is inept. Your conclusions about your teacher make you feel better—reduce your dissonance.

A second way in which you may respond when you experience dissonance is to *reinterpret* the statement made by the speaker. In other words, you hear what you want to hear—you focus on the part of the message that does not create dissonance.

Third, you may *seek new information* to support your position and attempt to find evidence to refute the position of the individual who created the dissonance. Imagine that you have just purchased a new car. You read in the newspapers that a recent test by a consumer organization has just found that make of car unsafe for highway travel. You experience dissonance. To help reduce your dissonance, you may seek additional information or studies about the safety of your new car to support your original decision to buy it.

A fourth possible response is to *avoid listening* to the information that is creating the dissonance. If you are a Republican, you will probably avoid going to Democratic party political rallies. If you are a Methodist, you probably will not attend a Unitarian church regularly. You tend to avoid those situations that do not support your attitudes, beliefs, and values.

A fifth option is the response that the persuader hopes you will make. You can *change your attitude, belief, value, or behavior* to support the position the speaker advocates. If a candidate for mayor convinces you that your city government is in a mess and only that candidate can provide an adequate plan to correct the problems, you may decide to support that person instead of the candidate whom you were originally backing. If the deodorant commercial convinces you that you may be the source of unwanted body odor that will invite scorn from all of your friends and associates unless you do something to correct it, you may decide that you should switch to the brand of deodorant that the advertiser is selling. The objective of the persuader is to cause you to experience dissonance that will motivate you to support a particular attitude or behavior change. The persuader must be perceived as credible. The message must be clear, so that the listener does not selectively interpret the message the speaker wants to communicate. And the information presented must be enough to convince the listener to make a choice in favor of the persuader.

NEEDS AS MOTIVATORS

In attempting to motivate your listeners to respond to your message, you should consider their needs. Appealing to the listeners' needs can help you hold their attention and ultimately persuade them. Abraham Maslow's often-cited "hierarchy of needs" suggests that more basic needs must be met before the listener will be likely to respond to appeals to higher-level needs.[3] Figure 9 shows a pyramid that illustrates the five categories of needs identified by Maslow.

At the base of the pyramid are *physiological needs,* those necessary for survival. They include such fundamental needs as those for air, water, food, and sex. According to the needs pyramid, if these basic physiological needs are not being met, it will be extremely difficult to motivate someone to take piano lessons, vote for a political candidate, or donate money to a worthy cause—unless the person believes that these actions will help meet the unfulfilled physiological requirements. Even though most audiences to whom you will speak will have few unmet physiological needs, if they missed lunch, find the room hot and stuffy, or have not had enough sleep, their response to your persuasive message will not be very good—unless, of course, you're trying to persuade them to eat something, turn on the air conditioner, or take a nap.

The second need category is called *safety needs.* Listeners must feel a sense of security and protection, the result of being able to predict what is going to occur. Insurance salespeople have long realized that the need to feel safe and secure can be a prime motivation in the purchase of life, health, and accident insurance policies. When the economy is unpredictable and people fear they can no longer afford adequate housing for their families, their jobs may be in jeopardy, and their savings accounts may soon be nonexistent, the audience needs to feel more stable financially and better able to predict what is going to happen to them in the future.

The third category is called *social needs,* which includes the need for love

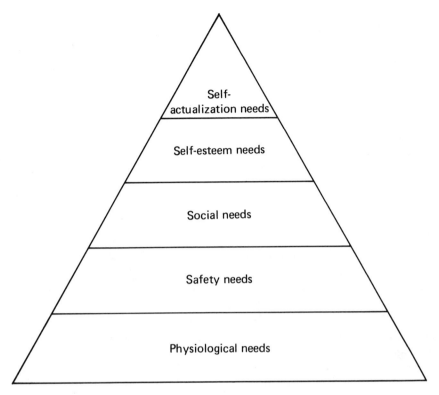

Figure 9 The Maslow hierarchy of needs.

and affection. According to Maslow, we each also need to feel a sense of belonging to a group (such as a fraternity, religious group, school, or place of employment). We need to feel that at least one other person cares for our needs, our happiness, and our well being. Until these social needs are satisfied, the needs for self esteem and self actualization will not be effective motivating forces.

Need for self-esteem is the fourth category. This includes our need for status, recognition, achievement, and influence. Automobile advertisements (particularly for high-priced cars such as Cadillac and Mercedes-Benz) usually appeal to self-esteem needs.

At the top of the need hierarchy pyramid is the need for *self-actualization,* which includes our desire to achieve our highest potential. Once the other four need categories are satisfied, we can be motivated to achieve the ultimate in personal satisfaction. We then strive for excellence because we want to make ourselves the best that we can be.

Maslow's hierarchy of needs, along with the theory of cognitive dissonance, helps to explain how listeners are persuaded to change their attitudes. You should realize, however, that persuasion does not necessarily occur as simply as we have described it here. It is not only creating the precise amount of dissonance and satisfying the specific unmet need that will cause an audience to change their attitudes or behaviors. Persuasion is not an exact science of applying a few simple rules and achieving immediate results. It is also an art, requiring a certain degree of talent and of sensitivity to both the needs and the feelings of listeners. Persuasion occurs gradually, in small increments. Dramatic changes in attitude can occur, but it usually takes repeated efforts before major changes result. Usually, though, it takes persistence, patience, skill, and human sensitivity before much success is achieved in persuading listeners to change their minds.

SPEAKER CREDIBILITY

Do you remember the story of the little boy who cried "Wolf!" once too often? His job was to watch the sheep to make sure that they were well protected from wolves. But when he was bored he thought it was fun to yell "Wolf" so that his father would rush out to the pasture to rescue the sheep. He did this several times. Each time his father believed him and came rushing out. Then when a wolf did show up and the boy shouted "Wolf!" his father did not come. The father had found that his son's cry lacked credibility, so he did not respond.

Credibility is the attitude that a listener holds toward a speaker. The persuader hopes that this attitude is a favorable one, because the more favorable an attitude the listener has toward the speaker, the more likely it is that the listener will respond to the persuasive message presented.

Aristotle felt that a speaker should possess good character and good common sense, and should be concerned for the well-being of the audience. The speaker who possessed these qualities was more likely to convince listeners of the point being made. Quintilian, a Roman rhetorician and teacher, similarly felt that an effective public speaker should be a "good man speaking well." From the advice of these ancient rhetoricans, it is clear that the speaker's search for audience favor is centuries-old. And it is still relevant today, for you may think of credibility as something someone either has or does not have. But it is not something that any speaker possesses or lacks. It is an attitude that the *listener* has toward the speaker. The audience gives credence to the message of a speaker if they judge the person to be qualified, honest, and dynamic.

Research using factor analysis reveals that credibility is not just a single factor. Aristotle's speculations as to those factors which influence a speaker's ethical character have been generally supported by these experimental studies. One major factor that emerges is *competence*—is the speaker knowledgeable and informed? Does the speaker have enough experience and possess the skills to be considered an expert on the subject? A second major factor that emerges is *trustworthiness.* To be perceived as trustworthy, the speaker should be honest and believable, and inspire confidence. A third factor of credibility is the speaker's *dynamism.* It is often said that a speaker has or doesn't have charisma. A person with charisma possesses charm, talent, and those other qualities that make an attractive and energetic person. The factor of dynamism embraces these charismatic qualities.

After reading about the definition of credibility and about the multidimensional quality of credibility, you may be asking, "How is this information going to be useful to me when I speak to others?" Once you know what credibility is, you can begin to consider ways to enhance your ability to be perceived as competent, honest, and dynamic. We will consider three phases of credibility and ways to enhance your image in connection with each.

The first phase is called *initial credibility.* This is the attitude that the listener has toward you before you begin your speech. Most listeners develop some preconceived notions about the speaker even before the person begins talking. Such impressions are based upon personal appearance, the reputation of the speaker, comments that others have made, and the nature of the introduction that the speaker receives. To enhance your initial credibility, consider the following suggestions:

1. Make sure your physical appearance does not violate the expectations of your audience. Don't dress informally, for example, if your audience expects more formal attire.
2. Before you arrive for your speaking engagement, prepare a list of your accomplishments or honors, if appropriate, so that the person who introduces you can help establish a positive image of your qualifications on your subject.
3. Don't rush up to the lectern and begin talking immediately. Appear confident by establishing eye contact with your audience before you begin your speech.

The second phase of establishing credibility with your audience is called *derived credibility.* This phase occurs while you are speaking to your audience. Here are suggestions for enhancing your credibility during this second phase:

1. Establish eye contact with your audience. Look at your listeners so you communicate your interest in them.
2. Maintain a varied vocal inflection that communicates interest, enthusiasm, and sincerity.
3. Communicate your enthusiasm and conviction in your topic. Don't slouch on the lectern, lean on a table, or distract the audience with unmeaningful gestures.
4. Present a well-organized message. Establish an overview of your major ideas, present the body of your speech, and summarize your key thought during the conclusion.
5. Use appropriate grammar.
6. Pronounce words clearly and accurately.
7. Use appropriate evidence to support your conclusions.
8. Research your topic so you convince your audience you are informed and qualified.

The third phase, *terminal credibility,* is the attitude that the listener holds toward the speaker after the speech. Terminal credibility is the result of the initial and derived credibility of the speaker.

Credibility, then, is the attitude that your listeners hold toward you. The more favorably you are perceived by your listeners, the more likely you will be to persuade them. If you carefully consider how you can enhance your initial and derived credibility, you will have more positive and lasting impact on your audience.

PREPARING THE PERSUASIVE MESSAGE

In the previous chapter we discussed the basic steps of preparing a public speech. The same overall process is employed in persuasive speaking as in informative speaking. But when attempting to persuade an audience, one must consider several additional principles. We will give special attention to (1) organizing the persuasive message, (2) appealing to the emotions of an audience, (3) using reasoning and evidence, and (4) adapting your message to friendly, neutral, and hostile audiences.

Persuasive speech organization

In Chapter 11 we identified several strategies for organizing a speech. The order in which your major ideas are presented to an audience can have a significant impact upon your communication effectiveness. For several years researchers have attempted to identify the most effective ways to organize information for maximum persuasive impact. Problem-solution, cause-and-effect, pro-and-con, primacy, and recency organizational patterns are particularly effective in presenting information for a persuasive speech. The following principles provide additional suggestions for organizing a persuasive presentation:

1. You will be more effective if you make the audience clearly aware of a problem that affects them before you present your solution to the problem.
   Rationale: This helps gain and maintain audience interest and attention and motivates your listeners to adopt your suggestions for solving the problem.
2. If you are speaking to an intelligent, hostile, or well-informed audience, it is a good idea to present both sides of an issue, rather than just stating the advantages of the position you are advocating.
   Rationale: If you don't identify arguments that your audience may have heard, they will be thinking of them anyway. It is better to acknowledge opposing points of view, and then to refute them, than to ignore other approaches to the issue.
3. Use the introduction of your persuasive speech to emphasize areas of agreement between you and your listeners.
   Rationale: This helps to establish common ground between you and your audience. They will more likely be favorable to your arguments if you have stressed areas of agreement.

4. If you are speaking to an informed, intelligent, or hostile audience, there is less need to identify explicit conclusions.

   Rationale: You run the risk of insulting informed and intelligent audience members, and further antagonizing hostile audience members, if you draw explicit conclusions from the supporting material you present.

5. If you feel you need to state specific conclusions to your audience so you can move them to take action, it is better to do so toward the end of your speech than in the early portions.

   Rationale: It is better to direct your audience's behavior at the end of your speech after you have presented your rationale and provided the evidence.

6. If you feel your audience may be hostile to your point of view, place your strongest arguments first.

   Rationale: If you save your strongest argument until the end, your audience may remain unconvinced and may no longer focus on the ideas you present.

In addition to these specific suggestions, a five-step plan for organizing a speech, developed by Alan Monroe, is a useful strategy.

Monroe's *motivated sequence* is based on the persuasive principles of cognitive dissonance and audience needs that were discussed earlier in the chapter. The five steps of the motivated sequence should help you organize a persuasive presentation.

1. Attention step   As in any speech, you should first capture your audience's attention. Beginning with a personal or hypothetical example, startling statement or statistic, rhetorical question, or well-chosen analogy is often an effective technique for gaining audience attention.

2. Need step   It is at this yet early point in your speech that you describe the problem to your audience. You must convince your listeners that the problem or issue you are addressing affects them. You can establish the need by citing examples or statistics to suggest how widespread the problem is. Personal examples and expert opinion can also be used to identify the problem.

3. Satisfaction step   After you have presented the problem and identified why your listeners need to be concerned about your topic, you should satisfy the need by presenting the solution to the problem.

4. Visualization step   Here, after presenting the solution, you help the listeners visualize the positive effects of your solution. You can also explain how the problem will continue or may even get worse if your solution is not adopted. In the visualization step you should refer to the need (the problem) and clearly demonstrate that your solution will help alleviate the problem.

5. Action step   You now ask your audience to take specific action to implement the solution that you have suggested to them.⁴

You may find that you will need to modify the motivated sequence to suit your needs for a particular audience. If, for example, you are speaking to a hostile audience, you may not include a specific action for them to take. If you can get your hostile audience to recognize that there is a problem (need step) and that your solution (satisfaction step) may have some positive benefits (visualization step), you will have achieved your purpose. If you are speaking to an audience that is apathetic toward your speech objective, you may need to emphasize the attention and need steps and not ask them to take specific action. The motivated sequence is a guide, not an absolute formula to apply in the same way to every persuasive speech that you ever deliver. Use it and the other suggestions about speech organization we have provided to help you best achieve your specific purpose.

USING EMOTIONAL APPEALS TO MOTIVATE LISTENERS

As you leaf through a magazine, you come across a picture that catches your attention. It is a photograph of a child, a young girl with big, beautiful, penetrating eyes. But the eyes are glistening with tears. The caption at the bottom of the picture reads, "Don't turn this page. Respond to the needs of starving children like this one. Send your check to Save Our Children today." It is not logic or evidence that makes you respond to this presentation; rather, it is emotional appeal. Our emotional reaction to our environment has an important effect on how we respond to what we observe. Using emotional appeals is one way a speaker may try to motivate listeners to take action or change their attitudes.

Emotional appeals consist of the statements, examples, opinions, and visual and auditory stimuli that trigger an emotional reaction in the listener. Emotional appeals can be verbal (e.g., a description of what may happen to us if we do not fasten our seat belts when we drive) or it can be nonverbal, like the picture of the child in the magazine promotion, or music accompanying a speech or rally.

Most psychologists feel that every human behavior is motivated by a need or desire. Often a persuasive speaker appeals to one of these basic needs by seeking to evoke an emotional reaction from his listener. One insurance company, for example, bases its television advertising campaign upon an appeal to the audience's need for security. The appeal is *not* made through facts or statistics, but through the portrayal of a young, busy family whose provider sighs happily, "They need me." He (and, the company hopes, the listener as well) is greatly relieved that he has life insurance to meet his family's needs, even if he should die.

We defined a value as an enduring concept of good and bad. That which we value highly can also be used by a speaker to stimulate an emotional reaction. Milton Rokeach feels that for many Americans the following list of values represents important goals that would motivate them to respond: a comfortable life;

equality; an exciting, stimulating life; family security; freedom; happiness; inner harmony; mature love; national security; pleasure; salvation; self-respect; a sense of accomplishment; social recognition; true friendship; wisdom; a world of beauty; and a world of peace.[5] Appeals to these values can serve to motivate an audience to support an idea you are proposing.

How can you use emotional appeals in a speech to motivate audience members to respond to your message? Perhaps the best way is to use examples and illustrations to which your listeners can relate. Imagine that you are speaking to a college-age audience, whom you want to persuade to make regular deposits in a savings account. You will be more successful if you tell them how their savings can have direct benefits to them in the immediate future (e.g., for a down payment on a house or car), rather than try to convince them to save for their retirement. An older audience, however, may find your appeal to save money for retirement more convincing, because they can more readily relate to the problem.

The Roman orator Cicero felt that if you want a listener to experience a certain emotion you should first experience the emotion as a speaker. If you want your audience to be excited and enthusiastic about a particular issue or proposition that you support, you must be excited and enthusiastic as you talk to them.

The language that you use should also be influenced by the particular feeling or emotional state that you want your listener to experience. Certain words can arouse an audience. Ministers and evangelists know that the words "Jesus Christ" evoke emotional responses in an audience. Patriotic slogans, such as "Remember the Alamo" or "Remember Pearl Harbor," stir strong emotions.

Considerable research has been conducted to determine whether motivating an audience by threats or appeals to fear is successful.[6] The research has focused upon how strongly a speaker should try to threaten or frighten an audience. The results suggest that high fear arousal (e.g., "You will get lung cancer and die if you don't stop smoking") will be better than moderate or low appeal if the speaker is perceived as highly credible. Doctors providing medical advice and lawyers providing legal advice, if they are perceived as highly credible, are among those who can use strong fear appeals to maximum benefit.

Other studies suggest that if you are not a highly credible source, a moderate level of fear arousal may be best. If you arouse fear too intensely, your listeners may find your message unbelievable or think, "That could never happen to me." They may even feel uncomfortable to the extent that they stop listening to you.

Then, too, the success of a fear appeal relies partly upon how likely the listener is to face the particular threat described. For example, if you usually do not drive or ride in an automobile, you will not be impressed or concerned about a speech trying to motivate you to wear seat belts. If you and your loved ones don't smoke, you will not be interested in a speech warning about the danger of lung cancer from smoking.

Emotional appeals can be effective if they are directed to the needs, values, and motives of an audience. Appealing to pride, fear, love, hope, or loyalty can be useful ways of persuading an audience.

USING LOGICAL ARGUMENTS TO PERSUADE LISTENERS

"Well, it certainly seems reasonable to me," Muriel says after hearing a proposal for a cable TV franchise. "I think we should adopt your proposal." How do we decide what "seems reasonable"? Or, phrased another way, exactly what is reasoning? Most of us like to think that we are logical individuals. How do we construct logical conclusions from the facts, opinions, statistics, and examples that we use to develop a persuasive presentation? Answers to the above questions can help us better understand how to prepare logical, reasonable, persuasive presentations.

Reasoning is the process of inferring a conclusion from evidence—examples, statistics, opinions, or facts. One of your primary objectives as a persuasive speaker is to prove to your listeners that the conclusion you have reached is a valid one. But how do you go about proving something? What is proof? *Proof consists of evidence plus the logic or reasoning that you employ to draw a conclusion from the evidence.* Evidence consists of the facts, examples, statistics, and opinions that you use to support your conclusions. To help you learn to develop more logical arguments, we will first discuss tests to determine whether the evidence you are using is valid and reliable, and then we will examine three major types of reasoning.

Facts

What makes a fact a fact? A typical response of most people is, "A fact is something that has been proven to be true." But this definition is only partially complete. How do you prove a fact to be true? Most scholars agree that a fact is something that has been observed to have happened or to exist. Technically, only eyewitnesses to an event can present facts as evidence. In a court of law, trial lawyers are primarily interested in facts—they want eyewitnesses to describe what they saw. They are less interested in secondhand information.

To help determine the validity of factual evidence, consider the following questions:

1. Do those who observed the fact agree that it actually happened or existed?
2. Are there contrary facts?
3. Is the report of the fact made by someone who observed the fact?

Examples

An example is an illustration that is used to dramatize or clarify a proven fact. A hypothetical example, fabricated to help clarify a point, cannot be used to prove a point, though it is useful for illustrative purposes. Real or personal examples help add interest to your speech and can also serve as useful evidence in persuading listeners if they meet the following tests:

1. Is the example typical?
2. Is it significant?
3. Is the source of the example reliable?
4. Are there contrary examples?

Opinions

An opinion is a statement made by another person, which you quote to add credibility to a conclusion you want to draw. The best opinions are those of experts or authorities who are perceived as unbiased, fair, and accurate. Opinions are usually most effective if they are combined with other evidence, such as facts or examples, to support the position of the authority or expert.

Consider the following questions to help you evaluate the opinions of others:

1. Is the source of the opinion reliable?
2. Is the source an expert or authority?
3. Is the source biased?
4. Is the source competent and qualified to make the statement?
5. Is the opinion consistent with other statements by the expert or authority?
6. Is the opinion consistent with opinions held by other experts?

Statistics

A statistic is a number used to summarize several facts or examples. It is simply not practical, and often not possible, to list numerous facts and examples when leading your audience to a conclusion. But statistics can express a number of examples in a concise way. Just as with other types of evidence, you need to be sure that the statistics you use are accurate and really reflect the point you want to make. Probably more than any other type of evidence, statistics are abused, misused, and often misgathered. The following criteria will help you determine the quality of statistics that you use in your persuasive speeches:

1. Is the source reliable?
2. Are the statistics recent?
3. Is the source of the statistics unbiased?
4. Is the sample from which the statistics were drawn a representative one?
5. Is the sample size adequate?
6. Do the statistics really measure what they are supposed to measure?
7. Are there contrary statistics?

Types of reasoning

Reasoning is the second half of proof. Reasoning involves drawing a conclusion from the evidence that you have gathered. Since antiquity, scholars have identified types of reasoning and have specified how to improve a public speaker's ability to draw meaningful conclusions from the evidence presented. We will discuss three general types of reasoning—inductive, deductive, and causal.

Inductive reasoning   Inductive reasoning is reasoning from specific instances to a general conclusion. There are several different ways to reach a conclusion inductively.

First, you can reason inductively by *generalization*—drawing a general conclusion from specific examples or facts. For example, Karl wore a seat belt during his recent car accident and was not seriously injured. Dorothy wore her seat belt, and she wasn't hurt when she was in a car crash, either. Steve came out of his accident unscratched because he, too, wore his seat belt. These examples, plus recent statistics from the National Safety Council that 10,000 accident victims who wore seat belts had significantly fewer serious injuries than did 10,000 who did *not* wear seat belts, point to the conclusion that seat belts help to prevent serious injuries. You have drawn a general conclusion based upon the specific evidence presented.

When reasoning inductively to a generalization, keep the following questions in mind:

1. Are there enough instances to prove your point?
2. Are the instances typical?
3. Are the instances recent?

Another type of inductive reasoning is the *analogy*. An analogy, you may recall, is a comparison, When we point out that two things have a number of characteristics in common, and that a certain fact about one thing is also likely to be true of the other, we have reasoned from one example to reach a conclusion about the example in question. You may reason that if Missouri has a highway safety program that saves lives, then Iowa will also find a similar program desirable. If a government health care system works in Great Britain, then it will probably be effective in the United States. In reasoning by analogy, you should consider the following tests to insure that you reach a valid conclusion:

1. Do the ways in which the two things are alike outweigh those in which they are different?
2. Is the assertion true (does the health care system in Great Britain really work)?

Deductive Reasoning   The process of deductive reasoning is just opposite to that of inductive reasoning: you reason from a general statement or principle to reach a specific conclusion. Deductive reasoning can be organized in the form of a syllogism, which is helpful in devising your specific conclusion. To formulate a syllogism, begin with a general statement, such as "Excessive campaign spending is undesirable." This is called your *general premise*. Next, move to a more specific statement, such as "Media campaigning requires that excessive amounts of money be spent." This more specific statement is called a *minor premise*. In reasoning deductively you need to make sure your first two statements (major premise and minor premise) can be proven or supported with evidence. On the basis of your general statement and your more specific statement, you are ready to draw a specific *conclusion*. In this example, your conclusion would be, "Therefore, media campaigning is undesirable."

Deductive reasoning, then, involves drawing a specific conclusion from a general statement. Tests of deductive reasoning include:

1. Is the general statement true?
2. Is the conclusion reasonable?

Causal reasoning   In *causal reasoning,* you relate two or more events together in such a way as to prove that one or more of the events caused the others. You can reason from *cause to effect,* moving from a known factor to a predicted result, or from *effect to cause,* knowing the effect and trying to figure out what caused it. For example, in reasoning from cause to effect you may know that there has been a shortage of rainfall in the past year. You can then reason that this shortage of rainfall, with the resulting drop in the water table, is probably the cause of the sinkholes that have formed in your community recently. In reasoning from effect to cause, you may know that inflation exists; it is an effect that everyone is experiencing. You then speculate that inflation is due to high energy prices and government spending. You have reached a conclusion about our economy by moving from a specific condition to the causes of that condition.

To determine whether causal reasoning is appropriate, ask yourself these questions:

1. Did the cause really produce the effect?
2. Do more causes exist than you took into account?

ADAPTING THE PERSUASIVE MESSAGE TO THE AUDIENCE

In the last chapter we began our discussion of the basic steps of public speaking by noting the importance of analyzing your audience. Audience members do not believe everything a speaker tells them. All listeners have certain attitudes, beliefs, and values that are going to affect their receptivity of the speaker's message. In persuasive speaking, audience analysis is particularly important to successful communication. One definition of rhetoric which nicely illustrates the role of audience analysis in persuasion has been formulated by Donald C. Bryant. He suggests that rhetoric is the "process of adjusting ideas to people and people to ideas." To be successful, you must know your audience members' positions on the issues you are presenting. Only then will you be able to adjust your ideas to theirs.

The predisposition of your audience to respond favorably or unfavorably toward your topic will affect your selection of evidence and supporting materials. It also has a bearing on your organization of the message. Before we suggest how your audience members' attitudes, beliefs, and values affect your specific strategies for preparing your persuasive message, let's consider several research conclusions that should help you better understand your audience.[7]

As a general rule, who do you think is easier to persuade, men or women? Research suggests that women are a bit easier to persuade than men, but you should keep in mind that this is a research generalization. While it is supported by several experimental studies, it does not mean that *all* women are easier to persuade than *all* men—only that there is a *tendency* for women to be more likely to change their opinions when confronted by persuasive messages.

A second research finding suggests that young audience members are more easily persuaded than older ones. Older listeners are more resistant to changing the positions that they have held for some time.

A third research finding indicates that listeners with less intelligence are more easily affected by persuasive messages than are those with higher intelligence. Greater intellect apparently keeps a listener from being easily persuaded by a message designed to change attitudes or behavior.

Fourth, researchers have found that listeners with low self-esteem are more easily persuaded than those with higher self-esteem. Audience members who feel others possess more intelligence, are more popular, and are more likable are more eager to respond to persuasion in general.

Finally, social scientists have concluded that the authoritarian or closed-minded listener is more likely to respond to a message supported with evidence that the listener feels is credible, rather than with well-constructed logical arguments and reasoning. If the closed-minded audience member (an Archie Bunker type) believes the *National Enquirer* to be a credible source of information, the statements of that publication can be more persuasive than an extensive, logical, reasonable argument.

These research generalizations about how certain listeners may respond to persuasive message should give you additional insight as to why certain audience members may or may not find your persuasive message convincing. But again, we caution you to keep in mind that these are research *generalizations;* they do not apply to every persuasive instance you will face. Use these research conclusions as guidelines, tempered by your own knowledge of the subject, your credibility, and additional information you may have about your specific audience.

Adapting to a friendly audience

With luck, most of the audiences you will face will be friendly and responsive to your persuasive message. Unfortunately, many, if not most, of your audiences may not be so supportive of you and your stand on the issues. But when you do face that group of friendly listeners, the following suggestions should help you adapt your message to them:

1. *If your audience is favorable toward your stand on the issues, try to suggest to your listeners some specific action to take.* Evangelist Billy Graham, who realizes that most of the people in his audience will be

supportive of his sermon, always asks his listeners to come forward to the front of the auditorium.

2. *Ask listeners for some immediate show of support.* Again, Billy Graham's invitation to his listeners to come forward in public gives them a specific way to support his message and to make a commitment to others. This public promise is more difficult to break than a commitment made privately.

3. *When speaking to a friendly audience, you can clearly state why you are there to speak with them and exactly what you want them to do.*

4. *Strong appeals to audience members' emotions are often effective with friendly audiences.* If the audience is already convinced of the logic of the position that you advocate, you can often move them to take action by evoking emotional responses, while reminding them of the evidence that supports your conclusion.

5. *Emphasize the degree of similarity between you and your audience. Identify with them.* If you are speaking to people who have children, and you have children of your own, mention this common bond if it is relevant to the issues you are addressing. What else do you have in common? Interests; education; stands on other issues; same hometown, state, or country?

6. *If your audience is already committed to the position you advocate, ask them to reinforce one another to support your position.* For example, if you are trying to motivate audience members to lose weight (and you know that they want to lose weight), ask them to reinforce one another when they are successful. Weight Watchers and other similar diet organizations use this technique successfully.

Adapting to a neutral or apathetic audience

While it would be great if most of the audiences that you faced were initially supportive of your ideas, many audiences to whom you speak will be somewhat neutral or apathetic toward your stand. Audience members can be neutral toward your position for at least three reasons.

First, they may not have enough information on your subject to be able to take a position. If you are trying to convince them that cryogenics is useful, you will first have to explain what cryogenics is.

Second, listeners may be neutral because, although they have enough information, they are simply undecided. During the 1980 Presidential election many people had heard the positions of President Carter and candidate Reagan, but they simply were not able to make up their minds and decide for whom to vote. The political polls revealed a large percentage of undecided voters.

Third, audience members may be unable or unwilling to take a stand on the issues because they do not see how the topic or issue affects them. If your listeners are convinced that the water shortage in the Southwest may eventually affect them, they may be more willing to accept your conclusion that steps must be taken now to conserve water in your community. Until they realize that the problem is relevant to them, they will probably be somewhat neutral or apathetic toward your water conservation message.

Let's look at some specific suggestions for adapting your message to a neutral audience:

1. *Make sure you have your listeners' attention.* It is going to be more difficult for you to help your audience focus on your message if they are not really interested in you or your topic in the first place. Ehninger, Monroe, and Gronbeck suggest that the following factors are useful in gaining and maintaining audience attention:

   Activity or movement. Physically move around or tell a story or example that has action and change in the story line.

   Reality. Listeners are concerned with what is real, tangible, and concrete.

   Proximity. Refer to events and examples that directly affect your audience, that are close at hand, or that are current.

   Familiarity. Things, people, and events that are common to your audience are easy for them to visualize and relate to.

   Novelty. Something unusual—a story, personal example, or visual aid—helps gain and maintain attention.

   Suspense. Withholding the key idea until the end of a story can maintain attention, just like the punch line of a joke. We know it's coming—so we keep listening.

   Conflict. Conflict of ideas, personality, or philosophical position helps maintain attention.

   Humor. Used effectively, humor can be an important asset.

   The Vital. Anything that affects a person's life, happiness, satisfaction, property, or employment is going to hold an audience's attention.[8]

2. *Make sure your listeners know how the subject you are addressing affects them or those they love.*

3. *Realize that the response from a neutral audience is not going to be as immediate or favorable as that of a friendly audience.* As we have noted earlier, persuasion does not occur all at once or upon a first hearing of the arguments and evidence. Several attempts may be required to reach a neutral audience successfully.

4. *Refer to beliefs your listeners have in common.* What are the issues or topics that your audience would find exciting or important? Speaking to a Parent-Teacher Association about children would be a better idea than talking about a recent vacation trip or other such topic that does not relate to the common needs of your audience.

Adapting to an unfriendly or hostile audience

Most speakers feel that the toughest audience to persuade is the group of listeners who are unfriendly or hostile toward either *them* or *their* stand on the issues. If the audience is unfriendly toward you, then you should consider how you can enhance your credibility. If the audience is hostile because they do not like your stand on the topic, there are several suggestions to keep in mind. Do not necessarily abandon your stand and try to be chameleonlike, telling your audience only what you know they want to hear. That is not persuasion; it is only patronizing your audience. Consider these suggestions if dealing with a hostile group:

1. *Don't tell your audience that you are planning to change their attitudes or behavior.* If you do, you may make them defensive. Imagine that you are a Democrat speaking to a Republican party meeting. You hope to win some converts to your political point of view. If you were to announce at the outset that you planned to change their attitudes, they would probably mentally say, "Oh, yeah? Just see if you can." It would be better to be more subtle in your intent to persuade your hostile audience.

2. *Don't ask for a major, dramatic change in attitude or behavior from a hostile group.* If you did, it could backfire and make your audience even more hostile. Set a realistic limit on what you can achieve. We're not suggesting that you be overly timid in your approach, only that you realistically assess your objective if your audience is unfriendly.

3. *Emphasize areas of agreement before you discuss those issues upon which you disagree.* Even if the group you are facing is not in favor of abortion, and you are, at least you can agree that the issue is a controversial one on which many people disagree. Your audience would probably also agree that individual free choice is important. Once you help your audience to understand that there are issues upon which you agree, they may be more attentive when you explain your position, even though it is at odds with their own.

4. *Acknowledge hostile audience members' points of view.* Be objective, so that your audience understands that you realize reasonable individuals may differ on the issues. Do not belittle your audience for taking a different stand on the issues than you have taken.

5. *Present both sides of the issue that you are addressing.* If you only present your side of the issue, your hostile audience members are going to be thinking about their stand on the issue anyway. Why not mention the reasons why others may take a different point of view and then use the appropriate arguments and evidence to show the relative advantages of your position?

6. *Take steps to establish your credibility with your audience.* Credibility is important, regardless of whether your audience is friendly, neutral, or hostile toward your stand on the issues. But when your audience is hostile, well-affirmed credibility is an important asset. Don't boast about your qualifications; simply let your audience know that you have the experience, interest, knowledge, and skills required for approaching your topic.

PERSUASIVE SPEAKING

PUTTING THEORY INTO PRACTICE

This chapter has focused upon speaking to persuade. We defined persuasion as the process of attempting to change or reinforce an attitude, belief, value, or behavior.

One theory that explains how persuasion occurs is cognitive dissonance. Cognitive dissonance is based on the assumption that we strive for consistency in our thoughts and actions. When we experience dissonance because we have been presented with information that is inconsistent with our attitudes, beliefs, or values, we may change our current way of thinking if we are convinced that the persuader's approach to a situation will reduce the dissonance.

Another approach that helps explain why we are motivated to change our attitudes or behavior is Maslow's hierarchy of needs. Maslow suggests that more basic needs, such as physiological and safety needs, must be satisfied before higher-level needs, such as those for social contact, self-esteem, and self-actualization, can serve as motivators.

A key concept in successfully applying the principles of persuasion that we've discussed in this chapter is to remember how important it is to adapt to your audience. Don't be in too much of a hurry to jump into the task of organizing information and rehearsing your speech until you have considered the attitudes, beliefs, values, and needs of your listeners. Remember, too, to be patient in your efforts to persuade. Attitude change occurs gradually; seldom does it occur in great leaps. To remind you of some of the more important suggestions for persuading others, we provide the following summary.

Suggestions for improving your credibility

- Prepare a list of your accomplishments or honors so that the person who introduces you can help establish a positive image of your qualifications on your subject.
- Your posture and gesture should communicate your enthusiasm and sincerity.
- Present a well-organized message.
- Research your topic so you can convince your audience you are informed and qualified.

Suggestions for improving the organization of your persuasive speech

- Present the problem before the solution.
- Emphasize areas of agreement between you and your audience early in your speech.
- Ask your audience to take some action in connection with your ideas toward the end rather than at the beginning of your speech.

- Use the motivated sequence to help you map your overall organizational strategy.

Suggestions for using emotional appeals

- For emotional impact, use examples and illustrations to which your listeners can relate.
- If you want your listeners to be excited and enthusiastic about your speech, you must be excited and enthusiastic as you talk to them.
- Direct emotional appeals to the needs, values, and motives of the particular audience.

Suggestions for using logical arguments to persuade listeners

- Use the appropriate tests of evidence to determine if your evidence is valid and reliable.
- Analyze the type of reasoning you are using (e.g., inductive, deductive, causal) to help you evaluate your logical arguments.

Suggestions for adapting the persuasive message to the audience

Adapting to a Friendly Audience:
- Suggest some specific action for audience to take.
- Ask listeners for some immediate show of support.
- Clearly state what your objective is.
- Use emotional appeals.
- Identify with your audience.
- Ask audience members to reinforce one another to support your position.

Adapting to a Neutral or Apathetic Audience:
- Make sure you have your listeners' attention.
- Make sure your listeners know how the subject you are addressing affects them or those they love.
- Bear in mind that a neutral audience is not going to respond as immediately or favorably as a friendly audience would.
- Refer to attitudes, beliefs, and values your listeners have in common.

Adapting to an Unfriendly or Hostile Audience:
- Don't tell your audience that you are planning to change their attitudes or behavior.
- Don't ask for a major, dramatic change in attitude or behavior.
- Emphasize areas of agreement before you discuss those issues upon which you disagree.
- Acknowledge hostile audience members' points of view.
- Present both sides of the issue that you are addressing.
- Take steps to establish your credibility.

SUGGESTED ACTIVITIES

1. Identify three nationally recognizable people who you feel are highly credible public speakers. Analyze their credibility on the three factors of credibility discussed in the chapter. Are they qualified, knowledgeable, competent? Are they trustworthy, honest, and sincere? Are they dynamic, charismatic?

2. Prepare and deliver a 5-minute persuasive speech in which you argue *against* your own convictions. Search for facts, examples, statistics, and testimony to support your speech purpose. Were you believable to your audience? Was it difficult to develop arguments for a speech about which you did not feel strongly?

3. After you have presented a persuasive speech in which you argued against your feelings, present a second persuasive speech in which you take the position you actually support. Again, search for convincing evidence to support your position. Compare audience response to and your own feelings about the two presentations.

4. Select five television or magazine advertisements. Analyze the persuasive strategies used to evoke a listener response. Consider use of evidence, message organization, emotional appeals, type(s) of reasoning, and adpatation of the message to the needs of the listener.

NOTES

[1] Leon Festinger, *A Theory of Cognitive Dissonance* (Evanston, IL: Row, Peterson, 1957).

[2] For additional discussion, see Wayne C. Minnick, *The Art of Persuasion* (Boston: Houghton Mifflin Company, 1967).

[3] Abraham H. Maslow, "A Theory of Human Motivation," in *Motivation and Personality* (New York: Harper & Row, 1954), Chapter 5.

[4] For an extensive discussion of the motivated sequence, see Douglas Ehninger, Alan H. Monroe, and Bruce E. Gronbeck, *Principles and Types of Speech Communication,* 8th ed., (Glenview, IL: Scott, Foresman & Company, 1978).

[5] Milton Rokeach, *Beliefs, Attitudes and Values* (San Francisco: Jossey-Bass, 1969), p. 124.

[6] For a discussion of fear appeal research, see Irving L. Janis and Seymour Feshbach, "Effects of Fear Arousing Communications," *Journal of Abnormal and Social Psychology,* 48 (January 1953): 78–92; Frederick A. Powell and Gerald R. Miller, "Social Approval and Disapproval Cues in Anxiety-Arousing Situations," *Speech Monographs,* 34 (June 1967): 152–159; and Kenneth L. Higbee, "Fifteen Years of Fear Arousal: Research on Threat Appeals: 1953–68," *Psychological Bulletin,* 72 (December 1969): 426–444.

[7] For a complete discussion of audience characteristics, see Gary Cronkhite, *Persuasion: Speech and Behavioral Change* (Indianapolis: Bobbs-Merrill Company, 1969), Chapter 7.

[8] Douglas Ehninger, Alan H. Monroe, and Bruce Gronbeck, *Principles and Types of Speech Communication,* 8th ed. (Glenview, IL: Scott, Foresman and Company, 1978), pp. 131–135.

EPILOGUE
SPEECH
COMMUNICATION
IN SOCIETY

In the beginning was Alpha and the end is Omega, but somewhere between occurred Delta, which was nothing less than the arrival of man himself and his breakthrough into the daylight of language and consciousness and knowing, of happiness and sadness, of being himself and being not himself, and of being at home and being a stranger.[1]

Without speech communication, there would be no society as we know it. Speech communication is at the center of who and what we are as individuals, groups, and societies. This book was written to help you understand how speech communication functions in your life. Without it, you would be little more than a responding animal.

> Language, symbolic communication, differentiates man from other life forms. . . . Unlike other life forms, humans are "time-binders" because language enables us to profit from the experiences of previous generations, to accumulate knowledge, and to establish complex systems and institutions. Modern society, with its intricate divisions of labor and its interdependent human activities, would be impossible if mankind did not possess the ability to symbolize—to communicate through speech and writing. In the words of Thomas Mann, "Speech is civilization. . . ."[2]

As we suggested at the beginning of the book, it is our capacity for symbol-making, speech communication, that most clearly sets us apart from the other animals. The individual human with his or her capacity for speech communication is the fundamental unit of society. Through speech communication, we build human relationships, form groups, make decisions, become educated, educate others. In a very real sense, the effectiveness of a society is a reflection of the effectiveness of the individuals within that society.

> Our social problems are often magnifications of our personal problems. The very personal conflicts of Herod and Hitler both worked havoc on the world around them. Speech communication functions are originally projected in the familial primary group. The family, in turn, is the organizational prototype which prepares (or

279

fails to prepare) the individual for organized roles in the larger society, so that eventually we see reflected in society as a whole the functions (whether adaptive or maladaptive) of speech communication in the individual.[3]

MASS COMMUNICATION IN SOCIETY

We do think together in a common mind, like it or not. There is a collective consciousness for human beings, and there may be something like an unconscious mind in which we hide parts of ourselves. We are linked together by speech and now we are becoming *wired* together by today's communication systems, all around the world. Is it anything like your mind or mine? Does it have hemispheres, east and west? It is a terrifying prospect when you think about it, for as we know, there is no way of controlling a human mind, least of all one's own. It does its own thinking, ungovernably. Thoughts pop in and out, on their own. Images go by, out of control. There is all that wishing, beyond restraint.

—*Lewis Thomas*[4]

It is becoming increasingly important that we understand the processes of human communication. Information and communication technology is progressing at such a rapid rate that it is not unrealistic to expect nearly instantaneous home-video contact with friends across the country, extensive computerized library and information services wired into the home, shopping at home through video-computer consoles, all within the next couple of decades. Already the rapid advances of telephone, radio, and television technology have made a dramatic impact on the way we live. Human-to-human contact, not long ago limited to face-to-face interaction and letters, which sometimes took months to arrive, now is possible through a variety of means, nearly instantaneously, almost anywhere in the world. To draw on an old cliché, the world is getting smaller, rapidly.

The term "mass communication" is actually somewhat misleading. When the anchor person of the evening news comes on the air, he or she is not really addressing the "masses." The receivers of the news are usually alone or with a small group, typically at home in their living rooms. *Individuals* comprise the "mass audience," and it is individuals who make decisions, such as whom to vote for, based on the communications they receive through the media.

Fundamentally, the process of listening to and understanding the evening news is no different from any other process of speech communication. It is still a transactional process in which senders and receivers of messages are engaged in an interpretive, meaning-assigning process, which is influenced by the nature of the interactants and the context in which communication occurs. What is different is that messages generated by so few can be received by so many.

In the midst of an information and communication technological explo-

sion, we must understand the process better. An effective communicator can influence the lives of millions of people. One who is also unethical can do a lot of damage. We cannot control a process we do not understand.

SUMMARY AND CONCLUSION

For the last time, we remind you that this has been a book about you, the reader, because you are one of the unique individual human beings who comprise interpersonal relationships, groups, families, organizations, cultures, societies, the world. This book is about the process of speech communication and how you use the process—effectively or ineffectively—to build those relationships, work within those groups and organizations, contribute to society and the world.

Our assumption—and there is considerable basis for it—is that conceptual understanding combined with practical skill development can help you to become a more effective communicator and therefore a more effective human being.

Unit I was designed to help you understand conceptually the fundamentals of human communication. In Chapter 1 we considered basic concepts, definitions, principles, perspectives, and the relationship between communication theory (what we can say about human communication) and communication practice (how that conceptual knowledge translates into increased effectiveness as a communicator). Chapter 2 presented a unified conceptual approach to the study of speech communication. The central question of Chapter 2 was: What is true about speech communication *wherever* it occurs? From this point through the rest of the book, we explored the effects of various contexts on the basic process of speech communication.

Unit II was devoted to intrapersonal communication, or communication within the self. Our concern there was with the spoken word as it relates to self-awareness.

Unit III moved outward from the self into the primary communication relationship, the interpersonal relationship.

In Unit IV, we looked at the spoken word as it functions within small groups striving to make decisions, reach consensus, and maintain satisfactory relationships within the group.

Moving outward, Unit V investigated our formal use of speech communication in the public setting.

We hope that you have found the book helpful and enjoyable.

NOTES

[1] Walker Percy, *The Message in the Bottle* (New York: Farrar, Straus and Giroux, 1975), p. 3.

[2] Gordon F. Hostetler, "Speech as a Liberal Study II," *Communication Education,* 29, 4 (September 1980): 332; Thomas Mann, *The Magic Mountain* (New York: Alfred A. Knopf, 1927), p. 602.

[3] Frank E. X. Dance and Carl Larson, *Speech Communication: Concepts and Behavior* (New York: Holt, Rinehart and Winston, 1972), p. 91.

[4] Lewis Thomas, "Still Surprised by the Secrets of the Universe," *Creative Living,* 8, 4 (Autumn, 1979): 2.

INDEX

A page number followed by an asterisk indicates a reference to boxed material in the text.

action language, 120, 121
Adler, Ronald B., 136, 154
Aronson, Elliot, 124, 133
Association for Communication Administration, 5
attitudes 69–70, 231
audience analysis, 230–232
demographic, 231, 232
environmental, 232
psychographic, 232
avoiding, as interactional
stage, 103, 106

Backlund, Philip, 95, 111
Backman, Carl W., 184, 189,
203
Bailey, Kenneth D., 17, 22
Baird, John E., Jr., 165, 173
Baker model, 92–94
Baker, Sidney J., 92, 111
Bales, Robert, 127, 133
Barker, Larry C., 13, 22, 24,
41, 66, 68, 86, 87
Barker model, 66–69
Barnlund, Dean, 9, 37*, 41,
154
B–A–V System 70, 214
Becker, Selwyn W., 127, 133
Beebe, Steven A., 108, 112,
221, 225
behavior:
affected by speech commu-
nication, 9, 25, 30, 31–32,
79–80
in interpersonal communica-
tion, 55, 107
and roles, 38, 58
beliefs, 69, 231
Benne, Kenneth D., 181, 184,
203
Berelson, Bernard, 70*, 87
Berlo, David K., 13–14, 22
Berlo model, 13–14
Blake, Robert, 124, 133
Bolinger, Dwight, 77*, 87
Bombeck, Erma, 139–140, 154

bonding, as interactional stage,
103, 104
Bradley, Patricia H., 165, 173
Brilhart, John K., 206*, 225
Brooks, William D., 48, 62

Cameron, Paul, 136, 154
Caple, Richard B., 193, 203
Cash, William B. Jr., 166, 173
certainty vs. provisionalism,
108
channel, 10, 12, 13
circumscribing, as interactional stage, 103, 105
Coakley, Carolyn Gwynn, 153,
154
cognitive dissonance, 258–259,
265
communication:
breakdowns in, 13
complexity of speech com-
munication, 8
defensive and supportive,
106–108
definitions of speech communication, 5–6, 13, 24
functional theory of speech
communication, 23–41
functions of communication:
development of higher
mental processes, 28–31;
linking function, 25–28,
48, 55, 91–92; regulation
of behavior, 30, 31–32, 55
group communication,
175–225
interviewing, 155–173
irreversability and unrepeat-
ability of, 8–9
levels of speech communication, 32–36: interpersonal,
33, 34–35, 36, 38–39, 48;
intrapersonal, 6, 33, 36,
39, 43–87; public, 33,
35–36, 48; small group,
33, 35, 36, 48

mass communication, 6
modes of speech communi-
cation, 39–40
nonverbal, 113–132
and perception, 76–77
persuasion, 256–277
principles of, 6–9
as process and product, 6–8,
9, 16–17: components of
process, 9–11; interac-
tional process, 13–15;
transactional process, 8,
15–17
public speaking, 229–255
relation of theory to practice, 20–21
and roles, 37–39
speech communication
models, 11–17
in society, 279–282
communication competence,
94
and interviewing, 162–163
communication context, 94, 96
communication performance,
94, 95
Condon, John C. Jr., 77*, 87
confirming and disconfirming
responses, 108–110
context, 15–16, 122
cultural, 16, 123
historical, 16
and nonverbal communica-
tion, 122
physical, 16
control vs. problem orientation, 107
courtship behavior, 125–126
Cronkhite, Gary, 272, 278

Dance, Frank E. X., 6*, 16, 22,
24*, 27, 28, 29*, 32, 38,
39*, 41, 58, 63, 68, 87,
215, 225, 228, 280, 282
Davitz, Joel R., 126, 133
decision making, 6, 127–129,

decision making—*continued*
206–213, 221
steps in decision making,
206–211
decoding, 10, 22
Delbecq, André L., 213, 225
description, 5
destination, 12, 13
DeVito, Joseph A., 94, 95, 111
DeVito model, 94–96
Diehl, Charles F., 126, 133
differentiating, as interactional
stage, 103, 104–105
displacement, 27
Dosey, Michael, 128, 133
dyadic effect, 100–101

Eadie, William F., 24, 41
Eckman, Paul, 117, 118, 132
Egan, Gerard, 100, 111
Ehninger, Douglas, 137, 154,
266, 274, 278
Emmert, Philip, 48, 62
encoding, 10, 22, 36
evaluation vs. description, 107
experimenting, as interactional
stage, 103, 104
eye contact, 124, 126, 128–129,
250

feedback, 11, 12, 13, 55, 216,
217
improving feedback,
149–150, 153
intentional and uninten-
tional, 148–149
intrapersonal and interpersonal, 148
and listening, 147–149
verbal and nonverbal, 148
Ferber, A., 125, 133
Festinger, Leon, 258, 278
field of experience, 95–96
field of language, 94
Fisher, Aubrey B., 193, 203,
204, 215, 222, 224, 225
Fredrich, Gustav W., 125, 133
Friesen, Wallace, 117, 132
function, 15, 16–17, 23–41

Gallup, George, 166, 173
gesture, 10, 39, 120, 127, 250
Gibb, Jack R., 106, 112
Glasgow, G. M., 126, 133

Goldberg, Alvin, 110, 112, 211,
225
Goyer, Robert S., 156, 173
Gronbeck, Bruce E., 137, 154,
266, 274, 278
group communication, 33, 35,
48, 127–129, 132,
175–176, 178–203,
204–225
group discussion
and decision making/prob-
lem solving, 213–214
and group perspective,
218–220
increasing effectiveness of,
214
and interpersonal perspective, 216–218
and intrapersonal perspective, 215–216
group dynamics
advantages of groups,
199–200
characteristics of a group,
180–195: group climate,
188–191; group phases,
193–195; group situation,
191–192; group structure,
180–186; group task,
187–188; individual group
member variable, 194–195
definition of "group," 178
disadvantages of groups,
198–199
increasing leadership effectiveness, 222–223
managing group conflict,
220–222
types of groups, 195–197
group structure, 180–186
interaction patterns, 186
leadership, 181, 185–186
roles, 181–184: functional,
181–182; group building,
181, 183; individual, 181,
183–184; status, 181,
184–186
Gusdorff, Georges, 79, 87

Hakuin, 45
Hare, A. Paul, 127, 133,
181, 203
Hart, Rod P., 125, 133
Hazel, Harry, 241, 255

Heidegger, Martin, 65*, 86
Hess, Eckhard, 117, 132
Heussenstann, F. K., 79, 87
higher mental processes
conceptual definition, 29
and speech communication,
28–31
Horney, Karen, 46, 62
Hostetlei, Gordon F., 279, 282
Howe, Reuel, 91, 111
Howells, Lloyd T., 127, 133

information, 10, 11
initiating, as interactional
stage, 103–104
integrating, as interactional
stage, 103, 104
intensifying, as interactional
stage, 103, 104
interactional perspective,
13–15
interpersonal attraction, 96–98
complementarity, 97
physical, 96–97
proximity, contact, and interaction, 97–98
similarity, 97
interpersonal communication,
34–35, 36, 38–39, 48, 89,
91–92, 96, 98–99,
102–108, 216–218
conceptual definition, 34
and group communication,
216–218
and relational stages,
102–108
and self-concept, 52–53, 91
interpersonal relationships, 6,
9, 13, 39, 89, 91
interpretation, as a stage of
perception, 71–72
interviewing, 115, 155–173
definition, 156
purposes, 157–160
responsibilities of interviewee, 169–171, 172
responsibilities of interviewer, 160–169, 172
intrapersonal communication,
6, 33, 36, 44–45, 65,
215–216

Jabusch, David, 15, 22
Jackson, Don, 105, 112

James, William, 49 (49*), 60–61*, 63
Janis, Irving L., 198, 203
Jourard, Sidney M., 99, 101, 111, 112

Kees, Welldon, 120, 133
Keller, Helen, 25–26, 41
Kelley, Harold, 97, 111
Kendon, Adam, 125, 133
Ketcham, H., 130, 133
Kibler, R. J., 13, 22, 24, 41
Kinch, John W., 54, 63
Kline, John A., 24, 41
Knapp, Mark L., 102, 103, 105, 106, 112, 125, 133
knowledge, 1–2
Korzybski, Alfred, 78, 87

Langer, Suzanne K., 64*, 66*, 86
language
  acquisition of, 6
  context, 6
  definitions of, 77
  as linguistic code, 12
  and perception, 30, 76–85
  and reciprocal identification, 94
  structure of, 6
Larson, Carl, 6*, 16, 22, 24*, 27, 28, 29*, 32, 38, 39*, 68, 87, 109, 110, 112, 211, 215, 228, 280, 282
Leavitt, Harold J., 148, 154
Lederer, W. J., 105, 112
Lefkowitz, M., 124, 133
Lilly, John, 69, 87
linking function of speech communication, 25–28, 48, 55, 91–92
listening, 134–153, 167–169, 170
  active listening, 150–152, 153
  improving listening, 144–147, 152–153
  and interviewing, 167–169, 170
  listening barricades, 141–144
  listening process, 136–138
  types of listening, 138–141
Littlejohn, Stephen, 15, 22
Luria, A. R., 32, 41

MacLean, Malcolm S., Jr., 71, 87
Malloy, John T., 124, 133
Maslow, Abraham H., 128, 133, 260, 278
Massarik, Fred, 185, 203
Masterson, John T., 108, 112, 221, 225
McGinnis, Joe, 78, 87
Mehrabian, Albert, 116, 119, 132, 133
Meisels, Murry, 128, 133
memory, 137–138
message, 10, 11–12, 13, 22, 39, 143–144
  delivery, 143–144
  intentional and accidental, 10
  verbal and nonverbal, 10, 39
Miller, Gerald R., 34*, 41, 99, 111
Mills, Judson, 124, 133
Minnick, Wayne C., 259, 278
Mintz, N. L., 128, 133
mode (modality)
  conceptional definition, 39–40
  modal contradiction, 39–40
  modal reinforcement, 39
  and speech communication, 39–40
Monroe, Alan H., 137, 154, 266, 274, 278
Morris, William, 25 (25*), 41
Morse, Ben W., 102, 112
motivated sequence, 265–266
Mouton, Jane, 124, 133
Mueller, Ronald A. H., 148, 154

neutrality vs. empathy, 108
Nichols, Ralph G., 136, 143, 144, 154
noise, 10–11, 12, 13
nonverbal communication
  in the classroom, 129–130, 132
  definition, 114
  dimensions of, 119–120
  and group decision making, 127–129, 132
  and impression formation, 123–126, 131
  interpreting, 122–123, 131

purpose of, 117–118
relationship with verbal communication, 117–118
and speaker effectiveness, 126–127, 131
note taking, 140–141, 152

object language, 120–121, 128
O'Connor, Flannery, 59*, 63
organization, as a stage of perception, 71–72

Parain, Bruce, 29*, 41
Pear, T. H., 126, 133
perception
  beliefs, attitudes, and values, 69–70
  and communication, 76–77
  definition, 70
  influences on perception, 72–76: contextual, 73–74; physiological, 73; psychological, 74–76
  as process, 70–72
  and reception, 67–78
  and stimuli, 66–67
perceptual processes, 68–69, 70–72
  cognitive, 68
  emotional, 68
  physiological, 68, 71, 73
  transmission of responses, 68–69
Percy, Walker, 3, 22, 26, 41, 279*, 282
persuasion, 256–277
  audience adaptation, 271–275, 277
  cognitive dissonance, 258–259
  definition, 257–258
  emotional appeals, 266–267, 277
  listeners' needs, 260–262
  logical argument, 268–271, 277
  speaker credibility, 262–264, 276
Pfeutze, Paul F., 52*, 63
Phelps, Lynn A., 102, 112
posture, 127, 129
Powell, John, 101, 111
practical knowledge, 1
prescription, 5

problem solving, 6, 206–213, 221
  problem-solving formats, 211–213: ideal solution, 211–212; nominal group, 212–213; reflective thinking, 211; single question, 212
  steps in problem solving, 206–211
process, 6–8, 9–11, 13–15, 16, 15–17
public communication, 33, 35–36, 48, 229–255, 256–277
public speaking
  audience analysis, 230–232
  organizing ideas, 240–248
  purpose, 233–235
  supporting material, 235–240
  topic, 232–233

questioning, 165–167
  closed questions, 165
  in interviewing, 165–167
  open questions, 165
  questioning sequences, 166–167

Rankin, Paul, 134, 153, 154
reasoning, 268–271
  deductive reasoning, 270–271
  examples, 268–269
  facts, 268
  inductive reasoning, 270
  opinions, 269
  statistics, 269
receiver, 10, 11, 12, 13
reception and perception, 67–68
reciprocal identification, 92–93, 94
Redding, W. Charles, 156, 173
relational stages and interpersonal communication, 102–108
Richey, John T., 156, 173
Reusch, Jurgen, 120, 133
Reynolds, Paul D., 17, 22
Robbins, Tom, 58–59*, 63
Rokeach, Milton, 267, 278
roles, 37–38, 58–59
  definition, 37, 181

functional roles, 181–184
role enactment, 38
role taking, 38
and self-concept, 58–59
and speech communication, 37

Satz, P. H., 126, 133
Schetlen, Albert E., 125, 133
Schramm model, 13–14
Schramm, Wilbur, 13–14, 22
Schulman, G. M., 125, 133
Schutz, William C., 97, 111, 193, 203
Secord, Paul F., 184, 189, 203
selection, as a stage of perception, 71–72
self-awareness, 43–63, 101–102
  material self, 49
  and roles, 58–59
  self-concept, 47–49, 54–57, 91: and interpersonal communication, 52–53; effects on communication, 57–58: selection of messages, 58; self-fulfilling prophecy, 57–58
  and self-disclosure, 101–102
  self-image and self-esteem, 56–57
  self-reflexiveness, 46–47
  social self, 49–50
  spiritual self, 51
self-disclosure, 99–102
  and the dyadic effect, 100–101
  interiority and exteriority, 99–100
  and self-awareness, 101–102
self-feedback, 68–69
Shannon, Claude E., 11–12, 22
Shannon-Weaver model, 11–13, 14
Shaw, Marvin E., 178, 194, 203
Sheats, Paul, 181, 184, 203
Sieburg, Evelyn, 109, 112
Siegel, B., 124, 133
sign language, 120
silence, 93–94
  in the Baker model, 93
  and psychic tension, 94
Sommer, Robert, 130, 133
source, 10, 11, 12
Speech Communication Association of America, 13

speech rate vs. thought rate, 143
speech pathology, 6
stagnating, as interactional stage, 103, 105–106
Steil, Lyman, 136, 154
Steinberg, Mark, 34*, 41, 99, 111
Steiner, Gary A., 70*, 87
Stenzor, Bernard, 127, 133
Stevens, Leonard A., 136, 143, 144, 154
Stewart, Charles J., 166, 173
stimulation, as stage of perception, 71–72
stimuli, 66–67, 137
  sound, 137
strategy vs. spontaneity, 107
superiority vs. equality, 108
supporting material, 235–240
  analogy, 236–237
  definition, 235–236
  example, 236
  illustration, 236
  sources, 239–240
  statistics, 237
  testimony, 237–238
  visual aids, 238–239
symbols, 24, 27–28, 30, 31, 32, 33, 39, 64, 84

Tannenbaum, Robert, 185, 203
terminating, as interactional stage, 103, 106
theoretical knowledge, 1, 2
theory, 3, 17–21
  definition, 17
  relationship to practice, 20–21, 23
  uses of, 17–20
Thibaut, John, 97, 111
Thomas, Lewis, 280*, 282
Thompson, Ralph, 5*, 22
Toch, Hans, 71, 87
Towne, Neil, 136, 154
transactional perspective, 15–17
transmissional perspective, 11–13, 14
transmitter, 12, 13
Tuckman, Bruce W., 193, 203

values, 70, 231
Van de Ven, Andrew H., 213, 225

vocal inflection, 126, 129–130
Vygotsky, Lev, 29, 41

Weaver, Warren, 11–12, 22
Wells, William, 124, 133
Weschler, Irving R., 185, 203
White, R. C., 126, 133
Willett, Thomas H., 129, 133

Wilmot, William W., 54–55
Wittgenstein, 27*
Wolvin, Andrew D., 153, 154
Woolbert, Charles, 126, 133
words, 78–85
   barriers, 80–85: allness, 82;
     bypassing, 81; fact-infer-
     ence confusion, 83, 84–85;

     overcoming word barriers,
     83–85; polarization, 81–
     82; static evaluation, 82–
     83
   power of, 78–80

Zajonc, Robert B., 98, 111